14003179

When Markets Quake

WHEN MARKETS QUAKE

QUAKE

The Management Challenge
of Restructuring Industry

JOSEPH L. BOWER

HARVARD BUSINESS SCHOOL

HARVARD BUSINESS SCHOOL PRESS

BOSTON, MASSACHUSETTS

Library of Congress Cataloging-in-Publication Data

Bower, Joseph L.
  When markets quake.

  Includes bibliographies and index.
  1. Petroleum chemicals industry—Management.
2. Business cycles.   I. Title.
HD9579.C32B69   1986   661'.804'068   86-18321
ISBN 0-87584-136-8

Contents

v

CHAPTER 4
What Role for Government?

CHAPTER 5
The Restructuring of Union Carbide Corporation
and Dow Chemical Corporation

CHAPTER 6
Other Forces in the Market: Oil Companies
and the United States Government

CHAPTER 12
A Restructuring Agenda for Managers

Preface

This book represents a continuation of twenty years of research into the strategic character of economic problems facing top managements. *Managing the Resource Allocation Process* describes how the process of making major capital investments determines the future character of the firm and argues that that process can be managed once it is understood. *Two Faces of Management* describes the problems that develop when political managers have to work with technocrats, a problem increasingly common as governments intervene in a wide range of economic activity. In that context, this book is an analysis of management work at the political/technocratic interface in one of the world's most important industries.

The book also represents one line in a series of investigations of business policy problems in that group of industries characterized by global competition which have been carried out at the Harvard Business School over the past decade. Although the research questions and findings are mine, the work has been substantially influenced by the other work done here.

Bruce Scott and George Lodge have played a major role with their project on U.S. competitiveness. Scott in particular with his analysis of national economic strategies, and Lodge whose work demonstrates the powerful role played by ideology have changed the way we think about international competition. In the research leading to the present book it was possible to expand on the considerable research they both have done in building the course "Business, Government and the International Economy," and in their individual research projects and writings.

Also important to the development of my thinking has been Malcolm Salter's study of the world auto industry, and the related work of William Abernathy and Robert Hayes. The works of Thomas McCraw on the evolution of regulation in the United

States, and Richard Vietor on regulation in energy and in telecommunications have also been useful. More directly, I am thankful for the comments provided by those who read and commented on the manuscript: Professors Kenneth Andrews, Joseph Badaracco, Richard Caves, Albert Chandler, George Lodge, Thomas McCraw, Richard Vietor, and Ezra Vogel of Harvard University; and Richard Foster of McKinsey & Co. Catherine Barre provided substantial assistance on France and the French companies, especially during the process of interviewing industry executives. Benjamin Gomez-Casseres contributed significantly to the research on Montedison.

The approach to the research reflects the context as well. Through friends and alumni of the Harvard Business School I was able to interview the leading managers of the chemical businesses at BP, ICC, Shell, Atochem, CdF Chimie, Rhône-Poulenc, ENI, Montedison, BASF, Hoechst, Mitsui Chemical, Mitsui Trading (Bussan), Mitsui Petrochemical, Mitsubishi Chemical, Mitsubishi Petrochemical, Mitsubishi Corporation, Showa Denko, Sumitomo Chemical, Takeda, Kanegefuchi, Dow Chemical, Du Pont, Exxon Chemical, Mobil Chemical, and Union Carbide. This was not a random sample; nor was it the population of petrochemical producers. By the estimate of industry participants, however, it was an extensive and representative group of the most important producers. In addition, I had access to the data bases of McKinsey & Co. and Parpinelli and considerable support from Chem Systems Ltd. A number of past leaders of the industry were also willing to be interviewed.

In all instances I tried to learn what was happening to the industry; how the companies were responding; and what special problems management faced. Since the companies were all familiar to each other, and the industry problems shared, I soon found that I was going over familiar ground. The managers I worked with were helpful and interested. After the field research was completed, I sent early drafts of the material to the managers interviewed for corrections and such vetting as they thought necessary. Generally speaking, the only changes were the elimination of factual error and the weakening of critical remarks about competitors and governments. In some instances, especially in Japan, managers were only willing to be quoted as "a company executive." Unless there is a specific reference footnoted, all quoted material in the text comes from company interviews. In my judgment, it is the best balance between retaining the use of valuable illustrative data and respecting the wishes of those who cooperated with the study.

The place where this approach was weakest was in dealing with the European Commission. I was asked by the European companies to avoid the Commission during my research. While in the end, I did have limited conversations with important figures, the discussion in the text may be biased by the lack of contact with Commission executives, especially those in the Competition Directorate. In fact, I do not believe that my argument is weakened, but the possibility must be acknowledged.

The same is not true for national governments. I interviewed key figures in the French Ministry of Industry, the Italian Ministry of State Participation, the British Department of Trade and Industry, the Japanese Ministry of International Trade and Industry, the U.S. Department of Commerce, and the U.S. Trade Representative. The only gap was the German government, where some of the same sensitivities existed as with the Commission.

I hope that the book is treated as a reliable description of what has been happening in the petrochemical industry. That description provides the basis of a somewhat controversial argument. Nonetheless, if readers find it persuasive, the study will have served its purpose. But it is important to understand that extensive as it is, this is not the definitive description of the world petrochemical industry. That has yet to be written. Nor are most of the company descriptions complete case studies of the restructuring that has been managed over the last decade. Those tasks would take a lifetime, and in the end, the policy problems would have changed.

I attempt, then, to step back and capture for consideration by managers a picture of an entire industry in transition, as environment and technology shift and company strategies are modified to take account of the sea change. From that detached but not remote perspective, I believe it is possible to see common features in the problems facing the companies and in their responses, features which carry important lessons for managers in other companies and in the governments of the free world.

Joseph L. Bower

January, 1986
Boston, Massachusetts

To Nancy

Introduction

A Story of Crisis

This book tells the story of how top managers in one of the world's largest industries responded to an upheaval in its markets. The quake is still going on, with aftershocks upsetting temporarily stabilized conditions, but a number of companies have already left the scene. New companies have arrived, taking advantage of changed circumstances, sometimes accelerating the departure of industry founders. This book draws lessons from the experience for policymakers in business and government.

The conclusions I reached are based upon a comparative study of the restructuring of the petrochemical industries of Europe, Japan, and the United States. As such, it is a contribution to the debate about the way the United States should manage itself in the economic competition of the last part of this century.

The book reflects my strong belief that how things are managed makes a difference. Good intentions and wise policies are not substitutes for effective action. Just as a company manager cannot improve his company's growth rate by simply announcing that he wants to enter a rapidly growing field, so no nation can improve its economic performance by announcing it wishes to do so. In each case, skillful use of the proper organizational structure and administrative systems is required. Department and divisional managers must understand the new direction sought by a company's leadership and have the imagination and skill to devise a successful strategy for entry into the new field. Company policies must facilitate rather than hinder the work of the manager, but they cannot solve the problem for him. The same is true for nations. Coherent macroeconomic policies that encourage investment and exports can provide the setting for a successful company, but if its management is incompetent, then there is no cure until a new team is installed.

To the extent then that the debate over industrial policy in the United States has tended to find answers at the extremes of national strategy or the free market, this book argues uncomfortably for the importance of the organizations and their managers. The lesson of petrochemicals is that the nations that intervened directly to help their industries made rather a mess of things. But the free market never existed and the economic jungle is an unacceptable state of affairs for a $400 billion industry of critical importance to national economies.

The question is not whether there should be government involvement *or* good company management. It is obvious both are required. What is quite unclear is the role that governments and companies should play in relation to each other.

The objective of this book is to use a comparison of business-government arrangements in France, Germany, Italy, the United Kingdom, Japan, and the United States to identify aspects of the relationship that seem to make sense. While my conclusions obviously have significance for public policy, my perspective is that of company managements. I interviewed a number of the top managers in the six countries to learn what were the special problems of managing companies in the middle of major transformations of their markets and competition.

The choice of topic and industry virtually guaranteed that the managers would be concerned with their governments and those of their competitors. The stakes were too high and the nature of the changes too great for governments to ignore the consequences of change. The petrochemical industry is not like the restaurant industry, where companies come and go without much impact on the environment. Indeed, the companies I studied are at the core of their nation's industrial economy. Governments could be expected to have a view. So the project also provided the opportunity to learn about the results of government action. From the perspective of managers and the market, what role could government play that seemed the most helpful and most important? What could managers do to help make sure that government involvement was constructive rather than merely disruptive?

A special problem that must be acknowledged at the start arises from the industry studied: petrochemicals. There has always been a special problem with the study of the industry. It may be huge and vital to modern life, but it is as unromantic as one can get.

Synonymous with "synthetic" it has a less interesting ring than steel and less attractive metaphoric implications. The importance of this casual cultural observation derives from its implication. It is not obvious to very many people that much can be learned from the achievements of the managers of companies that manufacture plastics.

Even researchers of management resist plastics. The products are hard to comprehend and, if comprehensible, boring. The processes of manufacture are impossibly complicated in theory and smelly, vast, and geographically distant in fact. One colleague of mine once called one of the companies a "five-legged cow," from which generalization was impossible.

In reality the popular image is undeserved. The companies and their products are fascinating. Involved are some of the oldest and largest firms in the world. Imperial Chemical Industries (ICI), Du Pont, Badische Anilin & Soda Fabrik (BASF), and Showa Denko have played key roles in the industrialization of Europe, Japan, and the United States. The procedures they developed to manage their complex operations provided the basis for what is today regarded as good management practice. Many of the companies were well run. The chemical industries in Europe and the United States have been bulwarks of the export sectors in the West. In fact, it is the very pervasiveness and success of "plastics" that make them boring to the general public.

But that era has passed. The firms manufacturing the leading plastics made major investments that far exceed the needs of today's markets. The excess capacity has been associated with severe price competition and large losses (see charts I.1 and I.2). In Europe and Japan, even the strongest companies have operated in the red for several years in a row, with aggregate losses of over a billion dollars a year. In the United States, the reputedly well-managed chemical industry earned more than its cost of capital less than half the time during the last decade (see chart I.2). The situation in Europe is worse. The losses in chemicals are severe. During the depth of the recession of the early 1980s it is estimated that the total business sector of France and Italy operated at a loss.[1]

The continuing losses pose a problem for the company managements and their host country's policymakers. But they also pose a challenge to the relevance of economic theory. It is conventional wisdom that when the supply of a product significantly exceeds

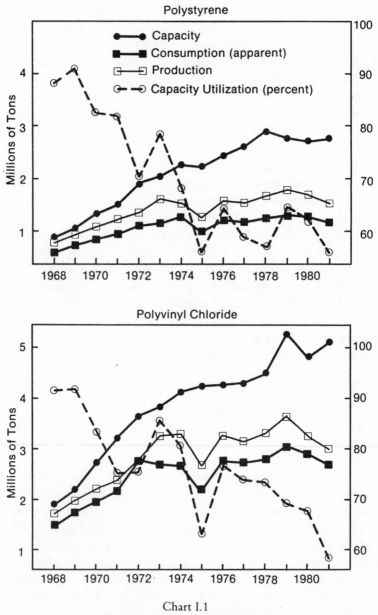

Chart I.1
Western Europe Capacity Utilization

From Etienne Davignon, vice president of the Commission of the European Communities, "Restructuring the European Chemical Industry: The Position of the European Commission." Paper presented at the annual meeting of the European Section of the Society of Chemical Industry, Brussels, 1982.

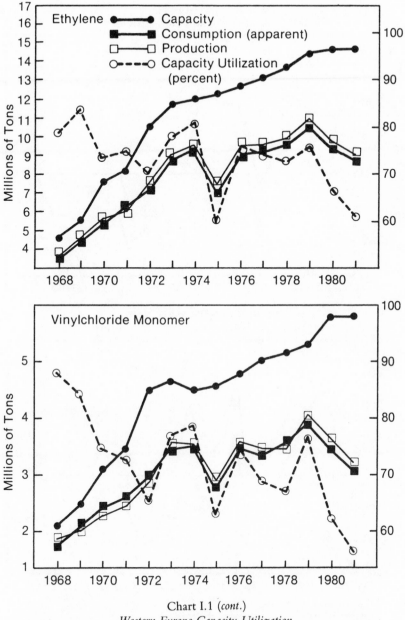

Chart I.1 *(cont.)*
Western Europe Capacity Utilization

From Etienne Davignon, vice president of the Commission of the European Communities, "Restructuring the European Chemical Industry: The Position of the European Commission." Paper presented at the annual meeting of the European Section of the Society of Chemical Industry, Brussels, 1982.

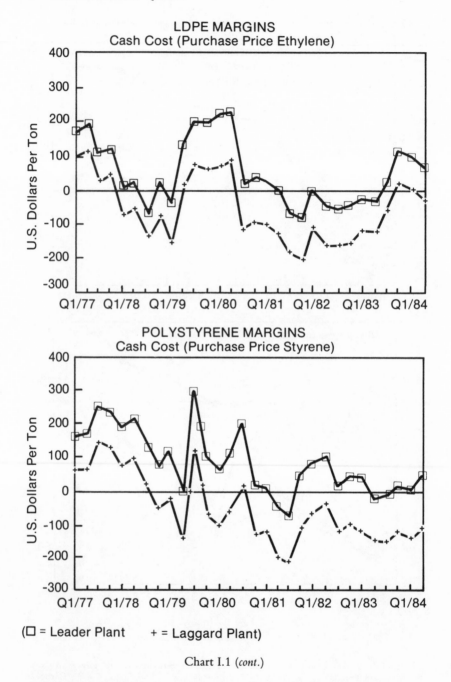

Chart I.1 (*cont.*)

Source: Chem Systems International Ltd., *Quarterly Petrochemical Business Analysis*, London, 1984.

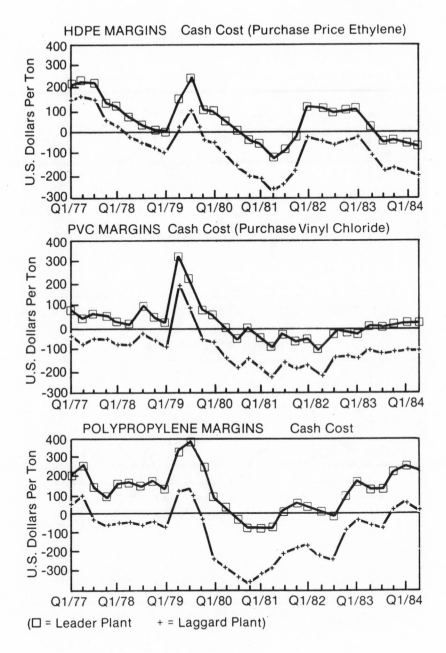

Chart I.1 (*cont.*)

Source: Chem Systems International Ltd., *Quarterly Petrochemical Business Analysis,* London, 1984.

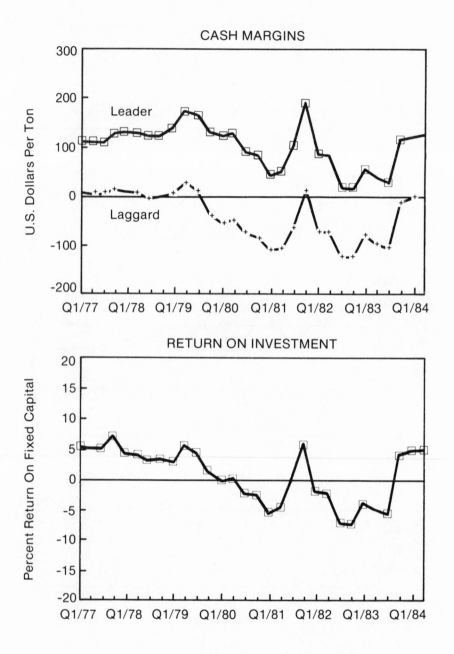

Chart I.1 *(cont.)*

Source: Chem Systems International Ltd., *Quarterly Petrochemical Business Analysis,* London, 1984.

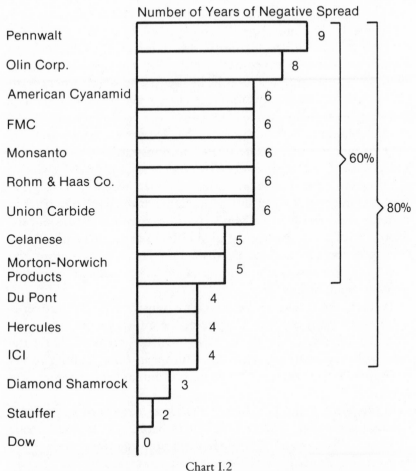

Chart I.2
Spread for the Top 15 U.S. Chemical Companies, 1971–1980[a]

Reprinted from Dan Connell, "The Chemical Industry's $100 Billion Opportunity" (McKinsey & Company, 1982), 1–12.

[a] Over 50 percent of total company's sales are chemicals; spread equals return on equity minus cost of equity.

demand, prices fall and the quantity offered is reduced by manufacturers unwilling to take a loss. In theory, the least efficient producers exit first, thus guaranteeing the market the lowest cost supply. Eventually, the exit of manufacturers balances supply with demand.[2]

In one industry after another, however, something different has happened. The market has not produced the results that it is sup-

posed to in steel, fibers, autos, or the industry studied here, petrochemicals. Instead, capacity is expected to exceed forecasted
demand for the foreseeable future. Moreover, the producers leaving the market first are sometimes the best managed or the ones
with the best alternatives, not the least efficient. Companies thrash
about, and the losses continue—cash losses that weaken the ability
of the firms to help themselves.

The consequent economic crisis has led governments to intervene in unusual ways. The Carter administration (through trigger prices), the Reagan administration (through orderly market
agreements), and European Commissioner Viscount Davignon
(through support for capacity reductions) have effectively tried to
cartelize industry. Japan's Ministry of International Trade and Industry (MITI) has vigorously tried to force depressed basic industries to restructure and has persuaded the Japanese legislature, the
Diet, to pass a new law providing the financial and legal opportunities to make it possible.

To date, the results of these rather extensive efforts by governments have been modest. In spite of the efforts of the Organization for Economic Cooperation and Development (OECD) the
steel industry is still a shambles. European fiber manufacturers
have shrunk their capacity by 40 percent but are still experiencing
losses.

In the petrochemical industry, the losses have been staggering,
running in the early 1980s to a billion dollars a year each in Europe
and Japan. While by 1985 the losses had been stemmed, progress is
expected to be temporary as new sources of supply are already
threatening the historical producers, and the long-term outlook
promises only more technological and economic turmoil. The
reasons for these results present a remarkably complex problem
involving the evolution of the world's economy, trade patterns,
national industrial policies, and corporate strategies.

For governments the situation is poignant. It certainly looks as
if the attempts of the French, Italian, and Japanese governments to
stimulate their petrochemical industry produced uneconomic results, not just that the decision makers guessed wrong about 1973.
Because of bad theory, or corruption, or poorly designed policy
they encouraged the development of an awkwardly structured
industry. This was not disputed by managers in either the govern-

ment or the companies. In Germany, the United Kingdom, and the United States the *relatively* noninterventionist industrial policy of government seemed to have fostered efficient producers, who, nevertheless, were losing market share to less capable companies that were better able or more willing to pour cash into chronically depressed businesses.

The companies were frustrated. Some, like Mitsubishi Petrochemical, had 90 percent of their business in these depressed markets. Cutting back meant liquidating in a situation where assets had little value. Others like BASF had a strategically sound position that would be profitless as long as the weak remained in the market. By 1983 the companies knew that all would benefit from an "orderly market," but national rivalries, geographic location, vertical integration, and the antitrust laws blocked many attempts at cooperative action.

Implications

What is one to make of this array of events? How can one interpret so much economic hardship? What does it mean for the theories we use to guide the development of government and corporate policy that an important modern industry can be in such disarray (petrochemicals, after all, is not a backward industry)? The chemical companies were some of the first to study the organization and economics of the firm (much corporate finance as well as its relation to the product divisionalized firm were invented by Du Pont). Hoechst, BASF, and Bayer together with ICI and Solvay invented the dyestuffs industry as well as much of the industrial chemistry on which our lives depend. The U.S. companies also made enormous contributions. The chemical companies are large, invest heavily in research and development, and have often been profitable. More important for the generality of any conclusions that can be drawn, this industry is not subject to a Japanese or East Asian takeover. The most successful companies are European and American—the most profitable are clearly American. What is happening reflects the economic circumstances of the last decades of the century.

This study focuses on the problem of building and managing corporate strategy in these apparently extreme conditions. These are described fully in chapters 5–11, but some summary observations here of crucial factors will provide a useful context for the more general conclusions of the book.

1. *National interest.* Much of what happens in the industry can only be understood in terms of the desires and plans of nation-states trying to improve their economic well-being by using their natural resources, their capital, and their buying power in a concerted, planned effort to help the nation prosper.
2. *State-owned enterprise.* When a nation will borrow or print money to fund a corporate national champion, a well-managed private competitor can be hurt or destroyed by that less efficient state-owned company. Good intentions are no more a substitute for good management at the level of the state than at the level of the company.
3. *Company advantage.* In petrochemicals, where employment is a less salient issue, raw material costs, technological advantage, or product development can neutralize the state's advantage.
4. *Competition.* Without great strength in raw materials, technology, or product development, there is every reason to expect that left to themselves privately owned competitors will withdraw in the presence of state-sponsored competition. Nonetheless, exit cost is high because plant write-offs are large and reduction in manpower may be illegal.
5. *Government policy.* Governments have urged simultaneously three different postures on their industry: retrenchment with more imports, rationalization, or protection of the status quo. These positions were built upon mixed foundations of ideology, analysis, and private self-interest.

The scope of the activity described in this book is vast. Europe, Japan, and the United States together constitute most of the developed industrial world that operates in what might be called enterprise capitalism. (There are far too many state-owned companies and government subsidies to talk about free enterprise.) The companies discussed are on *Fortune*'s list of the world's largest industrial corporations.

It is easy to drown in detail in studies of this scope or even to forget the purpose of the investigation which here is to see what can be learned from the tribulations of the chemical industry rather than merely to describe them. Nonetheless, it will be hard to understand why such fundamental changes as I propose are sensible unless one grasps the depth and complexity of the crisis facing industrial enterprise. While the behavior described is specific to these boring plastic companies the issues at stake are as important as any in political economy.

Because we are exploring what these problems mean for those who manage the companies and concerned government institutions, an important part of the data for this book was discussion with those managers. More than the extensive statistical record that was gathered, it is their interpretation of events, and their explanation of what is involved in formulating and implementing policy in response that provide the basis for the discussion here. It is their story that is told in chapters 5–11.

The chapters describe events of enormous import in the evolution of our modern economies. The decision of Union Carbide to depart from chemical markets in Europe reflects the end of a particular conjunction of economic forces in the post–World War II period that Servan-Schreiber called "the American Challenge." The swap of facilities by British Petroleum (BP) and ICI in the United Kingdom marks the reemergence of entrepreneurial professional management in the leadership of these two great companies. The privatization and restructuring of Montedison may mark the end of an approach to state control of the Italian economy that began with Mussolini. In turn, Japan's Law for Restructuring of Basic Industry represents an extraordinary attempt to see if the same governmental arrangements that were used to manage unending rapid growth can cope with the stresses of industrial decline. And the German effort to deal with new competition without social disruption represents only the latest scene in the continuing saga of German industry's effort to manage development without the intervention of a socialist government.

On the other hand, readers outside the industry will be more concerned with the lessons learned from its experience than with the details of the battle. Chapter 1 provides an overview of the changes that have taken place in the industry, focusing on the features common to the developments in the six countries studied. Chapter 2 identifies the patterns common to the very individual experience of the companies and countries. When similar features can be found in such diverse situations, a researcher can be sure that powerful forces exist that can be usefully explained. Once observed these common elements appear obvious. And because these common features can be found across culture and company, it is not surprising that they are important.

From the perspective of a manager reflecting on these events, two lessons stand out. First, the structure of an industry may be so dysfunctional to the results of competition that collective action is appropriate to fix it. In such an instance, the workings of the market produce neither efficiency nor profit. Second, the cooperative action that is required to develop and implement a remedy inevitably brings with it the involvement of government and politics. The necessity of dealing publicly with the sources of dysfunction and the means for developing and legitimizing remedies has dramatically increased the political content of top management's work. Chapter 3 argues that this important change in the role and task of the general manager must be acknowledged by contemporary executives whatever their ideology.

The kind of action I advocate in chapter 3 requires changes in the way public policy toward industry is developed. In chapter 4, I argue for changes in the approach to antitrust policy in the United States. But since the industrial crisis is upon us and public policy changes slowly, managers face the task of devising successful strategies for coping with the current turmoil. Chapter 12 suggests three basic approaches together with a new way of thinking about the work of top management.

NOTES

1. Michel Albert and James S. Ball, "Towards European Economic Recovery in the 1980's," *The Washington Papers-109*, edited by staff of the Center for Strategic and International Studies, Georgetown University (New York: Praeger, 1984), chapter 1.
2. The subject of exit has received increasing attention by economists. Richard Caves and Michael Porter were the first economists to discuss the extent to which "barriers to exit" interfered with the rather simplistic behavior hypothesized in the basic theory. "From Entry Barriers to Mobility Barriers: Conjectural Decisions and Contrived Deterrence to New Competition," *Quarterly Journal of Economics*, Summer 1977, 241–61. Since then Pankaj Ghemawat has also written on the topic. Pankaj Ghemawat and Barry Nalebuff, "Exit," *Rand Journal of Economics*, Summer 1985, 184–94. Business Policy researchers had begun exploring the topic even earlier, however; e.g., Clark Gilmore, *The Divestment Decision Process*, DBA diss., Harvard Business School, 1973 and Richard Hamermesh, *Corporate Response to Divisional Profit Crisis*, DBA diss., Harvard Business School, 1976.

1

The World Petrochemical
Industry in Transition

Background

The free-world petrochemical industry in 1980 manufactured goods worth $390 billion (32 percent of which was in the United States) and employed 857,000 (36 percent of which was in the United States). Using hydrocarbon gas or liquid as raw material, companies produced tens of thousands of industrial and consumer products such as polyethylene (PE) or polystyrene resin (PS) used for trash bags and coffee cups; polyvinyl chloride (PVC) used for pipes; and polypropylene (PP) used for furniture. While many companies are engaged in the entire chain of activity from oil and gas exploration to the sale of consumer products, the industry proper is usually considered to begin with the production of primary aromatics and olefins from the feedstock and to end with the manufacture of organic intermediates, such as vinyl acetate, polyethylene, ethylene glycol, and nylon resin and fiber. Any precise definition of the industry is problematic because products have multiple uses. For example, ethylene glycol is both an end product used by the consumer as antifreeze and a raw material used by the industry for polyester. Also, by-products of an intermediate stage may be recycled and used as inputs to an early stage.

Factors that aggravate the complexity of petrochemicals are: (1) there are generally several technological routes to a particular process and improvements can make obsolete much existing capacity; (2) production facilities are large, expensive, difficult to operate, and can become obsolete quickly; (3) no two companies produce the same product mix; (4) the products are often hard to differentiate while easy to transport, making the markets global; (5) shifts in currency value, therefore, are of great importance to relative competitiveness.

To understand how the industry functions, we will briefly con-

sider ethylene.[1] A key building block in the petrochemical industry, ethylene is "cracked" (that is, broken into simpler chemical
compounds) from ethane or naphtha feedstock by means of heat
and pressure in giant facilities called steam crackers. Ethylene and
its derivatives account for roughly 33–40 percent of the shipments
in the petrochemical category.[2] Moreover, because ethylene has
no use unprocessed, capacity to manufacture its derivatives is often built at the same time as new ethylene capacity. Consequently,
it is usually true that when there is excess ethylene capacity, there
is also excess derivative capacity. Ethylene capacity utilization is a
crude proxy for the health of the entire industry. In addition, some
70 percent of ethylene produced is used in the production of
four derivatives: low-density polyethylene (LDPE), high-density
polyethylene (HDPE), polystyrene (PS), and polyvinyl chloride
(PVC).[3] Finally, propylene is produced in the cracking of naphtha
to make ethylene (the proportion varies with the "severity" of the
process). If polypropylene (PP) is included in the studies, then
the major commodity plastics (accounting for more than half of
the petrochemical industry) are covered.

A sense for the flow and the economics of the industry may be
gathered from the impressionistic chart of a petrochemical facility
shown in chart 1.1.

For most countries, the development of a petrochemical industry has been relatively recent and rapid. Beginning in the 1950s
plastics and synthetic fibers quickly penetrated the world economy. The industry grew 30 percent to 50 percent faster than GNP
during much of the postwar period. With steadily declining real
costs to the user and an unending array of new applications,
growth seemed limitless. "Plastics!" were the frontier. The industry's original participants, the chemical companies, flourished and
many others entered. In the United States, the oil companies saw
an opportunity to invest their awesome cash flow profitably;
while numerous firms in mature industries, such as shipping,
tires, and steel, saw an opportunity to escape secular decline. In
Japan each of the major industrial groups entered the market,
sometimes with their long-established chemical producer
(Sumitomo) and sometimes with a newly organized venture (Mitsui Petrochemical). Later the original chemical companies all entered, as did some oil companies. In Europe the chemical companies were joined by oil companies, coal producers, and national

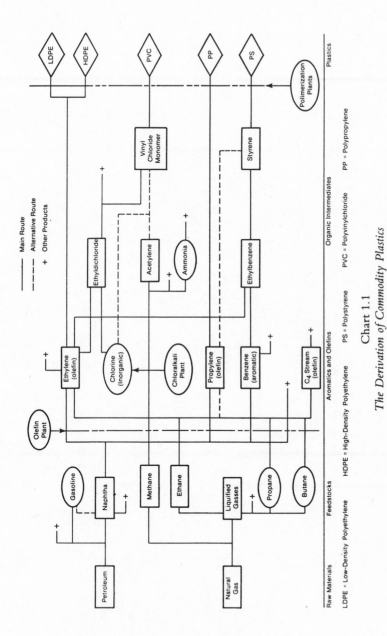

Chart 1.1

The Derivation of Commodity Plastics

LDPE = Low-density polyethylene; HDPE = high-density polyethylene; PS = polystyrene; PVC = polyvinyl chloride; PP = polypropylene.

Table 1.1

Number of Petrochemical Producers and Capacity, 1980

	Japan	U.K.	West Germany	Holland	France	Italy	U.S.
Ethylene							
No. of Producers	12	5	10	4	8	7	21
Total Capacity (1,000tpy)	6,227	2,090	4,608	2,670	2,700	2,132	19,745
Polyethylene							
No. of Producers	17	6	9	4	9	6	19
Total Capacity	2,558	728	2,386	673	1,369	1,270	9,600
Polypropylene							
No. of Producers	11	2	6	3	5	3	12
Total Capacity	1,175	340	395	178	265	1,750	2,750
Polystyrene							
No. of Producers	9	5	3	2	6	6	16
Total Capacity	801	253	605	—	555	500	2,315

Source: Data bases prepared by Industrial Bank of Japan and McKinsey & Co.

governments seeking to stake out a place in the sun of the new technology.

By 1980 the industry was crowded with giant producers poised to exploit the growth in demand (see table 1.1). But the tremors that some managements had perceived and responded to in the 1970s increased in intensity until a massive quake shocked the industry in 1980. Four major trends that had been slowly developing converged to convert what some managements had anticipated to be a prospect of prosperity into a scene of catastrophe. Feedstock prices increased, technology improved yields, the world economy entered a prolonged recession, and new sources of product were constructed in hydrocarbon-rich countries.

The Major Trends

Feedstock Prices

Prior to the escalation of oil and gas prices in the early 1970s, petrochemicals was a business of high fixed costs and low variable cost, roughly a seventy-thirty ratio. Several leading producers of the commodity plastics adopted strategies of building giant modern facilities and leveraging the financing of their cost with low-cost debt. By the early 1980s petrochemicals became a high variable cost business with feedstock and fuel cost eating up a much higher fraction of the final price. Variable costs were now 70 percent, total cost of a modern facility had increased, and the cost of debt was high. In other words, with the fixed cost of a facility unchanged or higher, the margin available to cover those costs and provide a profit was halved (see table 1.2).

Table 1.2
*Partial Recovery of Cost Escalation in
Final Price, 1970–1980*

	Percentage of Change
Fuel and Feedstock	+585%
Petrochemical Price	
Primary	+426%
Intermediate	+243%
Product	+161%

Source: Industry estimates.

A second major consequence of the rise in fuel and feedstock prices was that chemicals and plastics became more expensive relative to substitutes. Because penetration of the economy had already been extensive, the growth rate of chemicals dropped from 1.3 times the growth of GNP to 1.0—the same rate. In sum, higher prices meant lower profitability and slower growth.

Technology

At the same time that companies were scraping around for cash flow, new technology emerged that made dramatically better use of feedstock, fuel, and facilities. A leading example of such a break-through was Union Carbide's development of a low-pressure route to linear low-density polyethylene (LLDPE). The modified polyethylene molecule produced a stronger film, hence it was possible to substitute thinner film in existing uses. This in turn required less ethylene. Rapid penetration of LLDPE meant that ethylene would remain in excess supply even as markets grew. (In 1979, roughly 45 percent of ethylene was used in the production of polyethylene.) Because the new process was more efficient in the use of fuel and its capital cost was one-half a conventional facility, polyethylene producers all faced the potential obsolescence of their high-pressure capacity. Moreover, Dow, Du Pont, BP, and Char-bonnage du France Chimie (CdF Chimie) all raced to the market with alternative processes.[4]

Almost as challenging to capital budgets of companies already under economic pressure were tightening laws concerning the production and disposal of toxic substances. Although the indus-try's stance was supportive of improved health and safety, the diversion of scarce cash flow to modify new and existing facilities further depressed profitability.

Global Recession

A massive industry such as petrochemicals cannot grow when the GNP is stagnant. In the early 1980s the recession was espe-cially punishing—prolonged slow growth combined with de-celerating penetration, higher yields, and new capacity in Europe (built to meet the optimistic forecasts made in the mid-1970s) resulted in very sick businesses. For those companies such as

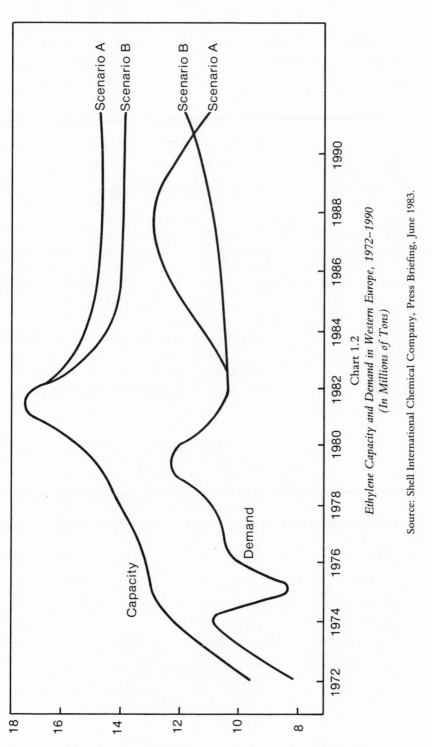

Chart 1.2

Ethylene Capacity and Demand in Western Europe, 1972–1990
(In Millions of Tons)

Source: Shell International Chemical Company, Press Briefing, June 1983.

Dow, who financed new capacity with debt, or Du Pont and Occidental, who financed acquisitions with debt, the low growth and high interest rates of the early 1980s were devastating. Chart 1.2 shows Shell's summary forecast of the European situation— excess supply into the 1990s.

Sources of Supply

As if these three forces were not enough, a fourth factor has developed in the last few years—new sources of supply. The nations that own the feedstocks—the Arabs, Canada, Indonesia, Mexico, and Norway—are all moving to capture some of the value added in the chemical industry by building ethylene crackers and derivative plants. Table 1.3 shows the plans of these countries in terms of capacity. While construction of some of these plants has been postponed, there is every reason to believe that when demand revives, these projects will be revived. Moreover, the Saudi projects are moving at impressive speed.

From a global economic perspective, it makes sense that a business 70 percent dependent on fuel and feedstock will develop where those raw materials are cheapest. All major studies of the industry's future trade pattern (e.g., Shell, U.S. Department of

Table 1.3
Planned Petrochemical Capacity
(In 1,000× Metric Tons)

	Ethylene	LDPE	HDPE	EDC**	Styrene	PP
Saudi Arabia	1,160	335	91	454	295	
Singapore	300	120	80			100
Indonesia	300	280	60	110		
Mexico*	1,600	360				
Canada*	2,000	910	375	190	510***	

*Mexican and Canadian figures are converted from billion lbs./year to metric tons/year.
**Ethylene Dichloride (polyvinyl chloride's precursor).
***Ethylbenzene (styrene's precursor).
Source: "Sabic Petrochemical Projects 1984," *The Economist,* 9 March, 1985, 68 and U.S. Department of Commerce, Office of Competitive Assessment, Assistant Secretary for Productivity, Technology, and Innovation, Technical Appendix to "The Medium- to Long-Range International Competitiveness of the United States Petrochemical Industry: A Competitive Assessment" (Washington, D.C.: Government Printing Office, 1982), sec. IV, 14, 15, 17, and 21.

Commerce, French Ministry of Industry, Chem Systems) forecast a shift in ethylene and derivative trade flows. OECD producers are expected to lose markets to the Arabian Gulf and Canada.

A more recent study by Chem Systems (a United Kingdom consulting group) commissioned by the Council of European Chemical Industry Federations (CEFIC) suggested where this new product would land. They estimated that 400,000 metric tons of commodity petrochemicals would reach Europe in 1987; 710,000 tons would reach Japan (as well as another 300,000 of other products); 540,000 tons would go to the rest of Asia and the Pacific; and 300,000 tons of methanol and ethanol would be imported to the United States.[5] In 1985, the first Saudi product arrived in Europe.

Both Europe and Japan are expected to become major importers of ethylene or derivatives. Together with the loss of export markets for all OECD producers, this means that growth in demand will be substantially constrained. For countries such as Germany and the United States that are major chemical exporters, the impact on companies and on the balance of payments can be severe. The U.S. petrochemical trade balance in 1981 was $8.3 billion (10 percent of shipments). Nonetheless U.S share of world organic chemicals[6] fell from 25.5 percent in 1970 to 16.9 percent in 1980. West Germany held just over 20 percent (see table 1.4).

The Need for Restructuring

The forces just described are large and sweeping in scope. Even the giant companies that populate the industry have been battered. One would expect some kind of restructuring to occur, such as some participants exiting so that over time capacity would come into rough balance with demand. This sort of shift in number and size of producers in an industry is what I mean by restructuring. Guiding this kind of shift in rough correspondence with indices of competitiveness (such as profit) is one of the most important tasks a market is supposed to accomplish.

But, if the market alone were at work, the industry has not behaved as one would have expected. While firms have exited the business, there seems to be a substantial willingness of companies to absorb major losses. This has been true in France and Italy where we have come to expect such things, and in Germany

Table 1.4
Percentage Share of World Exports—Organic Chemicals, 1970–1980
(Based on U.S. Dollar Value)

Year	U.S.	West Germany	Japan	Netherlands	U.K.	France
1970	25.5	20.7	9.5	8.8	7.7	6.6
1971	21.7	20.3	11.4	9.7	8.1	6.5
1972	20.4	19.6	12.1	11.2	7.6	6.5
1973	20.1	22.0	8.3	11.9	8.1	7.5
1974	18.0	21.5	10.1	13.2	9.0	7.0
1975	19.6	20.4	10.2	12.0	8.3	7.2
1976	19.9	21.1	9.3	12.7	8.6	6.5
1977	19.8	21.5	9.6	11.5	8.9	6.9
1978	14.8	21.8	9.6	11.5	9.3	10.8
1979	15.8	22.0	8.0	12.0	9.6	10.8
1980	16.9	21.2	7.8	13.8	10.3	10.6

Source: "Sabic Petrochemical Projects 1984," *The Economist,* 9 March, 1985, 68 and U.S. Department of Commerce, Office of Competitive Assessment, Assistant Secretary for Productivity, Technology, and Innovation, Technical Appendix to "The Medium- to Long-Range International Competitiveness of the United States Petrochemical Industry: A Competitive Assessment" (Washington, D.C.: Government Printing Office, 1982), 21, table 8.

where we have not. In Japan where we expect order and coherence there has been chaos and lack of cooperation (one chairman called it "stupid competition"). The willingness of major companies to bleed each other is awesome.

Companies have not only experienced accounting losses. Firms that invested in capacity prior to the changes in supply cost, technology, and demand growth might rationally conclude that they should continue operations as long as long-term prospects were brighter or they continued to earn positive cash contributions on their activities. But no brighter future exists and the current results have been dreadful. Even governments concerned with employment had to face the high cost of jobs in oversized state-owned companies. The research found that some, such as the Italians, were attempting to get hold of the situation to end the losses with capacity reduction and associated layoffs. But Charbonnage du France Chimie has plunged ahead, supported by government subsidies. On the other hand, firms in markets where governments had less of a role moved faster to change their position.

Table 1.5
Market Share of European HDPE Producers

	1970	1980
Hoechst	32.0	14.8
ENI	3.4	8.4
DSM	4.0	6.1

Source: Chart 1.3.

Table 1.5 and chart 1.3 which describe market share changes in HDPE help reveal some of what is happening in the industry as a whole. Chart 1.3 traces the evolution of HDPE capacity in Europe, Japan, and the United States from 1960–80. Table 1.5 notes the share of Hoechst in the European market for HDPE as well as that of key competitors. In interpreting the table, it is important to know that Hoechst is regarded as the leading producer in Europe based on its market position and technology; it is equally significant that ENI, the state-owned oil company of Italy, and Dutch State Mines (DSM) that so markedly increased their share are regarded as efficient but not leaders. Moreover, their new capacity was added when demand was stagnant.

A different picture can be observed in the United States. Here, certain chemical companies have lost position to others, but especially to the chemical company subsidiaries of oil companies. For example, chart 1.3 shows that U.S. chemical companies dropped from 70 percent of the high-density market in 1960 to 32 percent in 1980. In the process, Grace, Monsanto, Celanese, and Hercules exited the business. Finally, in Japan, the original three competitors now share the market with eight others, the smallest of which has significant absolute scale.

Restructuring has been taking place then, but it has involved more than the number and size of the competitors, it has involved the kind of company participating. There has been a shift from private chemical companies toward state-owned enterprises and oil companies. Despite the restructuring that has taken place, every forecast indicates that capacity will continue to exceed demand for a long time to come. Either the market is not working the way it is expected to, or it is taking a very long time to do its work.

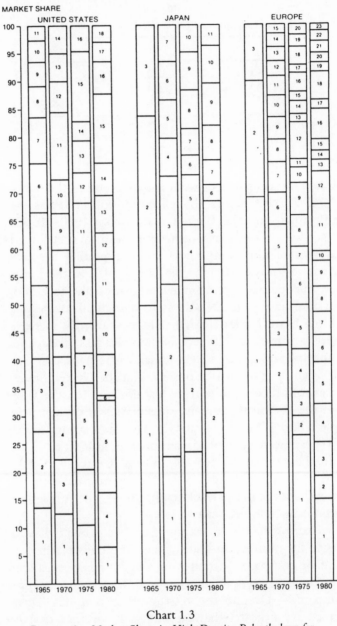

Chart 1.3
*Comparative Market Share in High-Density Polyethylene for
U.S., Japan, and Europe*

Source: McKinsey & Co. Chemical Industry Data Base; Mitsui & Co.; Parpinelli
Tecnon.

UNITED STATES (shaded area denotes oil companies)

Key	Company Name	Type
1	Union Carbide	Chemical
2	W.R. Grace	Chemical
3	Celanese	Chemical
4	National Petrochemical	Chemical
5	Phillips	Oil
6	Hercules	Chemical
7	Du Pont	Chemical
8	Monsanto	Chemical
9	Dow	Chemical
10	Sinclair Koppers	Oil
11	Allied	Chemical
12	Chemplex	Chemical
13	Gulf	Oil
14	Amoco	Oil
15	Soltex Polymer	Chemical
16	Atlantic Richfield	Oil
17	American Hoechst	Chemical
18	Cities Service	Oil

JAPAN

Key	Company Name
1	Showa Denko
2	Mitsui Petrochemical
3	Nippon Petrochemical
4	Mitsubishi Chemical
5	Asahi Chemical
6	Mitsubishi Petrochemical
7	Chisso Petrochemical
8	Shin-Daikyowa
9	Idemitsu Petrochemical
10	Nissan-Maruzen
11	Tonen Petrochemical

EUROPE

Key	Company Name	Country
1	Hoechst	Germany
2	Shell Row	Netherlands/UK
3	Dutch State Mines	Netherlands
4	Vestolen	Germany
5	British Petroleum Chemical	UK/France
6	Ruhr Chemie	Germany
7	BASF/Row	Germany/UK
8	Solvay	Italy/France
9	Belgium Polyolefins	Belgium
10	Manolene	France
11	Sarda Polemeri	Italy
12	Montedison	Italy
13	Calatrava	Spain
14	AtoChem	France
15	Rumianca Sud	Italy
16	Dow Iberia	Spain
17	Wacker Chemie	Germany
18	Unifos Kemi	Sweden
19	Anic	Italy
20	Sir	Italy
21	Taqsa	Spain
22	Norpoletin	Norway
23	Empresa de Polimeros	Portugal

Chart 1.3 (*cont.*)

The Response by Companies and Governments

During the period 1980–83, in response to the forces described, some 20 percent of OECD ethylene capacity was shut down; but construction added 12 percent. Reductions of derivative capacity were also significant. Perhaps equally interesting was the decline in the number of manufacturers. Chart 1.4 shows the European restructuring of polyvinyl chloride in detail.

Companies

For the producers of commodity petrochemicals the recent period has been a disaster, huge losses with no prospect of an end to competitive pressures. Many of these, however, faced high shutdown costs. As part of this study, I conducted interviews with top managers of the major companies of the industry. They *all* experienced the problems outlined below in the conceptual context of contemporary thinking about strategy. They knew that their task was to reposition their company so that strength in feedstock, technology, product, or market could be translated into profit. Otherwise, exit was appropriate. But whether they chose exiting or repositioning, they faced major problems.

1. *Integration Problems.* It is hard to shut down capacity for one product without hurting the economics of others that are linked by chemistry, marketing, or production site economics.
2. *Finance.* Many of the moves that firms needed to make required capital that they lacked because of the long period of losses, the high interest rates, and low stock prices. External markets were closed, and prices could not be raised to generate profit without a concerted suspension of competition.
3. *Competition.* There were too many firms with staying power.
4. *Regulation.* It has been traditional in the industrial markets of the West to cartelize when conditions made competition untenable and exit was unattractive or impossible, but the antitrust laws of certain countries and of the European Economic Community blocked efforts of this kind.
5. *Social Obligation.* In several countries, legal or moral obligations to the labor force or small customers seemed to block needed cost reductions and shutdowns.

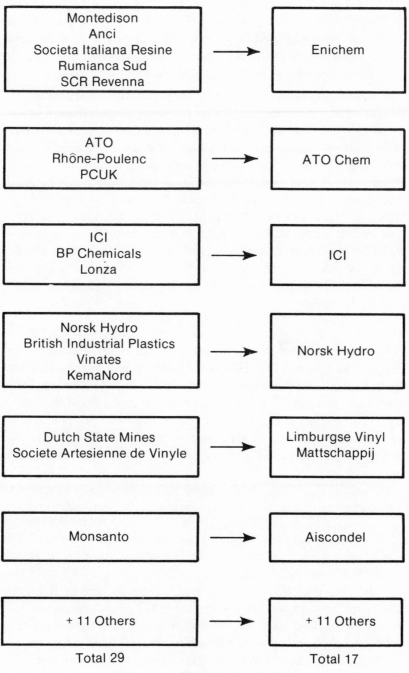

Chart 1.4
Examples of Restructuring of PVC Producers

6. *State Policies*. Either as owners or competitors, certain governments demonstrated a commitment to take a permanent significant position in the industry despite a weak initial—or only prospective—economic base in the industry.

As the companies organized to examine their portfolios, one firm after another recognized that they had to withdraw from all or part of the business. Others concluded that they must acquire their competition or remain ineffectively small. And still others sought profit in specialties or end-product businesses. Rhône-Poulenc (R-P) sold its petrochemicals to Elf Aquitaine. ICI and BP traded weak positions in LDPE and PVC so that they could be strong in the businesses they kept. Dow acquired the drug business of Richardson-Merrill; sold its petrochemical businesses in Japan, Korea, and Yugoslavia; and withdrew from its part of a Saudi polyethylene project. Union Carbide emphasized the licensing of its LLDPE process by organizing a service business to support its licensees.

Governments

For several governments the crisis of the 1980s was not something to be ignored. Initially, several intervened in the 1950s and 1960s to stimulate the development of the industry. These governments were owners, bankers, or observer/regulators of the industry. For them the existence and shape of their nation's petrochemical industry was not merely corporate, but an issue of national strategic significance. The excerpt below from a French study is typical.

> Therefore, there should be actions to promote adaptation of the [French] industry to the new environmental conditions and new developments in the chemical industry; these actions should aim to reduce the upstream dependence of the industry, to enhance new product development, and to reinforce the international position of French chemical companies.[7]

Moreover in 1983, Europe's economy was reeling from the effects of the two oil shocks, the extended global recession, and high U.S. interest rates. In steel and fibers there were examples of concerted action to take capacity off the market so that the remaining competitors might survive. The European Commission's Industry Directorate (DG IV) under Viscount Davignon was supportive when asked for help in restructuring by two major petrochemical producers. Most of the major producers cooperated in subscribing to a detailed analysis of their problems by the private consulting firm, Chem Systems, that explicitly displayed their relative position, cracker by cracker and derivative unit by derivative unit on what were called "survival matrices."[8]

In Japan, new leadership at the chemical desk in MITI collaborated with the prestigious Industrial Structure Council (ISC) to study the apparently permanent weakness of certain depressed industries in Japan such as aluminum, ferro alloys, fertilizers, fibers, and petrochemicals.

Inside the U.S. federal government, pressure built for protection of petrochemical producers, as studies of U.S competitiveness and trade were conducted by the Department of Commerce and the International Trade Commission (ITC). There was as well a major petrochemical dumping suit tried before the ITC and protectionist legislation filed on Capitol Hill.

For governments the petrochemical problem was similar but not the same as that for steel and fibers. Balance of payments and, perhaps, national security were involved, but the employment issues were quite small. Labor accounted for only 8–9 percent of chemical industry costs and consequently employment in the industry was less significant on a national basis. Nonetheless, regional issues could be important, as in Sardinia where 11,000 were employed by ENI or in Ludwigshafen where BASF employed 45,000.

The range of government response was dramatic.

France nationalized the entire French-owned portion of the chemical industry and regrouped the pieces into near monopolies. For example, Elf produced all the commodity petrochemicals discussed in this study except for some units of CdF Chimie and these were under consideration for movement to Elf.

Italy consolidated six companies into two, consolidated all of the commodity plastics save polystyrene and polypropylene into ENI, and reprivatized Montedison.

Germany's cartel office kept a close watch on the independent moves of gigantic BASF, Bayer, and Hoechst.

In sum, petrochemicals provides examples of the most extreme problems faced by manufacturing industry in the last decades of the century. For managements the lessons have been harsh, even bitter. With rare exceptions, no individual company could devise a competitive strategy that would make itself profitable. The entire structure of the industry had to be reshaped before individual action would suffice.

For the restructuring to be accomplished in ways satisfactory to the individual companies, managements found it necessary to deal directly with competitors to plan swaps or supply agreements. But as they contemplated or pursued action along these lines executives found themselves dealing with government politicians and technocrats in unaccustomed forums and in threatening circumstances. Although the conventional market provided no solution to their company's competitive problem, the behavior of governments over time has tended to aggravate rather than lessen their corporate difficulties. In fact the oft-criticized benevolent neglect of the U.S. government looked attractive to most chemical company managements everywhere.

The history, economy, and situation of Europe, Japan, and the United States that provided context for the companies are dramatically different. Nonetheless, it was striking how patterns emerged in the way managements dealt with their adversity.

In a first phase of activity, they went about recognizing the nature of the crisis and preparing their company for action that might rectify the situation. In this "preparation phase" of the restructuring process, the companies changed leadership, structure, and management systems; sought information; used consultants; and fenced with their governments in similar ways. Next, they devised plans, deals, and reorganizations that reduced the number of players in their markets. This "concentration phase" was accomplished in noticeably different ways in Europe, Japan, and the United States. Finally, once the structure of the industry provided the potential for profit, the managements moved to rationalize physical capacity by shutting down less efficient units.

As this book goes to press, the "rationalization phase" is still underway throughout the world. It is interesting that the progress is slowest where governments have intervened most in the past, and especially where the companies have not done the hard work of reorganizing themselves in preparation for industrywide restructuring.

A detailed understanding of the work involved in this three-part process constitutes the lessons of the study. They are important because excess capacity and global competition are the typical condition of today's markets for tradeable goods and services. If we can learn how managers dealt successfully with the tribulations of one industry, perhaps we can help the managers in another. It is to these lessons that we turn.

NOTES

1. A brief and simple description of ethylene and its derivatives as well as the processes by which they are manufactured is available in the Glossary.
2. Estimated from the U.S. Department of Commerce, Office of Competitive Assessment, Assistant Secretary for Productivity, Technology, and Innovation, Technical Appendix to "The Medium- to Long-Range International Competitiveness of the United States Petrochemical Industry: A Competitive Assessment" (Washington, D.C.: Government Printing Office, 1982), sec. I, 6, table 1.
3. Another 10 percent of ethylene is converted to ethylene oxide which in turn is processed to ethylene glycol. Glycol is used both as antifreeze and as the raw material for polyester fiber.
4. In the late fall of 1983, Union Carbide announced an advanced version of the process that permitted the manufacture of high- and low-density polyethylene and polypropylene with the same plant.
5. Chem Systems International Ltd., "Middle East Impact Study: Draft Report," prepared for CEFIC (January 1984), sec. III, 7, table III, B. 5.
6. A more inclusive category than petrochemicals.
7. Commission de l'Industrie, Rapport du Groupe de Travail: VIIIème plan "L'Industrie Chimique et Ses Prolongements Vers Les Bio-Technologies," (n.p., 19 June 1980), 2.
8. This unusual display of competitive position is discussed in chapter 10.

2

Patterns Observed

Introduction

Petrochemicals is a vital industry experiencing a massive crisis. The consequences of competitive behavior by the participating firms have been devastating. The usual result in such a situation is a call for industrial policy by individual national governments. If the call is heeded, protectionism and subsidies follow in short order.[1] But if we analyze the experience of the chemical industries described in chapters 5–11, we find the basis for a very different conclusion. Individual governments have not always helped. Their interventions are often associated with the sources of the problems rather than the solutions, especially when they have involved the application of detailed microeconomic tools of the sort associated with popular treatments of industrial revitalization.

The basic issue is that many nations are trying to increase their national wealth by growing industrial exports rapidly in circumstances where total world markets are growing slowly. Head-on competition is nonproductive. What is needed is an adjustment of growth objectives to the size of markets and a restructuring of product portfolios to the changing needs of the world economy.

Such a massive restructuring, however, requires basic changes in the way things have been done in the companies. But, the past represents a series of solutions to problems having to do with company strategy, organization, and patterns of staffing to which managers of existing companies are almost always committed as authors, designers, and participants. Acknowledging the need for significant change implies that the previous strategy has failed, that whatever equilibrium there is among the demands made by organizational subunits will have to be upset, that sources of finance will have to be alerted to danger. In short, facing up to difficulties means that top management may have failed. Much previous research suggests that for all of these reasons such changes rarely take place easily.

What we shall see in the companies examined later is that crisis forced on them a review of their management, and that new management then used new structure and portfolio systems for strategic analysis of the individual business units, relying on credible sources of outside information to make unpalatable conclusions legitimate.* Having done their homework, however, these managements then discovered that they could not cure their business problems within the context of the existing industry structure. Changing the structure of an entire industry posed a new sort of challenge since interventions of this kind are normally thought to be the prerogative of governments. Government politicians and technocrats take for granted their right to be involved in the decision making when issues clearly extend beyond the boundaries of a single company's interest and encompass an entire industry. But their competence seldom extends as obviously. For business leaders dealing with such situations, the engagements with government can be intensely frustrating.[2]

The most fundamental findings that can be derived from this study of the petrochemical industry are implied in the preceding paragraph. *Industry structure is strategic, in the sense that management action can alter industry configuration directly with consequences vital to the firm. Managing a change in industry structure means working in a highly politicized environment.* These arguments are developed in this chapter by focusing first on a sequence of actions observed in companies across Europe, Japan, and the United States. A cycle can be observed in which crisis is acknowledged, new management chosen, new company structure adopted, portfolio analysis carried out, and credible sources of outside information used to facilitate the recognition and diagnosis of the need for restructuring. Chapter 3 proposes how management should think about this sequence.

---

*In chapters 2–4, a number of examples are cited from the restructuring of the petrochemical industry. As well, managers are quoted. In most instances, there is no citation or note. Instead the examples are described more fully in chapters 5–11. This convention has been adopted to avoid breaking up the text with continual forward references.

The Role of Crisis

In Union Carbide, British Petroleum (BP), Imperial Chemical Industries (ICI), Montedison, Dow, Ato-Chloe and Rhône-Poulenc, and the various Japanese manufacturers studied, there were always individual managers who perceived the fundamental strategic problems facing their companies, but they were not necessarily the leaders of their company nor did their colleagues find them persuasive.[3] As is evident from chart 1.2 in chapter 1, it has often been difficult to make money in the commodity chemicals business. One U.S. executive called the business policies of the industry a "disease." The problem has been capacity in excess of demand coupled with marginal cost pricing. During those periods when there was order in the market, money could be made. The low-cost leaders, such as Dow, were able to make money during the entire period. For almost all companies there were some good times when they earned profits. When management asked about the bad times, they were told that things would improve as soon as "new technology" was assimilated or as soon as new competitors learned what their costs really were.

One by one the companies reached the conclusion that business would never get better unless there was fundamental change throughout the entire industry. Crisis forced the governing boards of companies to act. At Union Carbide, after a billion dollars of investment in the 1960s produced negligible incremental profit while Dow surged past them in size and profitability, new leadership was chosen. A decade later in European companies similar actions took place. At BP the horrendous losses of the chemical business provided the impetus for the selection of Robert Horton as managing director of the chemical company. At ICI John Harvey-Jones was called on to assemble a new team. Mario Schimberni emerged at the top of Montedison supported by a new assessment of the need for profitability by the Mediobanca. The socialist government acceded, faced by a disastrous drain on government-owned banks. Dow moved suddenly to reshape its portfolio in response to the squeeze on profits posed by high interest charges and lower relative energy prices. The French concluded that unbearable losses would not stop unless the industry was restructured and modernized. And Japan's MITI concluded that dramatic action was required before company managers would acknowledge the crisis and act to cut unsupportable losses.

What happened was that a fundamental shift external to the industry made it apparent to those within it that the industry would no longer produce the kinds of profits experienced in the past. No longer was it necessary to recognize that internal strategic analyses had been inadequate. Now one could face up to "the changes that began in 1973" and get on with it. An industrywide crisis is always easier to acknowledge than one whose genesis and effects are specific to a particular firm and management.

The Role of New Management

It is significant that the action taken by owners in most instances was to change leadership. As with other disinvestment situations, it was apparent that the same men who had made the commitments that led to the crisis could not find it in themselves to lead the way out.[4] It is characteristic of the chemical industry that the companies were rich enough in management talent that the new leaders often were selected from within the ranks. But just as frequently the new chief replaced an entire cadre. One described the changes as "a purge."

The new executives typically represented a different approach to management. Trained to think in terms of profit rather than engineering process they could bring more discipline to the analysis and control of what had become gigantic organizations. Whereas their predecessors had tended to be engineers who had grown up during the "can't do any wrong as long as you build" period of petrochemistry's growth, the new men often had financial backgrounds. The exceptions to this particular pattern are instructive in that they really do not contradict the point. Dow has had a financial management actively involved with operating management since the 1930s.[5] Orrifice, the present chief executive, has a strong financial outlook. Whereas other companies were losing money in commodities, Dow was winning. It was the leveraging of their position, the vertical integration, and the joint ventures that made their position vulnerable when conditions shifted in 1980. At that point they sought a rebalancing of their portfolio and shifted people and structure accordingly.

There is a point here worth addressing. It is fashionable to interpret authors such as William Abernathy and Robert Hayes to be arguing for the previous sort of engineering, and manufacturing, oriented managers who were removed and arguing against the profit-oriented managers that were critical to achieving change. Presumably there is no problem. Even if the signal of a problem is a financial projection of losses, the critics of a financial perspective would not argue for committing resources to projects that were strategically unsound.[6] An argument that environmental shifts change the profitability of economic enterprise in ways that production and product-oriented managers often miss is not a defense of shortsightedness. But those who argue that companies should continue to invest in industries for "the long run," regardless of any market justification, should seek employment on the staff of Arthur Scargill's British Mineworker's Union.

The Japanese are harder to interpret in the terms discussed here. Because of the way in which their business activity is managed, one would not expect dramatic change. Almost always the structure of Japanese companies is centralized. "Bottom-up" forces are powerful, but they are very sensitive to the wishes of top management. Consensus is indeed a critical prelude to action, but consensus will often form around top management's wishes and Japanese leaders are not reluctant to say no. During my research, Japanese managers commented frequently that there was less change in the way things were being managed than in Europe because there was less need for it.[7]

Moreover, the Japanese were not likely to change leaders in order to change direction. Things are not done that way unless there is a crisis clearly attributable to the weakness of an individual, (and even then there might be a face-saving way to avoid such a move). What had to be done was to change the leaders' perception of the circumstances they were facing and the order of magnitude of the changes needed so that the companies would then go about designing the appropriate specific responses. And since new law, especially forgiveness from antitrust provisions, would be needed, the public and Diet had to be educated so that they would accept the necessity for the dramatic moves the companies made. In other words, the management of the companies did change, but not because there were new managers.

Finally, there were new managers, not so much at the top as in the division or works management posts. But the reason they were new was not that there was crisis but because the Japanese companies tend to move upper-level managers with some frequency. To the extent that new skills were desired in a position, no purge was required. Rather, the right sort of man was selected at the next opportunity for rotation.

Looking to the Japanese results one finds the same reorientation of management as in Europe and the United States, but, as in most other things Japanese, the objective was accomplished by different means. The lesson, however, is clear: it takes some version of new leadership to exit a business.

The Role of New Structure

It is a basic tenet of management theory that the implementation of a new strategy requires a new structure. As well, it has been shown that a company's organization, resource allocation, and compensation systems substantially shape the new strategic options generated for top management consideration.[8]

In a large organization the analysis and planning required in order to produce actionable plans, the building of consensus and educating that have to go on so that plans can be accepted, and most importantly the inventing of new options for corporate action that bypass historic obstacles must all go on at divisional and departmental levels of the organization. But if it is a new strategic vision that must be articulated, such as one that involves restructuring the very activities being carried out by the divisions or departments, it is almost always necessary to reorganize first. In other words, structure shapes strategy by providing the context within which analysis and planning go on. "If you ask a Navy man, you get a Navy point of view."

If a new vision requires a new point of view, then reorganization is usually necessary. Union Carbide has been experimenting with the structure of its chemical businesses since the mid-1960s and may have been the first to use the "business team" concept. But it was only in 1969, after the crisis in profits was recognized and new leadership elevated, that the importance of breaking the influence of the traditional engineering, production, and sales functions was recognized. In the deepest sense, a profit orientation could not drive planning as long as concern for physical process dominated the thinking of those who managed resources.

This was the same problem Robert Horton of BP faced when an engineer showed him a wonderful facility but didn't know whether it was economic. The management of ICI quoted in Chapter 7 speaks to the same problem. The managers at Montedison reorganized in order to pin profit responsibility on the shoulders of division managements. The managers at Dow have been building worldwide product divisions alongside the commodity-oriented regional structure in order to manage agricultural chemicals, pharmaceuticals, and other specialties.

Again the Japanese have a different way of doing things, though in this instance not that different. Restructuring was less critical because the companies were less integrated. The production facilities are based on complex assemblies of individually owned and operated units, called "combinatos." This structure means that individual pieces of the petrochemical business were already separately incorporated and, perhaps, separately financed. Management structure did not interfere as much in the recognition or response to the profit crisis. On the other hand the financial/legal structure was paralyzing. It was most certainly the paralysis that led MITI to convene the Industrial Structure Council and the Diet to pass new laws.

Despite the legal restructuring of their companies, the French have not yet completed the reorganization of their producing units. In 1985 managers elsewhere in Europe were waiting patiently, but not with great hope. At this point, there have been changes in the legal and financial structure of the French-owned companies. But the kind of consolidation represented by a shift to profit-responsible subsidiaries with independent balance sheets (viz. Montedison) is not the sort of action currently expected in France. In the spring of 1985, Atochem claimed to be rationalized and in balance, but CdF Chimie remained independent. In fact, the Boston Consulting Group report commissioned by the French government emphasizes the rationalization of production platforms rather than businesses.

In 1983 one French company planner noted the role of government in his industry:

> We have had socialist presences for fifty years. So we never decided to close a plant. So now we have plants all over. It would take a very clever man to solve the problem. So far we discuss aggregating plants, not a strategy.
> We have no MITI. The technocrats try to control the industry. The

Ministry of Industry behaves as if it could control the industry. But there are too many forces: the ministers, the chambre, and the many companies.[9]

And a key manager in the French industry concluded that

We must be international. We try to manage as Europeans. But we are still French. Good engineering and good business must be simple. The American virtue is simplicity.

We will continue to move slowly because money is available. After you nationalize a company, you can't say that the state is bankrupt.[10]

In short, the situation of the French industry shows that it is hard to get attention paid to profit when business is not organized so that profit is measured or managers are held ultimately accountable.

The Role of Portfolio Analysis

Along with the structure to manage businesses independently has come the capability to analyze and control these subunits in their relation to the corporation's goals and resources. Perhaps the most recent advance in strategic thought, the business portfolio framework, has provided top management a way to understand the relationship among the competing needs and opportunities of its constituent businesses in strategic terms. Previously, managements had been asked by financial theorists to believe that the financial demands of their divisions were nothing more than a series of capital projects that could be analyzed independently in terms of expected rate of return on investment. Once managers came to understand that they had to allocate capital among businesses with different patterns of cash flow rather than among projects, then it was essential that a new framework for thought be created. The answer was the business portfolio.

In some sense, return on economic investment is obviously the goal any economic enterprise must pursue. But in an industry where major capital commitments have to be made over long time periods, the simple formulas for return on investment mask the complex judgments that underlie the estimates of future profitability. Each of the many approaches to portfolio analysis substituted a system that categorized business units according to market attractiveness and competitive position. The different frameworks all provided top management with a way of comparing the claims for funds made on the corporate coffers by widely differing subunits. At least as important, the use of the process quickly identified irredeemable competitive positions.[11] Although the framework was developed to help top managers with too many rapidly growing businesses, it turned out to be a vital tool for chemical company managements that were trying to establish priorities among too many businesses to fix at once.

It was in the process of portfolio analysis at BP that the long-term weakness of their polyvinyl chloride (PVC) business was revealed relative to the strength of their polyethylene position. With very limited financial resources, it was obvious that PVC should go. As carried out at Montedison, portfolio analysis was used to force exit decisions. It was clear that the cost of fixing each of their businesses exceeded any possibility of funding. Portfolio analysis at Hoechst generated the impetus for managers to exit from low-density polyethylene. At Union Carbide the recognition that other divisions of the company enjoyed strategically sounder positions in more attractive industries provided the impetus for withdrawal from plastics in Europe.

There is an essential point to be noted here. In principle, the calculation of return on investment ought to provide exactly the right basis for comparing the attractiveness of businesses. The problem is that it is too abstract and too gross. All the key assumptions about demand and supply are buried in a ratio. The various frameworks of portfolio analysis that are currently popular emphasize the strength (or weakness) of a unit's competitive position and the funds that will be required to maintain or strengthen that position as the market grows or shrinks. This approach helps managers at lower levels of multibusiness firms to see that no feasible sequence of incrementally profitable investments will restore the long-term strategic position of their division or department. It is only with this sort of understanding that cutbacks become legitimate. The issue of legitimacy is especially important where, for political or cultural reasons, permanent employment is the norm.

The Role of a Credible Source of Outside Information

In the previous paragraphs, portfolio analysis has been described in organizational terms as a force for objectivity in a situation where individual managers and groups within a company have parochial stakes in the status quo even when profits are meager. The same problem exists in much more virulent form between firms. It is virtually a disease among countries.

In the United States, when a company loses money we expect it to go out of business. Often the company first tries to get help from its bank or the government, but generally, if a business is losing money and there is no chance of its position improving it is shut down. The recognition of the existence of a crisis may take new management. But a large, free, competitive market and a vigorous stock market provide regular evidence of a firm's competitiveness and profitability. Some believe the measurement to be too shortsighted or short-term oriented, but the evidence is there and when a management chooses to act on it, there are few barriers.

The same is not the case in Europe and Japan. In both places companies are perceived to have commitments to their employees and their country that go beyond what is expected in the United States. A company is seen to have obligations to the communities where its plants are located to provide for their long-term livelihood. As well, their size, growth rate, and product mix may be part of a national industrial strategy. The clearest example of this is provided by the Japanese managers interviewed who discussed the problems of providing employment for workers in other parts of the company. But the most provocative insight was provided by a manager who noted that "Overcapacity was part of the reason for the Japanese miracle. We always had overcapacity."

Under such circumstances, managers' natural desire to improve or fix the portion of the business for which they are responsible rather than withdraw or cut back is reinforced by a sense of social obligation as well as a belief that one's effort, even if loss-making, is part of a long-term national strategy. Not only is cutting back unattractive, it is unpatriotic! Before managers in that sort of mind-set turn their effort to planning a withdrawal, they have to be persuaded that it is right to do so.

For this purpose outside, expert, and even government-sanctioned studies are often required. This was part of the importance in Japan of MITI's intervention and of the work of the Industrial Structure Council. It was also the role played by the Italian Ministry of Industry and the Mediobanca when they sanctioned layoffs. It was what people were waiting for in France. But as long as the published strategic plan of CdF Chimie includes the French balance of payments as a corporate objective, they may have to wait a long time.

Interestingly, in Germany where the key firms are private and committed to being profitable, some confusion around the politics of employment seems to have delayed their moves toward rationalization. The issue at BASF is clearest. They are the principal source of employment in Ludwigshafen, and they do not wish to aggravate a delicate political situation in Bavaria. In other German companies, dependence on the goodwill of the Ministry of Industry in profitable nonchemical businesses may affect the moves made in less profitable chemicals.

Under such circumstances, where national strategy or merely strong political forces seem to demand expansion or justify the status quo, it is very important to have a credible source of outside information documenting the need for exit. Something more than the profit calculations of managers will be needed to change the mind-set of committed parties inside and outside the company. In effect, there will be no crisis until a disinterested, credible source announces its existence.

If publicly acceptable data describing crisis can be very important for managers in individual firms wishing to cut back, it may be even more essential in persuading a group of competitors that it is in their collective interest to cut back. The problem is loved by theoreticians who call it the "prisoner's dilemma." Two actors who understand that they are best off if they cooperate will act selfishly as long as the payoff for competitive behavior is higher than the payoff resulting from unilateral, and therefore highly uncertain, attempts at cooperation. In a situation such as that existing in commodity plastics markets, a unilateral decision by one firm to cut back can have the effect of helping a competitor. True, the firm cutting back rids itself of losses, but unless it exits the business it may find itself faced with a stronger, even expanding competitor. In the worst case, strength gained by a competitor in the business one has exited is transferred to help with the attack on a new front. Unless a company can be assured that the competitor will also cut back, it makes sense to stay in the market and fight, despite the losses.

For all competitors to agree to cut back, assuming it is legal to do so, they must all be persuaded of the necessity for cutbacks.

Each firm must believe that there is a crisis. In the early 1980s a multicompany-sponsored study of ethylene and derivatives entrepreneured by the consulting firm, Chem Systems, and a similar study sponsored by nine producers under the dispensation of Viscount Davignon served to provide European companies with detailed objective evidence of a crisis. This was also the role of a trip to visit the distressed European manufacturers that MITI organized for the chief executives of the top twelve petrochemical producers in order to persuade them of the seriousness of the Japanese situation.

There were also more conventional efforts at exhortation, and, while they may have been useful, these appear to have been less important in bringing change. A European conference of chemical manufacturers sponsored by Dow in 1982 was certainly aimed at getting the producers in Europe to recognize that because of the structural origins of the overcapacity problem it would not go away. And a speech in 1982 to the annual meeting of the Council of European Chemical Industry Federations (CEFIC) by J. H. Choufoer, a top executive at Shell, had the same objective. But the call by strong firms for weak firms to get their houses in order seems to have had less impact than studies by credible, disinterested groups that documented the problem in detail.

The role identified here, that of the independent expert producing a comprehensive, objective view of the industry's condition, is one of the more interesting common features to be observed in this study. In two other important cases where cutbacks have been managed, the same function has been filled by an outsider—in the development of the European synthetic fibers agreement and in the U.K. foundry business. It is a vital function that needs much more consideration.[12]

For company managers the impact of credible descriptions of their industry in crisis is that it frees them for action. No longer is it their own incompetence that has hurt their company (although that may be the case), it is an industrywide problem. They can accept the fundamental findings of this study: (1) The structure of the industry must be altered before conventional competition will generate healthy consequences; (2) In order to change an entire industry's structure, it is necessary to deal with the government. Structure is strategic and strategy is political.

NOTES

1. Organization for Economic Cooperation and Development, "Positive Adjustment Policies: Managing Structural Change" (Paris: OECD, 1983), 7–8, 59, 111.
2. Joseph L. Bower, *The Two Faces of Management* (Boston: Houghton Mifflin, 1983), 46–66, 86–113.
3. In fact one European manager showed me a study prepared as early as 1972 by planners from five companies working jointly that anticipated the problems of the decade and called for collective capacity management.
4. S. Clark Gilmour, "The Divestment Decision Process" (Ph.D. diss., Harvard Business School, 1973); Richard G. Hamermesh, "The Corporate Response to Divisional Profit Crises" (Ph.D. diss., Harvard Business School, 1976); Brent D. Wilson, "Disinvestment of Foreign Subsidiaries by U.S. Multinational Companies" (Ph.D. diss., Harvard Business School, 1979).
5. Richard R. Ellsworth, "Corporate Strategy and Capital Structure Policies: A Descriptive Study" (Ph.D. diss., Harvard Business School, 1980).
6. Although Robert H. Hayes and David A. Garvin come perilously close to this in their article, "Managing As If Tomorrow Mattered," *Harvard Business Review* 60 (May–June 1982), 7–79.
7. The point is usually discussed by careful students of Japanese management. See, for example, M. Y. Yoshino. *Japan's Managerial System: Tradition and Innovation* (Cambridge, Mass.: MIT Press, 1968), 225–53.
8. Joseph L. Bower, *Managing the Resource Allocation Process: A Study of Corporate Planning and Investment* (Boston: Harvard Business School, 1970), 66–82, 281–319; Alfred D. Chandler, Jr., *Strategy and Structure* (Garden City, N.Y.: Doubleday & Co., 1942), 283–323; Paul R. Lawrence and Jay W. Lorsch, *Organization and Environment* (Boston: Harvard Business School, 1967), 185–210; Rosabeth Kanter. *The Change Masters: Innovation for Productivity in the American Corporation* (New York: Simon & Schuster, 1982), 69–102, 129–156; Robert A. Burgelman, "A Model of the Interaction of Strategic Behavior, Corporate Context, and the Context of Strategy," *Academy of Management Review* 8, no. 1 (1983), 61–70 and "A Process Model of Internal Corporate Venturing in the Major Diversified Firm," *Administration Science Quarterly,* 28 (1983), 223–244.
9. Interview with French planner, April 1983.
10. Interview with French manager, February 1983.
11. Philippe C. Haspeslagh, "Portfolio Planning Approaches and the Strategic Management Process in Diversified Industrial Companies," (Ph.D. diss., Harvard Business School, 1983). See also, Richard Hamermesh, *Making Strategy Work* (New York: John Wiley, 1986).
12. See R. W. Shaw and S. A. Shaw. "Excess Capacity and Rationalization in the West European Synthetic Fibres Industry," *Journal of Industrial Economics,* (December 1983), 150–166; Charles Baden Fuller and R. Hill, "Industry Strategies for Alleviating Excess Capacity: The Case of the Lazard Scheme for UK Steel Castings," working paper, London Business School, October 1984.

3
Lessons from Petrochemicals

Introduction

"Unity in command. Diversity in council."

Cyrus the Great

"Am I a Bureaucrat or a Manager?"

A French chemical company executive

At least from the time the words above were attributed to Cyrus, those concerned with the problems of management have echoed their message. The leader, working with his organization, is accountable for its success. The point is put quite starkly by Alfred Sloan, Jr., in his autobiography when he quotes from a 1919 organization study, "The responsibility attached to the chief executive of each operation shall in no way be limited. Each organization headed by its chief executive shall be complete in every necessary function and enable[d] to exercise its full initiative and logical development."[1] Fifty years later, the same point is argued by Kenneth Andrews in his classic treatise on corporate strategy, "Corporate presidents are responsible for everything that goes on in their organizations" and "Chief executives . . . are first and probably least pleasantly persons who are responsible for results attained in the present as designated by plans made previously."[2]

The most startling feature of the strategic situation facing chemical company managements is that they find it very difficult to devise any program of action their particular company can take by itself other than withdrawal from the business that has the prospect of returning profits on their investment higher than the cost of the capital. Sometimes, by trimming here and there they can make their way to break even. But the long-term competitive situation is so severe that long-term profits seem a very problematic prospect.

One manager summed up the strategic and organizational problems neatly:

> As we look ahead, conditions will not get better. The # 1's won't get bigger, and the 3–5's will fall out. The driving force will be inexpensive foreign material. You can be as lean and mean as you want. It won't change things.
>
> The guy who gets control of the channels of distribution; the guy who has an alliance with some offshore people; he will have an advantage.
>
> Right now we're all niching, value adding. It means with limited resources, you have a piece of something that is declining. You end up as traders.
>
> As this happens, all of the skill centers that make you low cost become questionable. It's bad news for them. But it's good news for traders, marketers, and distribution. Organizationally that means you get a patchwork quilt that can be a nightmare.[3]

To remedy the situation it is necessary to deal with one's competitors in order to change the structure of the industry so that normal competition yields healthy companies, not basket cases. But in some countries this is illegal, and in all countries, collective efforts to influence industry conditions means working with government managers. This often involves company managements in bureaucratic, legislative, and sometimes, electoral politics. For most company executives this necessitates acquiring a new set of skills.

The key ideas that help to make sense of the complex changes going on in the petrochemical industry are that industry structure has to be modified, and influencing that process brings business and government managers into the same arena during the process of restructuring the companies and the industry.

Structure Is Strategic

In the contemporary United States, it often seems that the notion of competition that permeates our thinking about the economy is derived from very simple models of conflict. In fact, it is common for the metaphor of competitive athletics to be used in describing business activity. Companies have "game plans"; the goal is "winning"; *Institutional Investor* ranks the "top ten" money managers; Coke and Pepsi have a "slugfest"; and so on. The eye of the press is focused on the week-to-week battle of the teams as they fight for top ranking. The playing field is our model of life in the United States where "winning isn't the best thing, it is the only thing" and tying is "like kissing your sister."

But at the end of each playing season, the owners of the professional teams in each league come together to examine the results of their competitive activities during the year to see if they make sense and whether improvement is possible. Do the rules need adjustment? Should the season be longer? Should there be a different arrangement for refereeing the contests? Most important, are the discussions preparing the groundwork for negotiations with the players and the TV networks? Although the nation's attention is on the contest between the Jets and the Raiders, the economic success of the teams is determined in large part by the negotiations among the league of owners, the union of players, and the TV networks.

Perhaps the single most important observation to be made on the basis of this study of the world petrochemical industry is that the metaphor of sports can well apply to the industry. But it is not the romantic idea of contest that describes accurately what is going on. It is the practical one of negotiation over the regulations. In a very real sense it is the rules of play that the companies are able to establish for themselves, as well as their relations with unions and government that determine the potential profitability of their industry.

As stated, the idea does not sound radical. In his very popular manual of competitive analysis, Michael Porter shows how industry structure determines potential company profitability.[4] But he makes that statement with the economist's premise firmly in place: industry structure is given—or it may be influenced by skillful implementation of strategy by an individual company. The finding of my study is that companies can cooperate with each other to create a healthy industry and that they should do so because it is in the public interest to have industry healthy.

This fact is the same one discovered by U.S. sports team owners which led them to create the draft system. The participants in the league had to be healthy for the competition to be interesting. In the predraft days, winning teams tended to get even stronger because the money coming from the ticket sales of successful teams funded the acquisition of the best players that in turn perpetuated that success. In the short term the rich got richer but in

the longer term the fans got bored. By instituting the draft system, the owners hoped to ensure that even the weaker teams
would have an opportunity to acquire leading talent and thereby
rebalance the league. In other words, the owners cooperated to
make the competition on the field more enjoyable to the paying
customers whose existence would assure the long-term financial
health of the league.

In industry the conclusion is similar. A society benefits when
the effect of competition is to keep companies from exploiting
customers, workers, or suppliers. The economists taught us that a
problem would arise only when there was too little competition.
What we have seen in petrochemicals (and what can be seen in
steel, forest products, aluminum, and most capital-intensive
manufacturing industry) are circumstances where there is *too much*
competition. Today's petrochemical industry structure is
configured so that conventional competition leads to a socially
undesirable result—chronic economic waste. Everyone loses. It
makes sense, therefore, for the managers to cooperate in restructuring the industry so that conventional competition can lead to a
healthy outcome.

Competition Can Be Destructive

The preceding argument prepares the way for a fairly unusual
proposal: there are circumstances in which companies should be
encouraged to cooperate. Much like the use of arsenic in the treatment of disease, this is a proposition that needs some justification.
What is it that requires so dangerous a remedy, so drastic a departure from conventional economic attitudes and laws concerning
competition?

The answer would seem to be obvious. Competition among
firms is assumed to involve frequent entry and exit with negligible
social cost. Perhaps that is still true in some industries, such as
restaurants, in which the cost of entry and exit is less. But the
evolution of technology made the mass market possible, thereby
encouraging the development of mass production. In turn, the
development of new techniques for production has raised the
minimum efficient scale in some activities to enormous propor-
tions. In steelmaking, for example, there is evidence that advantages from scale continue to accrue above 10 million tons, nearly

10 percent of the U.S. market. In theory, substantial excess capacity would not be built, but in the real world, it is clear that developing nations and diversifying or mismanaged companies build more capacity than the market requires.

In the many industries that experience this pattern of chronic overinvestment, one finds a fair number of large companies competing for a limited market. This structure has been described in theoretical economics as "monopolistic competition."

In this structural condition, firms find that if they raise price they immediately lose sales; but if they cut price to gain volume their move is matched by their competitor. In theory, prices should remain stable once firms learn the folly of moving away from an equilibrium condition. In fact, life is more brutal. The newest participant in the market has no volume. To fill up his new capacity—which is, or is believed to be, of lowest cost—he cuts price. Faced with the huge fixed costs of running their capacity, competitors match the cut. The ensuing price war stops when the bleeding is so great that bankers intervene.

Then capacity may be closed. But sometimes the entrant is a government-owned company or an oil-company-sponsored subsidiary or the first move into the industry of a rising keiretsu (in Japan, a family of companies related to a trading house).[5] In the first case, the government may be willing to print money to support its market position or the employment it supports. After all, the alternative would be welfare payments. The oil company may not do its accounting in a way that makes the problems visible. And the keiretsu may be well prepared to do battle with its lordly rivals.

Sometimes privately owned, well-managed competitors believe it wrong to be pushed out of markets by less efficient but subsidized competitors. Often they can use profits from other divisions to fund the battle.

In the 1980s it was common to find that each nation and each company wanted to grow rapidly by increasing their participation in the slow growth of the world market. They built global-scale facilities to compete even though their domestic markets could not absorb the output. Under those circumstances losses can be predicted for years.

The consequences of competition in situations like those caricatured above can be very destructive. The losses weaken indi-

vidual companies so that eventually they do not have the strength
to heal themselves. They can only lumber about and die like di-
nosaurs after a change in climate. Their death, however, involves
the loss of thousands of jobs and in some instances, the competitive position of nations. Perhaps the United States economy could
tolerate the loss of 500,000 jobs in shoe manufacturing,[6] but it is
less likely that the British economy could remain unscathed from
loss of 200,000 in autos.

The obvious remedy in a healthy economy is for the resources
to move from the sick industry to another one where growth and
competitive position are better. But chronic losses wipe out the
capital required for funding research or building new facilities.
Convalescence requires a benign environment that the envisioned
industry structure does not provide. In other words, when a large
capital-intensive business experiences many years of operating
losses, it also loses the ability to seek out and exploit new opportunities. Radical surgery is required before anything like recovery
is possible. And the company that emerges is almost always a
shrunken version of its former self. It is a very unpalatable decision to make.

The hardest exit to plan, the unkindest cut, is one which leaves
the market to the competitor whose irresponsible moves or government subsidies caused the problem in the first place. (Hoechst's
1985 deal with ENI on low-density polyethylene has some of this
character. ENI's facilities are efficient but poorly located.) Even
worse is when the reshuffling of position leaves the exiting competitor dependent on the miscreant for product. And worst of all is
when the competitors are nations not companies. (This is the view
some take of the French in commodity plastics or of the Italians in
fiber.) At least in Europe, most producers and governments remember the consequences of their dependence on I. G. Farben for
fine chemicals and dyestuffs as World War I began. In the chemical
industry, companies do not have to reach far to find reasons not to
exit.

Cooperation Is Required to Escape the Dilemma

For most companies, it is not hard to go through an analytic
exercise that demonstrates the positive economic consequences of
abandoning uncompetitive capacity. The preceding discussion

also makes clear that serious political and social consequences might pose high barriers to exit.

In Europe, the recurrent answer to the problem of destructive competition has been the cartel, legal and otherwise. In Japan, cartels are regularly used as a tool of government economic policy. In the United States their use violates the antitrust laws. In recent times governments have organized international cartels such as the trigger-price agreement in steel. Trigger prices—also referred to as "reference" prices—are "a schedule of prices for imported steel which would act as a checklist against which the U.S. Customs Service could compare the actual prices of imported steel. Should a price drop below the trigger price for any given shipment, the Treasury could initiate an anti-dumping investigation, shortening the protracted 13-month anti-dumping procedure already in place and eliminating the need for aggrieved companies to compile and file complaints."[7] Trigger prices have been used as a kind of economic disarmament treaty whenever conventional competition produces unhappy results. And like disarmament agreements, the cartels often have broken down. The urge to compete seems far more powerful than the urge to cooperate.

It is easy to see, nonetheless, that open markets are a rare occurrence. In one way or another, leagues have formed to organize the terms of trade. Agriculture is the clearest case, with the giant cooperatives in the United States being perhaps the most consistently successful deviants from free market structure. The agreements among the Seven Sister multinational oil companies lasting from the 1930s until the 1970s constituted one of the most efficient and effective arrangements ever known.[8] The Multi-Fiber Agreement in textiles is a more ambitious project, but is modestly successful.[9] The International Air Transport Association seems less helpful in controlling the competitive aspirations of international airlines.

The underlying logic of cartels is well understood, and failures are easy to predict. There are three rules: (1) the organization of production must be separate from the organization of sales; (2) there must be compensation for the losers; (3) there must be means to punish cheaters.

The first rule reflects the fact that facilities must be managed on a decentralized basis but that successful division of the market requires some centralized management and control. The second rule is obvious. Voluntary agreement is not forthcoming when significant players lose as a consequence. The third caveat is an obvious corollary to the competitive instincts of man.

Many of the contemporary efforts to organize European markets have broken down over the third rule. Sovereignty provides the basis from which contracts can be broken. In turn, the first two requirements have not been met in many international agreements.

In the industries studied here, it is apparent that the only successful, publicly acknowledged cartelization took place in Japan. And even there, the principal rationalization was accomplished unilaterally or with bilateral swaps. In the United States, cartelization was not attempted, so that overcapacity still depresses the profitability of the commodity businesses. The well-positioned majors do not expect to lose money, but look ruefully at the competitive effects of the companies that will not quit. Although there has been no objective, comprehensive study of the U.S. industry of the kind Chem Systems did for European companies, managers have a clear sense of which units should be off the market because of high cost or weak market position. But each exit comes as a wrenching decision for management since, as noted by Robert Cacheux, president of Amoco Chemicals, "Commodity chemicals will be the meat and potatoes of the chemical business for the foreseeable future."[10]

In Europe, effective cooperation has taken the form of merger or swap. Rather than attempting a long-term relationship among independent parties, they have used the direct control of a single management to achieve rationalization. The managerial simplicity achieved is obvious, but the approach tends to be limited to physically proximate facilities. With some exceptions starting in 1984, most rationalization has taken place within the borders of one country. The consequence is unhappy, for while private action has succeeded in reducing overcapacity in ethylene, for example, by more than two million tons, there remain some two million tons in excess over the market. Meanwhile, the Exxon-Shell project at Mossmoran, Scotland nears completion and Saudi product arrived in the European market in early 1985.

There are endless discussions among the European players but effective stabilization of the market along the lines of the Japanese seems a pipe dream. The problems are numerous. To begin, as put succinctly by Christian Stoffaes of the French Ministry of Industry, "There are too many countries in Europe." The point is obvious but serious. Modern sovereign states are not keen to do without a chemical industry, and, putting the issue of dependence aside, the volumes are such that trade balance and competitiveness would be affected.

The second problem is geographic. As is apparent from the maps below, the European industry is spread all over. France has petrochemical activity in all six corners of the state. Product is often transshipped in situations where transport cost exceeds value added. It is easy to say "shut down the inefficient units," but these are often the ones that make sense from the perspective of trade. For example, the Carling complex is often cited as an appropriate candidate for rationalization. But it sits across from Hoechst in Cologne and BASF in Ludwigshafen. Similarly, the Italians must have mixed feelings when they consider what to do with the inefficient complexes in northern Italy.

In the United States, the enormous web of feedstock and product pipelines all along the Gulf coast facilitates rationalization. It is not unusual for a company to "toll" its product through the more efficient unit of a competitor sitting across the fence.[11] But with the exception of the grid along the North Sea and up the Rhone from Marseilles, the connections in Europe are poor. Complexes tend to have been built up around a port, or coal fields, or gas, or brine. (The same is true in Japan where the combinatos were expected to be self-sufficient and where popular resistance to pipelines crossing populated areas has been extraordinary— witness the uproar when a line was planned to bring fuel to the new Tokyo International Airport at Narita.) Poor geographical connections make it that much harder to design agreements for cutting back capacity that make economic sense.

The third problem taxing European companies is the behavior of the European Commission. The Directorate of the Commission that is responsible for enforcing the antitrust laws, DG III, is described by various executives in the industry and other parts of the Commission to be full of narrow-, literal-minded technocrats who actually believe to be true the theoretical propositions under-

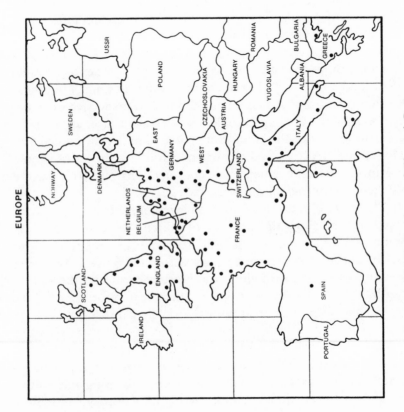

Location of Major Petroleum and Chemical Centers

JAPAN

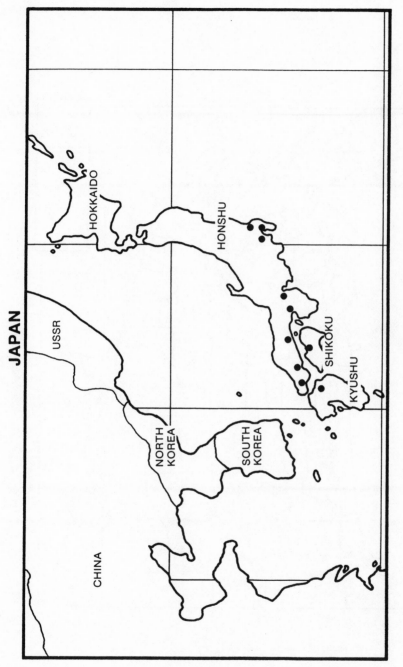

USSR

CHINA

NORTH KOREA

SOUTH KOREA

HOKKAIDO

HONSHU

SHIKOKU

KYUSHU

Map (*cont.*)

UNITED STATES

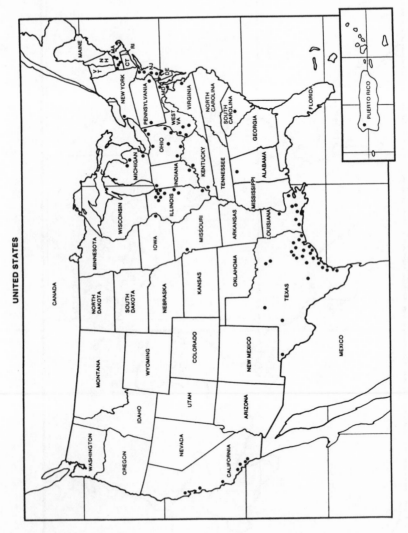

Map (cont.)

lying the antitrust law laid out in the Treaty of Rome's Articles 85 and 86. Their zealotry has virtually defeated the efforts of companies to construct cross-national deals that reduce capacity.

The subject is extremely sensitive and very difficult to research rigorously, but the highest ranking managers in companies and the European Economic Community (EEC) were unanimous in their criticism of Commission competition policy. Certainly it seems paradoxical that Viscount Davignon at the Industry Directorate argued for the rationalization of European industry through individual and collective action at the same time that the Competition Directorate investigated the major companies and blocked them from these same deals.

There is no doubt that collective action will be required to deal with the "excess country" problem even if the individual countries do a reasonable job of rationalizing their national positions. When one thinks of the extraordinary conflicts that divide the parties, and then considers the role that will be played by the major multinationals such as Shell, Essochem, and Dow, it seems clear that what is needed is a MITI pointing the way and encouraging progress rather than a group of lawyers threatening criminal action on the basis of laws grounded in the history and the ideological premises of nineteenth-century industry.

Strategy Is Political

The dramatic changes described above pose extreme alternatives for those managing the development of strategy in the petrochemical producers. The options seem to range from exit to aggressive expansion in an energy-rich nation, but also include merger, joint venture, specialization and radical tailoring of product mix. Both the Department of Commerce study and the International Tariff Commission report note the importance of a move toward "specialties" in the United States. Chart 3.1 reveals, however, just how dramatic a change is needed if a shift to specialties is to have any impact. If the twelve major commodity producers acquired the twelve major specialty producers, the impact would be positive but negligible. The problem for commodity producers will continue to be prices.

Moreover, there is a more fundamental problem. If all the major producers shift to specialties, these products can quickly be-

Millions of Dollars   Percentage of Margin

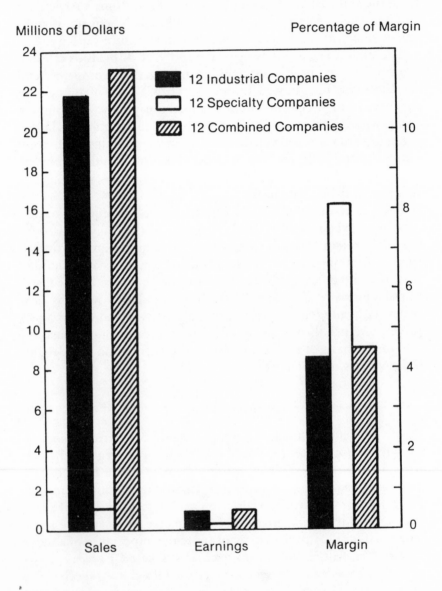

Chart 3.1
Margins for Industrial, Specialty, and Combined Companies
(Results Second Quarter 1982)

Reprinted from Peter Godfrey, "Speciality and Fine Chemicals, A Panacea for Profit?"
prepared for the Energy Bureau Petrochemical Conference (n.p.: Chem Systems, Inc.,
November 1982), 26.

come commodities. The point was asserted directly in *Chemical Week*'s thirty-page survey of the chemical industry entitled "Restructuring." Estimating total specialty sales in the United States at $40 billion in 1982, they forecast an increase at 5 percent a year to $61 billion in 1990.[12] After a discussion of various moves being made into specialty materials as well as chemicals, one author confirmed that "chances are that the competition in specialty materials will be every bit as intense as it is in specialty chemicals. In fact, most players expect a shakeout in all the specialty areas."[13] Nonetheless, all the major chemical companies throughout the world were in various stages of progress toward a reshaping of their portfolios away from the profitless commodities.

When they addressed the long term, however, most managements believed that they could not or should not abandon the commodities where they had some strength. But to improve these businesses they had to participate in the process by which governments were altering the rules for the industry. As they faced that task, the company managements I interviewed reflected the uncertainties one might expect from managers responsible for changes of this order. In particular they tried to understand the different demands that were associated with the different games they were asked to play and to understand which of these games they had to play. They were especially concerned with what it might mean to make strategy in a politicized environment.

Which Game to Play?

The top managements of most companies find themselves in the middle of several dilemmas.

Stopping the Bloodbath. The years of recession, the apparent end of further penetration of the GNP by petrochemical substitutes, coupled with the growth of capacity and the large number of competitors has produced a situation in which no one makes money at present prices. In order to reach profitable prices, cooperation is necessary—either to fix prices illegally or reduce capacity to bring it in balance with demand. The problem is that unless the agreement is enforced, it is in the interest of individual companies to cheat.

In the United States, long-term losers quit—up to a point. Excess capacity still hangs over the market. But in Europe the biggest losers are often state owned and will not exit; to the contrary they expand. Efficient private manufacturers do not wish to stand aside so the competitive battle proceeds. Like the players in the prisoner dilemma game, they lack the trust to cooperate.

Winning the Endgame.   At the same time, the same managers look ahead and realize that the world economy is likely to recover, there will be rationalization, and petrochemicals are among the largest markets in the world. Some companies will be making commodity plastics, and there is the potential that they will make profits. To be one of those players, it will be necessary to have the lowest costs and the best technology. Competition is the way to win the endgame, especially fierce, threatening competition.

Maintaining Employment.   The governments of consuming and producing nations have multiple interests. In 1983, employment and balance of payments dominated most policy discussions. The most elegant attempt at a solution was probably to be found in Japan. Their policy treats the worker as a fixed cost for the economy and seeks to help companies maximize value added per worker. If the chemical industry were to be restructured, that would require a transition period during which major companies could earn profits necessary to fund the migration to new higher value-added businesses.

In Italy and France the government intervened much more directly. Companies were reorganized and huge sums invested toward the intended objective of a world-class, competitive industry. In Italy workers were laid off and plants closed, but in France it was not clear what would be closed or whether the government would permit closings. The resignations of the heads of two major French companies (M. Gandois from Rhône-Poulenc and M. Chalandon from Elf Aquitaine) were directly related to disputes over commerical issues.

Maximizing Profits.   On the other hand, if one was trying to provide economic results that satisfied the objective of private capital markets for a return on investment competitive with other uses, then the requirement for regular return on investment led most managers to conclude that the government ought to be kept at arm's length. Otherwise the very natural need of the government to protect its political constituencies would interfere with the need to rationalize by shutting plants and laying off workers.

Playing Two or More Games at Once

These different objectives were also associated with different time pressures. The world of politics is day to day. Each morning's headlines and evening's TV news is important to the strength of a government and the position of individual politicians. A management seeking to ally itself with a government must have a very short-term view. If the government bank that owns your shares needs a dividend this month in order to shore up its balance sheet and perhaps the currency, then the opportunities in the capital budget to use those funds over the next year are irrelevant.

But the *world of return on investment* is also demanding. Stock markets may have a longer-term view than the headlines, but they are only loyal to the last eighth of a point, and they have a healthy understanding of present value. If the cost of money is 15–20 percent, then commercial investment should yield that plus some premium—next year if not this.

In contrast is the *world of market share*. If a management believes that there is a long-term future to a large market, then it may pay to stick out the period of low or cyclical returns during competitive battles in order to build up the cumulative experience and scale that permits one to dominate an industry. After all, if there is growth, there may be positive cash flow even if profits are meager. And over time, well-managed market share position will generate profit.

Each of these situations has its own structure or logic. A management trying to compete in each one can develop a strategy that makes sense. The problem is that any move a company makes in one game is a move in all the others. What helps in one situation may well hurt in another. The simplest example is where the competitor fighting fiercely in an endgame, finds that other firms are uncomfortable dealing with it in a cooperative industry-level effort to develop a coherent aggregate position.[14]

If one could deal with these games sequentially, the task would be difficult but feasible. It is not unusual to meet conflicting demands one after another. The problem is that all of these "games" are being played out simultaneously; there is no space or slack.

Under the circumstances, it is extremely difficult to move forward with any clear sense of direction. Some companies more or less ignore all but one of the games and treat their demands as if they did not exist or were unimportant.[15] There are U.S. companies, for example, that treat all noneconomic problems as constraints affecting the simpler problem of maximizing return. Some European companies simply try to meet the objectives of employment and balance of payments specified by their government.

But most managements interviewed were struggling to move forward in several games at once: cooperating while competing, shrinking while surviving, making profit while maintaining or increasing market share, using government support to strengthen long-term international position while avoiding where possible short-term political costs.

Managing in a Politicized Environment

Inevitably managements facing these dilemmas are confused. This sense of confusion is illustrated by the following comments of a U.S. company manager:

> I think the basic problem of the business is that we fall in love with our production process. It is such a miracle to make the whole thing work, that we sometimes forget that it is a business. That is the only reason I can think that we put so much capacity into markets whose size we know well.
>
> Today that disease is compounded by change. Things are moving so fast that it is absolutely necessary to avoid heavy commitments. For example, in ethylene there is so much capacity. As a result, you can see Dow buy Richardson-Merrill and move toward pharmaceuticals. But it is stuck with a heavy debt load from its old strategy.
>
> The third thing is that we're now subject to the political arena. I guess it's the politicizing of the business. Look at what Trudeau did to us in Canada. They passed a national energy act and we woke up with our margins reduced from 22 percent to 8 percent. Why? It's income redistribution among the provinces. Take another example, Mexico. The government runs the country broke and we get hit. I think all over, you're in control of about 10 percent of your activities.
>
> When we meet in the management committee, I sometimes feel that the facts don't mean anything. Take the problem of synfuels. Eight years ago the president gave a speech. We knew it had to be an important area; you had to move ahead. Where is it today? What we've had to learn is that the public is your peer group, not the other managers in the company.

In the present situation, it is a war of attrition. Each day the action of a competitor or a government body poses serious problems. The aid of one's home government is tantalizingly attractive. But with support comes dependence and potential politicization. Even government-owned firms shun the direct intervention of political leaders whenever possible.

Fundamentally, there is something unattractive to a professional manager about paying hard currency for feedstock and managing a large, complex, high-technology machine that produces a high-quality product only to sell at an economic loss. A manager can deal with multiple objectives; but it is hard to cope with what he perceives as intentional waste.

But what is waste? Key to the political world is awareness of the day-by-day consequences of operations. Where the carefully guided commitment of resources toward long-term objectives cuts across the fine balancing act of political leadership, the long-term view may have to go. At such times, enormous pressure can be brought to bear on a corporate manager. In one instance, the French Minister of Finance allegedly brought all his influence to bear on the manager of Rhône-Poulenc the night and morning before a board meeting to get him to pay a dividend despite an extremely weak financial condition.[16] The dividend was not paid but a manager can only "win" a few such battles. In another industry, in another country, the author witnessed the chief executive officer of a vast state-owned enterprise learn from the minister of industry that a friend who ran another major state enterprise had been fired for blocking a series of appointments in the company—"and you're next," he was told.

For managers in such settings, every day is a battle. The best one can hope for is incremental progress on strategic matters and a containment of political pressure at the boundary of the firm. Political coalition building requires a kind of equity that defeats the selectivity in resource allocation, organization, and reward required for efficiency and effectiveness. For politicians, everything a company does can be traded away in day-to-day maneuvering: executive position, local jobs, plant location, construction contracts, maintenance contracts, all kinds of equipment purchases and raw material sourcing that bring benefits to someone can be traded for votes on an immediate issue. These benefits rather than the needs of the firm can become the central criteria by which action is guided in the politicized organization.

Where a company can predict that its activities will be politically salient, it is possible to build defenses. Long-term costs of unwise proposals can be made visible. Politicians who disagree with a proposal can be alerted to the problem. More useful, carefully constructed working relationships can be built between the technical staffs of a company and relevant government counterparts. It is then possible to use company expertise to inform the public policy-making process.

The problem comes when the wind shifts so rapidly that a manager is caught unprepared. For example, in the United States, strong, long-term relations at staff levels did not help Allied Chemical's nuclear reprocessing plant when President Carter's election led to a shift in policy and a reorganization of the Nuclear Regulatory Agency. The plant died at a cost of over $100 million.[17]

In the petrochemical industry the basic problem has been adjustment to a new set of circumstances in a situation where many players

1. had inadequate capital to invest in modernization or new products, or
2. had only recently perceived the structural nature of the problem, or
3. could only get government help by reinvesting in mature areas where jobs would be maintained, or
4. were blocked from negotiating to stabilize markets and reorganize capacity for fear of antitrust prosecution.

In the United States and Europe many of the leading firms were worried that the economic recovery would take the pressure to exit off marginal producers. One manager put the point rather bluntly: "This recession has done what none of us had the courage to do for ourselves. Another year and we would have really cleaned up the industry."[18] The consequence of delay is political pressure for protection from the weak producer and from the unions. So far, conservative administrations have held the line in Italy, Germany, Japan, the United Kingdom, and the United States. But governments can do more than allow the weak to be winnowed out.

Where government policy could help company managements most would be in freeing them from the legal and other restrictions that prevent them from discussing their shared dilemmas and cooperating in their solution. Governments could help by providing them with legitimate forums for their discussions and by providing (or commissioning others to provide) useful data describing the situation.

Ignorant players are the most dangerous factor in the condition of excessive competition. The Chem Systems report, subscribed to by several European companies, was clearly useful in relieving ignorance to the extent that its findings were accepted as accurate. Studies of this sort provide the basis for intelligent intracompany strategic planning and intercompany negotiation. Their production need not be an accident of entrepreneurship. But for the study to be used, the changes noted above need to be made. A new approach to competition policy is required.

For the executive thinking about the sort of problems analyzed above, the complexity can be daunting. But further consideration suggests that where leaders succeeded, they dealt with the problems identified to the extent that they could manage them in sequence rather than simultaneously. In short, even where crisis meant that there was no slack, they maneuvered and dealt with events so that for their subordinates there were priorities. First, the bloodbath was stopped; then, the long term was addressed through negotiations with competitors and the government; and finally, there was rationalization of capacity for the endgame. Using the cycle outlined in chapter 2, we can examine how the three phases of restructuring can be planned and managed separately.

Three Phases of Restructuring

From a public and a business policy perspective, perhaps the most striking lesson from successful managers in petrochemicals is that restructuring is a time-consuming process that can usefully be seen as involving three phases. During the first, the individual companies must go through the difficult work of getting their organization under control with all this means for new management, new structure, planning systems, and strategy. I have called this phase *preparation*. The second phase may simply be called *concentration*. We can see that in each country, the key step on the way to balancing capacity with demand was a reduction in the number of competitors. The final stage, called *rationalization,* occurs once the individual players who have large blocks of capacity under their control that are in excess of the market need, carry out optimization programs, including the shutting down of inefficient units.

Preparation

From a company perspective, management must accomplish an enormous amount of work before taking part in the restructuring game. In essence, the studies in chapters 5–11 reveal that the hardest kinds of tasks a top management can face—reorganizing, changing people, reassessing the corporate strategy—have to be carried out *before* the company can start influencing its industry structure with any hope that the intended effects of its efforts are in its long-term interest. Without a clear strategic view of strengths and weaknesses measured against long-term market conditions, the result of intercompany negotiations can be a real nightmare.

Perhaps the clearest example studied was Enichemica, the subsidiary of the Italian state-owned oil company. Chapter 9 describes how Montedison walked away from the government negotiations with something resembling a potentially profitable business portfolio, while Enichemica emerged holding awkwardly located commodity businesses. Only time will tell whether its leadership will be able to clean house. It is the judgment of industry observers that the results reflected the relative strengths of the management team at the time of the negotiations, i.e., the preparation they had completed.

There is an important public policy lesson to be learned. The competitiveness of an industry, measured by its ability to compete in a free-trading global system, depends in the end on the strength of the individual companies. Improving structural conditions only creates the potential for profit. In a setting where demand, feedstock supply and price, technology, and competitive strategies are all changing, and where commitments involve hundreds of millions of dollars and evidence of success is long in coming, the difficulty of thinking through how a company's resources ought to be deployed cannot be exaggerated. For the outcome of a restructuring effort to make sense, there must be some mechanism insuring that company managements have done their job in the preparation phase.

In principle, the market ensures that companies are well managed. But in the petrochemicals situations the market is not working. Some companies are politicized, some are run as extensions of oil companies, and some managements have been unable to cope with the hard times.

There is also an argument that the financial markets of some countries, especially the United States, put so much pressure on management to generate current profit, that they cannot afford to put their house in order. Worse still, goes the argument, the management that endures a tough preparation phase and emerges lean and ready to play will generally have a strong balance sheet, an improving strategic position, and low current earnings—the perfect target for stock market raiders. The very act of getting ready to restructure makes the management vulnerable to a takeover.

This book is not the place to explore this last set of problems at length. The reason for mentioning them here is as a caution to public policymakers. Industry cannot be restructured successfully without well-managed companies. Good management performance, in turn, depends upon the right incentives as well as the right personnel.

Concentration

Once companies turn from getting their own houses in order to the problems of their industry, the problem they face is the number of players. There are too many to avoid the costs of excess competition. But no one seems willing to exit. The barriers are too high. In petrochemicals we have seen that these included important national objectives such as defense and balance of payments. The effects of physical integration in multiplant complexes were also important, as were the social effects of shutdowns at single plant locations. At least as powerful a barrier, however, was the emotional trauma of exit from a traditional line of business. Even where the cash benefits of a unilateral cutback were clear, it was galling to managements to make a move that would help the surviving players.

Some companies were tough enough to make major exits on

their own, abandoning businesses that had no prospects. But the most dramatic shifts involved concentration in a given product line, either through acquisition of the whole or part of a company, or through deals that represented specialization by previously full or broader line companies.

Chart 1.3 in chapter 1, showing the concentration among European manufacturers of PVC producers, illustrates the phenomenon perfectly. Reflected are the BP/ICI swap, ICI acquisition of Lonza, the French restructuring, Norsk Hydro's takeover of most of Scandinavia, and so on.

Following this concentration, the surviving companies went about optimizing their own properties. The key to understanding the concentration phase is to look for the way the exit barriers were overcome. The easiest approach to understand, if not to execute, was where a privately owned company chose to exit a weak position on economic grounds without being blocked by a government (e.g., Carbide in Europe). More interesting to the present discussion are the virtues of merger, swaps, and acquisition as routes over the barriers to exit.

Mergers. In a horizontal merger, two competitors join forces to face the rest of the industry. The benefits are clear: the number of competitors is reduced, the market share may be preserved for the amalgamation, and the manufacturing capacity can be optimized. The usual obstacles to this approach to rationalization are legal and human. The resulting company's size or market share may be deemed too large according to some law. And the prospective partners may be uncomfortable as they contemplate what will happen to management after the consummation. Efficiency can mean fewer managers as well as fewer workers and only one president.

Swaps. I suspect that consensus about who serves as president is one reason that swaps have proved so appealing to managers in Europe. The operating units get rearranged under new management, but the top management groups remain intact, responsible for more narrow, specialized portfolios. There may be cutbacks, but there is no surrender. The principal obstacles to swaps seem to be legal and physical. The resulting market shares can be challenged (the BP/ICI deal was reviewed for more than a year by the European Commission), and the manufacturing units involved may be too entangled in an integrated chemical complex to be hived off.

Acquisitions. Still another approach is acquisition, one company simply buys the business of another. Where a large company simply sells off one of its units, this can be thought of as a swap for cash. The obstacles are the same as for physical swaps. But entire companies may be acquired as when Occidental bought Getty, or Du Pont bought Conoco. Here the obstacles to be overcome are legal and human. Assuming that legal challenges can be overcome, the principal problem is that managements of major companies seldom wish to be taken over; they have to be failing (Getty) or captured in the stock market (Conoco).

It is quite apparent that swaps and mergers are the prevalent approach in Europe, where governments are encouraging or tolerant and the European Economic Commission occasionally permits them, and where financial markets are relatively small. In the United States unilateral exit and acquisition have been the more common approaches since the government is less tolerant of cooperative ventures, and the stock market has the scale and incentive to finance gigantic amalgamations.

Takeovers. There has been much discussion of the spate of takeovers of companies by "raiders." From the perspective of restructuring, takeovers pose interesting questions. A raid that leaves a new, talented management holding old but efficient assets at a new, *lower* price can contribute to the industry's strength. This might happen if a financier bought a sound but mismanaged company on favorable terms and restructured its costs. (Frank Lorenzo appears to have done this with Continental Airlines in the United States.)

A second sort of raider makes his money by stripping value from a company, rather than creating it. Just like the value-creating raider, he takes over a company using assets of the acquired company as security for large amounts of debt that covers the purchase price. But then, instead of repaying the debt by improving earnings, he repays it by selling assets. Even here, if the final result is a leaner industry, the fact that assets have been stripped may have been a good thing for the economy.

Cartels. The final approach to concentration is the formation of cartels. These are less common than one would expect and not just because they are often illegal. Contrary to Adam Smith's dictum about how much businessmen like to fix prices, a good number of managers enjoy competing. Cooperation seems to be a more difficult state to achieve than competition and, consequently, cartels are extraordinarily difficult to manage. The rules for cartels (spelled out earlier in the chapter) are seldom satisfied. Whether organized by the European Commission or privately, they are hard to police. Managers have learned that governments encourage their companies to cheat. Sovereignty interferes with effective cross-border cooperation in Europe.

In Japan, the powerful competitive drive of the firms seems to have been overcome to a certain extent, but the physical and financial configuration of the industry makes rationalization brutally difficult to achieve.

In other words, concentration through ownership is a much simpler administrative proposition than concentration through cooperation. It follows that under circumstances of excess competition, government policy should encourage constructive mergers, acquisitions, and swaps as well as facilitating experiments with cooperative forms.

Rationalization

Once a single management gains responsibility for the operation of a group of previously independent facilities, it is possible to go through the studies of plant sites, customer needs, logistics, and supply on the basis of which costs can be reduced and which operations improved. This is hard work for engineers, cost accountants, and marketers. The quality of their effort will have a great deal to do with the future prospects of the company, but it is not intrinsically difficult. The hard problem for top management, as discussed earlier, is to manage these changes in a politicized environment. The most difficult situation is one such as that of France where managers ostensibly responsible for profit have to negotiate every move to close facilities or reduce employment with inexpert government technocrats. The happier situation, though still challenging, is where social and political needs are defined by the government and discussed with the company, but where strategy formulation and implementation are left to the company managers—with the presumption that they would not ignore the community's needs.

France, Italy, and Japan are working directly on this problem, experimenting with new law and new arrangements. But to a significant degree, this represents an effort to find cures for previous government-prescribed remedies. And the ability to cut employment is a constant political question. In Germany and the United Kingdom private managements invest great time and effort in devising company strategies that fit the political setting. But they go to great lengths to avoid presenting the occasion for intervention by the government doctors.

In the United States, the leading companies have used a variety of industry associations to achieve cooperation in their dealings with the government, have linked themselves with pipelines within regions to achieve further economic efficiencies, and have otherwise competed vigorously. The result has been a slow transfer of market share from the chemical companies to the oil companies and nearly profitless growth in the commodities. While protectionism needs to be managed, and while the strong dollar has hurt, the industry's efforts over the decades could be a model of how to work with government. More likely to be a problem for companies in the immediate future are environmental and safety issues. The cost of cleanup is proving to be a major barrier to shutdown and its dimensions and consequenes are not yet well understood. But overall, from the perspective of companies trying to rationalize, the United States government has not been a significant problem.

The comparison suggests that the rationalization of industry is most easily carried out by well-managed private companies. The cuts in employment that are implied are very difficult for legislatures to accept. Governments are better off participating in a broader discussion of what sort of concentration is needed, examining the mechanisms available for managing concentration, and making sure that there are incentives for companies to do their own work well.

NOTES

1. Alfred P. Sloan, Jr., *My Years With General Motors* (Garden City: Doubleday, 1963), 55.
2. Kenneth R. Andrews, *The Concept of Corporate Strategy,* revised edition (Homewood, Ill.: Richard D. Irwin, 1980), 4, 5.
3. Interview with U.S chemical company executive, spring 1983.
4. Michael E. Porter, *Competitive Strategy: Techniques for Analyzing Industries and Competitors* (New York: Free Press, 1980), 3–33.
5. For a description of keiretsus, see James C. Abegglen and George Stalk, Jr., *Kaisha, the Japanese Corporation* (New York: Basic Books, 1985), 162.
6. The U.S. International Trade Commission found in 1984 that the loss of 500,000 of an original 700,000 jobs had not injured the industry. In 1985 injury was found, but President Reagan chose to ignore the ITC finding and to attempt to punish unfair traders selectively.
7. Allan Gray, "The Steel Industry and Imports (C), 9-379-043. Boston: Harvard Business School, 1979, revised 1980.
8. Anthony Sampson, *The Seven Sisters: The Great Oil Companies and the World They Shaped* (New York: Viking Press, 1975).
9. David B. Yoffie and Jane Kenney Austin, "Textiles and the Multi-Fiber Arrangement," 9-383-164. Boston: Harvard Business School, 1983.
10. "Commodities: Stuck with Low Growth?" *Chemical Week,* 26 October 1983, 31.
11. A company shuts down an inefficient unit and has that step in the process performed by a neighboring company in return for a fee—the "toll" on volume passing through.
12. "The Urgent Rush to Specialty Markets," *Chemical Week,* 26 October 1983, 44.
13. Ibid., 50.
14. The phenomenon is documented in Manesh Shrikant's "Managing the External Competitive Context: Management Function in the Regulated Environment of India," Ph.D. diss., Harvard Business School, 1979. He argues that companies must organize specifically to deal with the issue so that both a consensus and a cooperation are provided.
15. These are managements, such as the ones studied by Gordon Donaldson and Jay W. Lorsch in *Decision Making at the Top: The Shaping of Strategic Direction* (New York: Basic Books, 1983), who keep the government out of the set of forces they balance.
16. Interview, spring 1983.
17. George C. Lodge and Joseph L. Badaracco, "The Barnwell Nuclear Fuel Plant (A) and (B), #9-379-143, 9-379-144. Boston: Harvard Business School, 1979.
18. Interview with U.S. chemical company executive, fall 1982.

4

What Role for Government?

Introduction

The preceding chapters emphasized the extent to which potential profits are determined by industry structure. I have also stressed that some sort of cooperation among competitors was required for an early end to structurally induced destructive competition. In the process, the company managements have come to recognize the importance of a broader set of constituencies than those active in the market. The strategic problem of the companies thus becomes politicized. In order to make these points, the activity in Europe, Japan, and the United States has been compared.

Comparison revealed the common elements in the diverse approaches taken to restructuring by managements in the countries studied. Also illuminated, however, were the efforts made by governments to monitor and influence the process of restructuring according to their satisfaction with the way the needs of the community were defined and respected. Indeed, the relative success of restructuring activity is clearly affected by the different postures and policies adopted by the several governments who intervened to define national objectives. It is instructive, therefore, to compare the governments studied, including the institutions of the nascent government of Europe. There are interesting contrasts in the way the several producing nations have treated their chemical industry, and the implications for policy are worth noting.

It is especially important to consider the attitude toward competition that is embodied in the antitrust laws of Europe, Japan, and the United States, for some of the premises contradict directly the conditions required for improvement in the industry described in the preceding chapter.[1]

Europe: The Need for a Regional Perspective

In 1983 and 1984 there was considerable reporting of the disarray in the Common Market in the popular press.[2] The fact, of course, is that there is a European Economic Community, not a "common market." The Community's survival and development in the face of divisive economic forces is remarkable. The discussion of Europe's chemical industry in this book is evidence of the potential usefulness of being able to take a European view of industry. But the behavior of the Commission's Competition Directorate (DG IV) in chemicals cannot reassure anyone that the view taken would be enlightened. There is no evidence that in Europe (or in the United States) a MITI-type organization could function as it does in Japan. Careful comparative study suggests that the Japanese approach is based on a very different view of economic development than is held in the West.[3]

The great advantage of a European perspective would be the scope that it would give individual European-based firms in their own rationalization. Without the borders of nation states to worry about, bilateral deals might be more imaginative and swap agreements easier.[4] Industrywide agreements might also be more feasible because there would be less concern for the impact of national industrial policy.

On this point it is worth mentioning what several executives interviewed called "the lesson of the fiber agreement." In 1978 and 1982, nine European synthetic fiber producers were organized through the efforts of Davignon into a capacity-reducing cartel. The situation was considerably simpler than that in petrochemicals because the absence of vertical integration and important by-products increased the symmetry of the stakes of the participating companies. The problem was that the Italian producers actually expanded capacity during the period of rationalization. There is much debate among the participants as to whether they had any prior understanding that this would happen.

In any event, European petrochemical executives were wary of the "benefits" to be gained from such broad agreements. The strongest rejected the legitimacy of symmetry, and all were suspicious of the enforceability of such agreements.

It would be very difficult for any European institution to play a leadership role in industrial rationalization in any instance where an economically attractive solution does not involve a fair share for each member nation. There really is no rationale that has been constructed that justifies a selective approach to resource allocation except the market mechanism. This may in fact be why the Commission has been so obdurate in trying to enforce the Community's antitrust laws. They are the only politically legitimate tool available for fighting mercantilist national policies that create and maintain excess productive capacity. While they surely play havoc with company attempts to reach agreements, they do at least keep manufacturing free from the extremely uneconomic consequences of the Common Agricultural Policy that has led nation after nation in Europe to subsidize excess agricultural production to the detriment of trade.

Within the individual countries, the impact of structure on strategy is quite clear. In effect, the national strategies of the nations are reflected in their institutional arrangements. These posed obvious problems for participating companies.

France

In chemicals, France has pursued an aggressive national industrial policy from a geographic position at the center of Europe that is destabilizing to all of Europe, especially since almost all the major players are stronger than the French participants and several of them (such as Shell, BP, and Essochem) have important positions in France. From a purely commercial perspective, it is not clear why France would not be better off in multinational alliances that traded access to her markets for joint venture positions, than she would be if ambitious government investment schemes proceed.

On the other hand, as discussed in chapter 5, a purely commercial perspective is perhaps the least useful one for understanding what has, and most likely, will happen in France. The country has a political and economic history that bears directly on the present situation, and the chances of the government changing its approach soon seems unlikely.

It is not the fact that the companies are state owned. They might be returned to the private sector and the situation would not fundamentally change. It is rather the role played by the government, first, in rejecting the dependence that comes with true international interdependence and, second, in managing toward complex commercial objectives with a very top-down approach. It is almost as if the accomplishment of legal concentration and specialization were thought to be the same thing as rationalization of the production capacity. Concentration, stage two of the restructuring process, was mandated by the government, but without the preparation phase that would permit successful rationalization. The deep polarization between socialists and the right serves to aggravate an already difficult situation.

France might do well to see what its companies would propose if left to their own devices. There certainly should be coordination between CdF Chimie and Ato. But Ato might well find deals to make with BP and Solvay.

Germany

The role of the government in German industry is at least as subtle a question as it is in Japan. It is easy to note the conservative commitment to the free market in German politics and ignore the equally powerful themes of social welfare and nationalism.[5] At the same time that the foundations of BASF, Bayer, and Hoechst were being constructed, Bismarck was laying the foundation of the German welfare state.

At least as important, the giant Commerzbank, Deutschebank, and Dresdnerbank play a role in the German economy quite unlike the banks of any other country. Through controlling blocks of proxies and seats on the governing boards, the big three banks play leading roles in the industrial life of the country. Together with a powerful central bank, a strong economics ministry, strong unions, and a tight employers federation, they lend a coherence to economic activity that reflects a shared commitment to the economic success of the country and a painfully developed sense of the importance of cooperation.

The big three chemical companies are a piece of this industrial fabric. Because they are large and profitable and because they are outstanding exporters, they are more independent of the banks than many other companies. But precisely because they are leaders, their actions are viewed carefully as a critical piece of the German political economy.

There is widespread expectation in Europe that Hoechst will

reduce its commitment to petrochemicals,[6] that the Erdolchemie venture between Bayer and BP will somehow be revised, that Huels will make only modest rationalizations, and that BASF will remain a powerful player in the endgame. For a host of reasons the Kartellamt scrutinizes the companies' behavior, so much so that the German managers were described as valuing European industry meetings simply so that they could have freer discussions than were possible in the German context. Thus although it might be useful, cross-company agreements are unlikely. Moreover, there has already been a good deal of specialization among the companies, especially in the products studied here. In fact, Germany looks more like the United States: big powerful companies, waiting out an unprofitable decade in a posture that maximizes freedom from government intervention and minimizes the progress of socialism.

The German companies, however, are hedged. An August 1985 *Financial Times* study reported that more business of BASF and Bayer was now in the United States than in Germany. The role of government in Germany could not be more different than France. Except to enforce their antitrust laws, the government has confined itself to a benevolent macroeconomic policy, succumbing only lately on environmental issues under terrific pressure from the voters. Labor relations in the industry have been relatively quiet compared to those in autos or steel. The government has kept its hands off, even though the companies have continued to invest aggressively overseas, especially in the United States. This may well be because of the power and success of the companies. It is not clear what a German government would do that wanted to strengthen its national position in chemicals.

Italy

Italy seems to be at a crossroads as a group of talented managers and politicians in their forties and fifties take over positions of power in the Christian Democrat, Republican, and Socialist parties. Across the spectrum they reveal a desire to make Italian industry strong and competitive, and this means breaking up and/or privatizing the huge publicly owned and politicized combines in steel, telecommunications, and chemicals. But they are also rivals for political power, and they all have to deal with the Communists, who can choose to defend "the interests of the workers." Other factors that cannot be ignored are the great family empires such as Agnellis, that have shown no interest in sharing power with any new large private groups.

A revealing glimpse of the nature of this latter battle was provided when Montedison tried to free itself from the hands of the old families by buying a controlling block of shares in the company that controlled Gemina and thereby Montedison. An uproar in the newspapers indicated that the great families that collectively control Gemina thought it was wrong for Montedison to seek to control its own future. The battle now continues beneath the surface.

Italy is different from France and Germany in that the government technocrats must operate in an evolving world in which the stakes of some families are as important as, and interact with, the stakes of political parties. The record of Italian industry has been relatively good in the last two decades, suggesting that if the management of Enichemica can devise a plan or alliances that will give it a chance for a competitive future, it will get government support. Neither ideology nor nationalism will block a pragmatic strategy.

Japan: The Issues Addressed

The situation in Japan is quite different from that in Europe. A strong cohesive network of business and government institutions has worked effectively during the last three decades to make Japan the most competitive industrial economy in the world. Japan has had the mechanisms in place that permitted action; the only question is how successful they were.

In petrochemicals, the answer is mixed. Technocrats have determined that unless the long-term energy price drops to something below an equivalent of $25/barrel for Arabian light, the Japanese are at a fundamental disadvantage in comparison with hydrocarbon-rich producers.[7]

Perhaps the most dramatic lesson from the Japanese experience is how hard it can be—even in Japan!—to get competitors to cooperate in the recognition of and adjustment to structural economic change. It is also apparent that even such wise planners as those at MITI can lead companies to create structures, such as the combinatos, that have unintended negative consequences. In retrospect, it seems clear that where there has been unified management (e.g., Sumitomo Chemical), it has played an important part in maintaining profitability and taking relatively prompt steps toward rationalization.

But the most important lesson, surely, is that when the companies and bureaucrats finally turned to the task of fixing the industry, the companies acknowledged their role in dealing with the entire problem posed by a redeployment of assets (including employees and small customers), while the government always took the view that only healthy, profitable companies could plan and carry out the changes necessary. Several authors are attempting to interpret for Western audiences the implications of this different approach to thinking about the economy. It is vital, both in Europe and the United States, for academics and policymakers to pay attention. The attitude of reciprocal respect, not the specific institutional arrangements, would seem to provide the foundation for any cooperative industrial readjustment.[8]

The United States: Toward a New Competition Policy

The U.S. government has played a reasonably constructive role over the chemical industry's life, protecting its development during infancy, its exports during its preeminence, and now encouraging, by informed benevolent neglect, the migration of capital and management toward higher value-added materials that began in the 1960s as oil companies entered the field.

The company managements have been remarkably sophisticated in devising for themselves a wide array of industry associations that are used for different purposes. They range from the Chemical Industry Institute of Toxicology which studies toxic substances to the Organization of Chemical Industry Trade Associations (OCITA), the umbrella organization that has managed the industry's participation in trade negotiation. OCITA's working philosophy exemplifies what might be called an intelligent or constructively selfish approach to public policy. First, multinational members try to approach trade issues as U.S. companies and, second, they try to avoid protecting inefficiency.[9]

While obviously U.S. government trade negotiators might disagree on the interpretation of these points, they appear to have provided a basis for the building of an effective coalition within a very heterogeneous industry. In turn that coalition has been able to contribute its expertise and analysis to the formulating of policy in the United States Trade Representative (USTR) and Department of Commerce and to the making of legislation in Congress. The coalition is almost Japanese in character.

Stepping back and taking a broader view, the United States must recognize that the playing out of foreseeable economic shifts will cost it billions of dollars in trade in the commodity plastics. The question is not, How shall we prevent the loss? but, Is there a useful role for government institutions to play in facilitating the development of new materials and their markets?

For example:

1. Are patent laws adequate to protect process development associated with high-volume production of the raw materials?
2. Is there a way that the government could assist the funding of studies on toxicity?
3. Are there other areas where methods for testing could be advanced?
4. Can government support for basic research in chemicals and materials be increased or made more effective?

In other words, the government might help by improving the context for product and market development. In considering such activity, the industry's associations again ought to provide useful guidance.

The temptation will inevitably exist to provide more vigorous protection or assistance. But here the record of the French, Italians, and Japanese ought to be clear. Unless a legislature has the discipline to produce something like the Japanese Basic Industry Restructuring Law, government ought to be interested observers only. What the United States does not need is politicization of petrochemicals.

The problem, of course, is that both companies and the government are constrained in their actions by the antitrust laws. A group of companies that wanted to work together to rationalize part of the industry, would have to fear that their activity would attract a lot of attention from the Justice Department. What is needed is an approach to the structure of industry based on an understanding of how modern industrial economies operate.

The antitrust laws of the United States are the clear descendants of the antimercantilist arguments of Adam Smith. Drafted in the late nineteenth century in reaction to the awesome transformation wreaked on the U.S. economy by the powerful forces of industrialization and the opening of the national market, the laws were even then a politically reactionary program designed to protect small businessmen from the tide of technology.[10] Both Europe and Japan adopted versions of these laws in the period of reconstruction after World War II.

From the perspective of the petrochemical industry, they are anachronistic. The small operators imagined by the drafters of the law simply do not exist. The scale of efficient activity dwarfs anything even Senator Sherman, exercised as he was by Standard Oil, might have imagined. But already by 1890, the resources required for major industrial activity, the time required for large investments to pay off, and the introduction of new products and new processes contradicted directly the premises of the theory that presumably provided foundation for the laws.

To the extent that economic theory may be said to provide footing for the laws, the basic premise is that the structure of an industry determines the conduct of its members, which in turn determines the performance that can be expected.[11] If there is a large number of small participants, they will compete vigorously, driving prices down to the marginal cost of the most efficient group of producers. If there are only a few producers, they will compete less vigorously, and consumers will be charged monopoly prices; that is, higher than the marginal cost of the most efficient producers. These higher prices will generate monopoly profits which are presumed to be consumed in a specially wasteful fashion. Certainly, there is no discussion as to whether these profits are necessary to fund research or the massive investments required for future operations.

The problem, of course, is that the operations and development of industry seldom work that way. The structure of an industry does not determine the conduct of the participants in that industry. Instead it determines the boundaries of what might be. The actual pattern of performance depends upon the interaction of firms participating in the industry, suppliers, customers, and those adjacent to the industry who might enter.[12] In other words, one cannot even speak about the potential effects of the structure of an industry without knowing the structure of the industries where its participants buy and sell. From the time researchers carried out the first comparative case studies of companies in the same industry, and then proceeded with comparative studies of different industries, it has become increasingly clear that performance can vary widely even within a similar industry structure.

The work began in the late 1950s when Kenneth R. Andrews studied three manufacturers of watches in Switzerland. The anomaly to be explained was their variance in performance, given superficially similar company size. The answer found that differences in objectives and the appropriateness of functional policies to those objectives led to the development of the concept of corporate strategy. Later, in 1972, Michael Hunt demonstrated that industries could be distinguished according to whether the participants adopted symmetric or asymmetric strategies.[13] In the latter case (petrochemicals is an example), competition may be much more severe. Howard Newman extended Hunt's work with a study of drugs and their distribution,[14] and Michael Porter established the general significance of these findings for industry.[15] Depending on the structure of prior or subsequent stages of industry, performance in the adjacent stages can be substantially affected.

Beer provides a simple but illustrative case. The rivalry of Budweiser and Miller would seem to consist of relatively similar companies with almost indistinguishable products, bashing each other in the market with advertising and price competition. Occasionally one would introduce a new product such as light beer and improve position in the market, but this would be matched as soon as possible. And this was almost the way the industry was evolving. Schlitz and Pabst fell back under a superior marketing assault, and small firms dropped by the wayside. But Heileman took a different view of the industry. Recognizing the importance of distribution and the loyalty of consumers to local brands, they began a program of acquiring some of the small dropouts, but kept their brands. Instead of competing on the basis of national advertising and size, they competed on the basis of strong distribution. Today they are a profitable third in the industry.

Even if the structure of the industry and all adjacent ones are known, it is still only possible to speak of potential behavior. The reason is that structure, by itself, does not determine conduct. The intermediate factor is the corporate strategies of the companies participating in the industry. Where strategy is symmetric so that the firms are look-alikes, then it may well be that the economists' predictions are correct. But where there are differences in strategy, it is very difficult to anticipate the outcome of competition.

In chemicals, for example, Dow's decision to make aggressive use of debt financing enabled it to grow much faster than its competitors expected, both because the leverage permitted adequate profit at lower prices and because more cash was available for investment. In industrial gases, Air Products used financially leveraged on-site facilities to crack into and grow in a very difficult industry. In computers, Digital Equipment Corporation's early decision to produce small computers for use at the bench by engineers led them to a path of great growth away from head-on competition with IBM, while those mainframe producers who sought direct competition floundered.

An unsystematic but powerful piece of evidence revealing the difficulty of predicting the effectiveness of a strategy is provided by the work of Wall Street's security analysts. While the relationship between company performance and share price is unclear, analysts do have an incentive to predict the impact on future performance of present strategy, and therefore, to determine as best they can the shape of a company's strategy. The relatively low value attributed to most such research attests to its difficulty.

If there is anything general to be said about an industry, it is that performance varies more widely when there is more variety in the strategies of the participants. Some of the industries where "me too" competitors adopt as best they can to the status quo provide the best examples of the type of collusive behavior that can be successfully attacked with the antitrust laws (steel in the United States prior to significant imports, for example). On the other hand, studies of industry behavior by the Boston Consulting Group suggest that even in classically oligopolistic industries, the only force that substantially interrupted the decline of cost with experience was antitrust prosecution.[16] If they are correct, the implication would be devastating: antitrust intervention led to higher costs, rather than the reverse.

In fact when, as a result of this suggestive observation, inquiry was made at the policy analysis shop of the U.S. Federal Trade Commission as to whether any studies had been made of the price performance of an industry over time to see whether experience effects were being shared with customers, the answer was negative.[17] Oddly enough, with the exception of certain criminal investigations, the trigger for antitrust is not poor performance but the squeals of defeated competitors or the objections of the Justice Department to structure. The government's case against IBM, as well as the derivative private suits, all failed precisely because IBM was a successful competitor rather than an exploitive monopolist. Simpleminded structural analysis failed to reveal the obvious.[18]

It is remarkably easy to conclude that for making public policy, performance should be measured directly. The trouble is that it is very hard to do. In the United States it is not common even for companies to keep good records of their performance in relation to competition. The records kept by the government are far too gross for the sort of analysis contemplated here.

Moreover, there are fundamental difficulties facing anyone who tries to develop the measures. Companies define their business in very different ways. One company, for example, may take the view that its business is to sell telephones. Another sells telephone service but in the process provides customers telephones. Are they in the same business? The major home appliance business consists of the design, manufacture, distribution, retailing, and service of refrigerators, freezers, washers, dryers, stoves, and dishwashers. Sears and GE perform four of the five functions and are the dominant forces. Yet Sears is not treated as an "industry participant" by conventional economists. Why? This kind of problem is not trivial. Most statistics describing the production and use of semiconductors in the United States leave out the chips manufactured by IBM and AT&T for themselves. That this is a very significant share of the business does not seem to bother the users of the data.

But how would one go about getting the data? Do we want the government to be able to require companies to report on strategically sensitive transactions? How else would one get the data? One possible answer is the example of the Transportation Research Center of the Department of Transportation. Independent of the automobile manufacturers they have built up a considerable body of expertise that has proved useful in formulating policy. For instance, their reconstruction of Japanese auto manufacturing costs was an important weapon in the debates over small car strategy in Detroit.[19]

In fact, the question of where the data would come from is academic. It is apparent from this study that an outside source of accurate information appears to be a necessary ingredient of a successful restructuring for reasons having to do with the need to neutralize bureaucratic forces internal to the companies and to provide legitimate grounds for action in the external political context. Sources of data will be either serendipitous, as with the Chem Systems report, or part of some long-term continuing effort to have good information available for policymakers.

Once there is data, it is possible to measure the acts of companies by their consequences. Over time it should then be possible to develop an understanding of business behavior based on observation of action and reaction rather than on ideology, which is our present approach. It should also be possible to avoid blocking any company action (other than criminal) on the ground that it violates antitrust law per se. Instead, all sorts of company action can be accepted on the grounds that it is likely to generate constructive economic performance: waste will be eliminated, costs will be lower, the consumer will be better served.

Unfortunately, for those who take an absolutist view of the value of "getting government off the people's backs," this does not imply that anything goes. While it is not hard to argue the social usefulness of a reduction of competition in certain circumstances, it is also easy for the forums of cooperation to be used in an exploitive way—primarily to take from others rather than to create value. There needs to be some mechanism for testing or clearing structural moves or conduct that appears on its face to be exploitative.

Precisely this problem has been worked through with some care in the drafting of the National Cooperative Research Act of 1984 that permits research joint ventures. While the result rests too heavily on conventional antitrust thought in the tests applied— they are still structural rather than performance oriented—the basic spirit of the bill is "here's a useful form for firms to experiment with. Let's not block their efforts unless the effort is clearly anticompetitive." The Department of Justice has agreed to review proposed joint ventures with the premise that they will be approved unless they can be shown to be bad. The penalties for performance later determined to have violated the law have also been reduced.

This argument represents a first step in a revised way of thinking about how the economy should be policed. If we can tolerate research joint ventures, then perhaps we can consider capacity swaps. If several companies can share a pipeline, perhaps two or three companies can share a new generation steel operation. If IBM appears to be reasserting its dominance, perhaps we should discuss what objectives we would like it to achieve through its strength. Then we would be in a better position to consider the inevitably forthcoming claims of competitors that it has abused its dominance.

It should be clear to any business manager reading this argument that the proposal is for a different kind of government rather than a weaker one. Instead of having a regulator that applies nineteenth-century thought to present-day competitive problems, there will be a partner with the power to intervene on a case-by-case basis. The shift is enormous and controversial. In a fundamental sense it represents an abandoning of adversarial legal structure for an administrative one. The task of the relevant government body would not be enforcement of a code of law, but the encouragement of effective competition. It would not be antitrust but properformance.

But to the extent that government was active, business managers would find it obnoxious. Small companies would find it excessively tolerant of big ones. Big companies would find its standards of judgment biased toward one industry or another.[20] The real difference would be a freeing up of corporate imagination to invent arrangements that would help deal with the severe economic, social, and political problems posed by overcapacity and obsolescence in our heavy manufacturing industries. Judging by successes such as the BP/ICI swap or the restructuring of Montedison, that would be a very healthy result for the world's economy.

NOTES

1. It should be clear to the researcher that this study made no independent effort to examine the problems and policies of countries. Instead, it has drawn extensively upon observations of individual countries made earlier by others.
2. "How the EEC Could Still Have a Future," *The Economist,* 23 June 1984, 29–32; Scott Sullivan, "The Decline of Europe," *Newsweek* 9 April 1984, 44–48,

51, 55–56, 58; Scott Sullivan, "The EEC: On the Brink," *Newsweek* 19 December 1983, 54–55; "Three Days That Shook the EEC," *The Economist* 10 December 1983, 41–42.

3. Bruce R. Scott, "National Strategies: Key to International Competition," in *U.S. Competitiveness in the World Economy,* eds. Bruce R. Scott and George C. Lodge (Boston: Harvard Business School Press, 1985), 71–143. Also Miyohei Shinohara, *Industrial Growth, Trade, and Dynamic Patterns in the Japanese Economy* (Tokyo: University of Tokyo Press, 1982).

4. The increasing pace of cross-country deals in 1985 and 1986 may mean that market forces are powerful enough to overcome nationalistic barriers.

5. Wilfried Kohl and Giorgio Basevi, *West Germany: A European and Global Power* (Lexington, Mass.: Lexington Books, 1980); Andrea Boltho, *The European Economy* (Oxford: Oxford University Press, 1982); Andrew Schonfield, *Modern Capitalism* (New York: Oxford University Press, 1965).

6. It exited low-density polyethylene in 1984.

7. Interviews with Japanese producers, MITI officials, and bankers. The picture is confused today because of the collapse in world oil prices. While strategically a cutback may still be appropriate, the role of crisis as a motivation for cooperation is gone.

8. Joseph A. Badaracco, *Loading the Dice: A Five-Country Study of Vinyl Chloride Regulation* (Boston: Harvard Business School Press, 1985).

9. Interview with Richard Brennan, previously executive director of OCITA, December 1982.

10. The emergence of giant corporations in the American economy is well described in Alfred A. Chandler, Jr.'s *The Visible Hand* (Cambridge, Mass.: Harvard University Press, 1978). The development of regulation and antitrust laws in response to the large corporation is described by Thomas K. McCraw in *Prophets of Regulation* (Cambridge, Mass.: Harvard University Press, 1984) and by George C. Lodge in *The New American Ideology* (New York: Alfred A. Knopf, 1982).

11. Carl Kaysen and Donald F. Turner, *Antitrust Policy: An Economic and Legal Analysis* (Cambridge, Mass.: Harvard University Press, 1959).

12. See Michael E. Porter, *Competitive Strategy* (New York: The Free Press, 1979); and Frederick M. Scherer, *Industrial Market Structure and Economic Performance* (Chicago: Rand McNally, 1970).

13. Michael S. Hunt, "Competition in the Major Home Appliance Industry, 1960–1970," (Ph.D. diss., Harvard University, 1972).

14. Howard H. Newman, "Strategic Groups and the Structure-Performance Relationship: A Study with Respect to the Chemical Process Industries," (Ph.D. diss., Harvard University, 1973).

15. Michael E. Porter, "Retailer Power, Manufacturer Strategy and Performance in Consumer Goods Industries," (Ph.D. diss., Harvard University, 1974).

16. Boston Consulting Group, "Perspectives: Antitrust Policy," (n.p., 1968).

17. Interview at U.S. Federal Trade Commission, spring 1978.

18. Franklin M. Fisher, John J. McGowan, and Joen E. Greenwood, *Folded,*

Spindled, and Mutilated: Economic Analysis and U.S. v. IBM (Cambridge, Mass.: MIT Press, 1983), 1–7, 339–52.

19. Davis Dyer, Malcolm Salter, and Alan Webber, *Changing Alliances* (forthcoming, Boston: Harvard Business School Press, 1987).

20. Anyone interested in hearing a vitriolic attack on an agency should ask a ranking executive of Japan's consumer electronics companies what he thinks about MITI.

5

The Restructuring of Union Carbide Corporation and Dow Chemical Corporation

The histories of Union Carbide and Dow parallel that of the petrochemical industry in the United States. The problems that Carbide faced in the seventies were typical of those that plagued all of the large chemical manufacturers; and the dilemmas facing Dow in the eighties exemplify how dramatically conditions in the industry have worsened.

Petrochemicals in the United States

In the United States, the petrochemical industry of the 1970s and early 1980s posed a paradoxical picture of nearly profitless prosperity. A number of giant, technically innovative, and commercially sophisticated companies dominated the industry. Much portfolio pruning had already been accomplished as a result of strategic resource redeployment by the individual company managements, and the trade figures reflected a steady ability of the U.S. manufacturers to penetrate foreign markets (see table 5.1).

For these exports, the biggest customer was Western Europe with 30 percent; Latin America followed with 21 percent, and then Asia (excluding Japan) with 12 percent, Canada 12 percent, and Japan 11 percent. The biggest sources of imports were Western Europe, Canada, and Japan.

Despite these evidences of success, the financial results of the companies over the last decade have been poor, with the exception of the post-1973 years when scarcities permitted prices to move up faster than cost. Table I.2 showed the results for the fifteen most significant producers of commodity chemicals.

Table 5.1

U.S. Trade (Exports—Imports) in Petrochemical Derivatives*

(In Millions of Dollars)

	1972	1977	1979	1981	1982	1983[1]	1984[2]
Chemicals and Allied Products	2,150	5,432	11,250	13,734	11,844	10,530	11,070
Plastic Materials and Resins	382.5	950.9	1,936.9	2,236.8	2,179.7	1,940	1,970
Nitrogenous Fertilizers	0.0	0.0	202.5	249.8	67.7	-151	-301
Agricultural Chemicals	193.5	661	938	909	1,018	954	1,063

Source: U.S. Department of Commerce, Bureau of Industrial Economics, *1984 U.S. Industrial Outlook* (Washington, D.C.: Government Printing Office, 1984), 9-1, 10-3, 10-6, 11-3.
*Respectively, SIC codes 28, 2821, 2873, and 2879. Plastics Materials and Resins are closest to the products studied. The other groups are included for discussion and contrast.
[1] Estimated.
[2] Forecast.

The lack of profitability needs to be qualified as well as explained. The post-1973 decade was a peculiar period during which few U.S. firms earned more than the cost of capital. Growth in demand slowed faster than supply; raw material costs soared; the cost of capital moved from negative to historic highs; and inflation undermined the strength of capital-intensive industries that were pricing and accounting for depreciation based on historical cost.

But other more peculiar factors hurt the industry. It was infected with such severe competition that even during periods of product scarcity, price was often at marginally profitable levels based on historical costs. Entrants misunderstood the industry, competitors were exceedingly dissimilar and truly misunderstood each others' economics, and aggressiveness eroded value added in the chain of activities from raw material to the end user.

Misunderstanding by Entrants

To illustrate how newcomers to the industry misunderstood it, imagine that a large oil company decided to enter a part of the chemical industry. Technical analysis would reveal that a facility using the most modern process available tied to one of the company's gas lines or refineries would give lower product cost than the industry average. In fact, utilizing the proper scale facility, price could be set so as to enter below prevailing industry levels and still make a good return on investment. Technology could be licensed, and it would cost "only" $250 million to build the facility. Moreover, it would require "only" 10 percent of the forecasted U.S. demand for the product to utilize the facility efficiently.

Four years later, with $350 million or $400 million invested, the management would face the problem of selling the output expected in nine to twelve months. Without a sales force it would be hard to sell, and a sales force could not be created overnight. So before the plant was opened, new salespeople would be out trying to sell out the new capacity, and with what as an inducement? Price. The entrant would cut price in order to break into existing buyer-seller relationships. But most of the time existing companies would be likely to have plans for capacity underway themselves. They would cut price in order to defend market share. As a consequence of such behavior, prices for commodity petrochemicals were sometimes soft even when the U. S. market was tight.

Misunderstanding by Competitors

Now imagine that in order to make plywood a forest products company generates a great deal of formaldehyde—or something a step away from formaldehyde. What is the cost of the product? In fact next to nothing. It is a by-product that inevitably is made and must be disposed of. A very modest investment will put the forest products company into the business with a very different cost position than the chemical company whose formaldehyde must bear the full cost of a different process. The forest products company should always cut its price as long as the financial return is attractive.

Or suppose a tire company earning 4 percent or less on its assets notices that chemical companies report earnings of 10 percent. It is not too hard to figure out that modern capacity and lower expectations might make one price competitive.

The consequence of these patterns of thought is that many chemical businesses were invaded by outsiders with very different expectations from the old-time chemical companies. Table 5.2 reveals the important role played by newcomers.

Table 5.2
Leading U.S. Manufacturers in 1983

Low-Density Polyethylene	High-Density Polyethylene	Polystyrene	Polyvinyl chloride	Polypropylene
Union	Union	Goodrich	Dow	Hercules
Carbide	Carbide	Diamond	Monsanto	Shell
Dow	Phillips	Shamrock	ARCO*	Amoco
ARCO*	Soltex*	Conoco*	Gulf**	ARCO**
Mobil*	Cities	Shintech*	Mobil**	Gulf**
	Service*			

Source: Derived from McKinsey & Co., Chemical Industry Data Base.
*Entered the market in 1970 or later.
**Entered the market in 1975 or later.

Aggressiveness

Finally, the staggering volumes produced by the industry put a premium on finding end-user market segments protected from competition. In effect everyone sought a "Scotch Tape" in order to add value to cellophane. But most of what they found could not be patented: sandwich bags, trash bags, and blown bottles. Each emerged as a specialty item with high margins and then submerged as a near commodity under the pressure of excess capacity built to capture the profits of end-use products. As competition at retail drove down the final price, less and less value added was available for raw material producer, resins manufacturer, and converter.

The consequence of this intense competition has, finally, been exit. As revealed in table 5.3, the major commodity plastics have seen companies with good alternative opportunities (e.g., Dow in PVC) or very marginal positions (e.g., Cities Service in polyethylene) leave the business. Relative to Europe and Japan which began considering exit in the 1980s, the table shows dramatic early moves.

As a consequence of this pattern, the survivors have tended to perform notably better than their European and Japanese competitors. While they may not have returned the true cost of capital, they have been moderately profitable as shown in the list of the eight largest chemical producers and chemical groups of oil companies (see table 5.4).

Overall the dilemma of producers in the United States can be understood if all producers are taken into account. Although there has been a net exit since 1980, since 1974 there has been an increase in the number of producers of ethylene (from 24 to 26), of propylene (from 34 to 38), and of two of the plastics studied (HDPE from 12 to 13; PP from 9 to 12). On the other hand there were exits in LDPE, PVC, and PS and this has been a source of stability.[1]

In sum, the picture in the United States is mixed. As markets grew and changed in character, companies were quick to respond to the potential opportunities. Building on technical strengths developed before World War II, the chemical companies opened up the vast markets for synthetic products. But not long after that

Table 5.3
Entry and Exit in U.S. Commodity Plastics

Companies Exiting	% of Market Share		Companies Entering	% of Market Share	
	1965	1980		1965	1980
LDPE			*LDPE*		
Allied	1.0	0	Atlantic Richfield	0	4.3
Dart	6.4	0	Chemplex	0	4.5
Du Pont	17.1	7.6	Cities Service	0	7.9
Eastman Kodak	6.4	4.0	Dow	9.4	14.6
Monsanto	5.5	0	El Paso	0	6.0
Sinclair-Koppers	3.2	0	Exxon	0	7.2
Union Carbide	31.1	16.4	Gulf	8.4	9.3
USI Chemicals	11.5	7.8	Mobil	0	3.3
			Northern PC	0	7.1
HDPE			*HDPE*		
Celanese	13.2	0	Allied	2.6	9.8
Du Pont	8.2	7.6	American Hoechst	0	3.6
W. R. Grace	13.7	0	Amoco Chemical	0	5.7
Hercules	8.6	0.3	Atlantic Richfield	0	5.3

(*cont.*)

Table 5.3 (*cont.*)

Company		
Monsanto	5.5	0
National PC	13.2	9.9
Sinclair–Koppers	3.8	0
Union Carbide	13.7	6.6
PVC		
Air Reduction	4.7	2.8
Allied	5.1	0
Diamond Shamrock	11.1	7.7
Dow	3.5	0
Ethyl Corporation	3.3	2.1
Firestone	5.1	0
Goodyear Tire	3.3	0.9
Great American Chem. Co.	2.9	0
Monsanto	6.1	0
Pantasote	4.3	1.8
Union Carbide	10.3	2.3
Uniroyal	5.5	0
Other companies	9.7	0

Company		
Chemplex	0	4.7
Cities Service	0	3.1
Dow	4.3	7.4
Gulf	0	6.9
Phillips	13.2	16.8
Soltex Polymer	0	12.3
PVC		
Air Prods. & Chems.	0	2.6
Borden	2.5	6.8
Certain Teed	0	2.4
Conoco	0	7.1
Georgia Pacific	0	9.0
B. F. Goodrich	12.4	17.6
Kensor Century	0	0.7
Occidental Petr.	0	11.8
Rico Chem.	0	1.9
Shintech	0	4.1
Stauffer	0	5.4
Talleyrand	0	0.9
Tenneco	7.8	9.6

Source: Derived from McKinsey & Co., Chemical Industry Data Base.

Table 5.4

Return on Operating Assets and Sales of Leading Chemical Producers, 1981
(In Billions of Dollars)

Chemical Companies	% of Operating ROA	Chemical Sales	Oil Companies	% of Operating ROA	Chemical Sales
Dow	7.1	9.4	Gulf	—	2.4
Celanese	8.1	3.7	Shell	0.4	3.6
Union Carbide	9.7	5.6	ARCO	0.6	2.7
Allied Chemical	10.4	2.7	Exxon	5.5	8.5
Hercules	11.1	2.3	Occidental	5.6	2.4
Monsanto	12.9	6.3	Mobil	6.8	2.3
American Cyanamid	13.3	1.9	Std. Oil of Indiana	7.6	3.1
Du Pont	14.0	12.2	Phillips	9.1	2.5

Source: U.S. Department of Commerce, Office of Competitive Assessment, Assistant Secretary for Productivity, Technology, and Innovation, "The Medium- to Long-Range International Competitiveness of the United States Petrochemical Industry: A Competitive Assessment" (Washington, D.C.: Government Printing Office, 1982), 7, table 2.

they were joined in the market by competitors with different degrees of understanding and different objectives. As time passed and managements were able to comprehend the forces at work, most devised strategies that focused their resources on those areas where their distinctive competencies promised profits. The pattern of exit and entry in table 5.3 is the consequence. But because conditions sometimes revealed themselves slowly and some managers never learned, profitability suffered. (See tables 1.2 and 5.4.)

Union Carbide was the petrochemical industry's chemist and Dow perhaps the most commercially successful member of the industry. Thus the way they dealt with the forces of the market is instructive. The last sections of this chapter are devoted to their stories. Exxon and Shell are good examples of how oil companies changed the competitive conditions in the market. Exxon is treated in chapter 6 and Shell in chapter 10.

The Restructuring of Union Carbide

In 1985, Union Carbide was a diversified manufacturer of industrial and consumer products. Its Linde division was first in industrial gases; its Carbon Products division was first in electrodes for electric furnaces; it was the leading manufacturer worldwide of dry cell and alkaline batteries; and it is a major producer of chemicals and plastics for industry and consumers. Glad Bags and Prestone, two of its products, are well-known brand names.

Union Carbide conceived itself in the 1930s to be the "Chemistry Industry's Chemists." A leading developer of vinyl and phenolic plastic, Carbide after the war was the dominant force developing polyethylene in the United States. Until the oil companies took over the business Carbide dominated ethylene, and until Dow began to push them aside they were leaders or important in PVC and polystyrene as well as low- and high-density polyethylene. What Carbide did not understand until the 1970s was the importance of market share, the economics of the experience curve, and the potential advantages of leverage.[2]

Having seen its position erode under competitive onslaughts, Carbide committed itself in the 1970s to defend its still dominant position in polyethylene and ethylene oxide. It has succeeded in these objectives, but the cost has been the deteriorated profits available. Nonetheless, Carbide developed the most widely accepted linear low-density polyethylene process (called Unipol) and appears to be using that as a basis for a move toward a technology and service business. Partly because of royalty fees, Carbide may be the only company to have operated a profitable polyethylene business in 1982.

At the same time that Carbide focused on polyethylene and ethylene oxide, it withdrew from a series of weaker positions in vinyl chloride, styrene, polystyrene, and all of its commodity chemicals in Western Europe (selling the businesses to British Petroleum and its position in Unifos to Neste Oy). The dramatic changes in Carbide's product portfolio are shown in table 5.5.

The process of managing this change involved two new chief executives, a major reorganization, the introduction of portfolio planning, a series of reassignments of top executives that broke down traditional walls among historical product groups, as well as extensive analysis of the entire chemical business and its components.

Union Carbide, the outcome of a series of post–World War I mergers, was one of the inventors of petrochemistry. Its Bakelite plastic division produced phenolic resins and Union Carbide divi-

Table 5.5
Union Carbide Capacity Share in Ethylene and Derivatives, 1965–1980

	1965	1970	1973	1974	1975	1980
Ethylene	30.5	24.3	17.4	18.2	16.4	10.7
LDPE	31.1	23.2	18.6	20.2	10.1	16.4
HDPE	13.7	12.6	5.4	5.4	10.5	6.6
PS	10.7	5.8	6.8	7.6	—	—
PVC	10.3	9.4	6.3	6.1	6.1	2.3

Source: McKinsey & Co., Chemical Industry Data Base.

sion produced acetylene for automobile lamps from calcium carbide. In close relation with the Mellon Institute, Carbide was responsible for the development of vinyl plastics and, working from ICI technology, introduced polyethylene to the United States. In the 1950s, Carbide's chemists were masters of the chemistry of ethylene, while in 1960 the company held a market share of 30–40 percent in ethylene and 50 percent in low-density polyethylene. The company was strong in styrene and in vinyl chloride; it was the leader of the ethylene oxide market. In fact, much of the competition in ethylene and derivatives to emerge in the 1950s built their facilities with technology purchased from Scientific Design, a company headed by an ex-Carbide chemist. Carbide had key positions in important specialties, as well.

It is harsh, but probably fair, to say that during the sixties Carbide gave that favored position away or allowed it to be taken away by Dow, several oil companies, and others diversifying from mature basic industry into the explosively growing plastics business. Obviously, Carbide could not have held virtual monopoly positions once its products became mass market necessities. But the managers who inherited the company in the late 1960s looked back sadly at the way resources and technology were diffused and market share left undefended.

When under new leadership they turned to examine their strategies closely, they found that resource allocation had been guided by a poor understanding of the economics of the business. Because depreciation on new investments depressed reported profits in rapidly growing businesses, they had been underfunded. Meanwhile, competitors—especially Dow—had borrowed at the negligible interest rates of the 1960s to chase cost down the experience curve. To change the situation required more funds than were available to restore position in all components of the portfolio. Moreover, other parts of the corporation than chemicals had attractive opportunities for investment.

In order to make choices among the opportunities, new information systems had to be built that more clearly reflected profit by product line. Systems for measuring and rewarding management had to be implemented that reflected a strategic orientation toward profit, and procedures had to be developed to provide managers a new way of assessing their strategic position. Especially important to this research was an international perspective because petrochemicals had become a global business during the 1960s, with exports rising and overseas opportunities for investment more than competitive with those in the increasingly crowded U.S. market. The number of competitors in the markets for the five commodities studied peaked in the 1970–75 period, with net exits increasing after 1973.

At the same time that the chemicals and plastics group transformed itself, the corporation introduced new systems for strategic evaluation of businesses and planning. In the process of studying the business, management consultants introduced the concept of experience, as well as business attractiveness/position matrices.

The scarcity of resources and an improved understanding of their competitive position led Carbide to exit a number of businesses: polyvinyl chloride in 1977 (share/cost was too weak), styrene in 1976, polystyrene in 1978, as well as other smaller product and geographic positions. Funds were then reallocated to major opportunities such as ethylene oxide and polyethylene. Perhaps the most dramatic event, however, was Carbide's sale of its European chemical activities.

Carbide had arrived in Europe by the usual assortment of steps. Bakelite started BXL, its UK subsidiary, before World War II. Carbide began production of higher alcohols in a joint venture with Distillers Ltd. in the late 1950s. Carbide also constructed on its own a major polyethylene facility at Antwerp in 1959. The final major facility was producing polyethylene at Stenungsund, Sweden in a joint venture with Essochem. There were smaller production activities as well as sales and service subsidiaries.

The new structure and planning systems were well suited to reveal the strategic problems facing these facilities, and a new chairman of Union Carbide Europe, drawn from the financial staff, was well suited to use them. The process revealed that the surge of the state-owned companies and the major oil companies was irresistible, unless Carbide wished to invest huge sums in new low-cost facilities. Even then, the problem of feedstock would remain, as would the tendency of competition to price at levels returning negligible margins on assets. The very powerful German companies were content to earn 2–3 percent on assets during the late 1960s and early 1970s, further depressing the competitive situation.

Carbide discussed the situation with its British partner, Distillers. Distillers' management, at once concerned by the apparently boundless demands for capital from the ethylene and derivatives businesses and intrigued by the opportunities available elsewhere in their portfolio, declined to participate in new investments—especially the large investment required to buy out Carbide's interest. But British Petroleum, the source of feedstock for the Carbide ethylene cracker at Grangemouth, was concerned that withdrawal would seriously harm the development of their North Sea properties. At the same time, the prospect of acquiring a going petrochemical business and expanding onto the continent through Antwerp made sense. Whereas Carbide feared the state-owned firms and the oil companies, BP was a 30 percent state-owned oil company.

The deal was made at $400 million. Carbide has since reported that it would have lost $100 million annually had it kept its European chemical businesses. It remains enthusiastic about its European gas, carbon, and consumer businesses.

The point here is not that Carbide appears to have made a sensible decision. The more interesting observation is that the same process of careful analysis of the profitability and prospects of their portfolio led them to exit a number of major commodity plastics positions both in the United States and in Europe. On the other hand, they vigorously supported their North American position in low-density polyethylene and ethylene oxide. The strong funding of the research leading to Unipol LLDPE was confirmed at this same time. It was the ability of Carbide to assess its position accurately and allocate resources accordingly that distinguished the 1976 company from its 1966 progenitor. The difference was what I have called the work of "preparation."

The Restructuring of Dow

Dow Chemical Corporation is a paradox. Headquartered in Midland, Michigan with huge integrated complexes there, in Freeport, Texas and Plaquemines, Louisiana, it prides itself on its small-town, family atmosphere. At the same time it is the most multinational of companies.

Until very recently Dow's strategy might be crudely summarized as follows: to be the world's largest and most profitable producer of commodity chemicals and plastics based on low-cost leadership and aggressive marketing in the businesses where it competed. Low costs, in turn, were achieved by vertical integration, technical excellence, near or maximum scale, and leveraged financing, all on a worldwide basis. When oil prices skyrocketed, Dow sought integration further back to reduce cost. For years, the Boston Consulting Group used the contrast of Dow and Du Pont to illustrate the power of an experience, curve–driven strategy financed with debt to generate rapid, profitable growth. And, over the decades from 1960 to 1980, Dow's performance was outstanding.

Dow Chemical Company is another example of an American chemical company that restructured itself in response to economic pressure. Perhaps because it had experienced breathtaking success with its strategic focus on commodities, its redeployment of assets came later than Carbide's. And because it had been able to construct a formidable base of profitable subsidiaries in Europe during the 1960s and early 1970s, it retained a larger international position in petrochemicals even after restructuring.

For Dow, the shift was wrenching. As early as the 1930s, top management had concluded that inflation would be a fact of life in the U.S. economy, and therefore, that financial leverage made sense. Dow's steady postwar growth was fueled by a far greater use of debt than its rivals at Union Carbide or Du Pont would countenance. As a consequence, during the 1970s expansion was occasionally fueled by capital with a negative real current cost.

When 1973 changed the relative value added in feedstock and chemicals, Dow was ready and willing to use debt to fund a program of backward integration into oil and gas. It was only the high interest rates and declining real energy prices of the 1980s that precipitously altered the attractiveness of Dow's portfolio. All of a sudden, they had to scramble to generate funds to eliminate debt. In the process, a number of problematic investments were liquidated: Asahi-Dow, Dow's Saudi venture, most of Dow's oil and gas ventures, Dow's Korean joint venture, and Dow Yugoslavia; also some less-favored diversifications, such as Dow's BioScience Enterprises, were terminated. Resources freed by these measures were used to reduce debt and increase the investment in agricultural chemicals, pharmaceuticals, and specialties.

In contrast to the problems facing many others, the problem for Dow was not the introduction of a new decentralized way of managing business. The reverse was true. In the view of at least some of its management, the success of its leveraged global growth in commodities during the 1960s and 1970s made it that much harder for the company to recognize the fundamental shifts in the industry that began in the 1970s. With power dispersed in strong geographically based organizations that were competing for resources to grow their commodity businesses, it was hard to pick up and react quickly to the shifts under way. Moreover, because many of Dow's businesses were low-cost leaders, the developing secular decline in profitability was not immediately obvious. One Dow manager noted that

> We faced three major strategic problems. The elasticity of demand has caught up with the chemical industry. That's the fundamental change. Second, we were back integrated. But today, you only make your profit at the forward end. You can't afford to back integrate. And third, we learned that under bad business conditions our joint ventures were harder to operate.
>
> I think what's happening to us, and happening to the industry, is that we never took out depreciation. And we invested in rebuilding our old plants. What's really happening is that the new plants are replacing the old plants. We're shutting down. I think this is going to be the decade of rationalization. There may be some mismanaged companies that might expand if we have a good year or two; the chemical industry has been famous for lousy planning, but I think everyone sees the fundamental change.[3]

Dow management suggested that the key issues they faced in dealing with this change had to do with strategy, organization, and people. Initially, it was no longer as obvious on which distinctive skills Dow would rely to beat the competition. For years, Dow management had relied on process technology, operating skills, and marketing to large customers as the foundation for their company's growth surge. Looking ahead, it was not obvious that these same skills would propel Dow forward. In the words of a Dow planner,

> I think the history of our company is that we are much better managers when we have a technological base. For the future, there has to be a fit between where Dow's technological strengths are today, or could be, and what we or our consultants perceive to be the emerging technologies. And Dow's strengths have always been in chemistry rather than physics or biological science.[4]

Another manager noted that the growth of the service economy threatened Dow: "Doctors and lawyers are now the ones whose profits survive recessions," not chemical companies.

The organizational challenge was equally interesting. During the previous phase of Dow's growth, the critical resources required by the geographically based businesses were technology and money. Both were more or less easily managed centrally from Midland. In agricultural chemicals, pharmaceuticals, and specialties, capital was a less critical element—because requirements were not so massive—and cross-licensing led to very different arrangements among competitors. To manage these new demands, Dow was creating worldwide product organizations.

Even in its commodity businesses, Dow in the mid-1980s was operating in a more centralized mode. In order to gather the resources to reallocate toward specialties, more power had shifted to the center. Previously the corporate product department had played an important but limited role in resource allocation. Strategy was driven regionally. Now managers reported that the geographic areas were only free to operate day to day.

Finally, the new strategic thrusts were changing the human equation in another more profound way.

> People in a company like Dow [are] really more of a fixed asset than a variable cost. We don't hire and fire and lay off. We don't treat people like garbage. That becomes increasingly difficult when we get more people-intensive businesses.[5]

Managers were not sure how Dow would behave as the structure of its balance sheet and income statement changed with the shifting business portfolio.

For all their concerns, Dow management expressed great confidence in the company's future. While they were less than happy with competitive conditions in the petrochemical industries of the United States and Europe, they assessed their position to be outstanding based on feedstock and facility cost. The long-term growth might have vanished, but market share could be defended against both oil company and government-owned competition.

On the other hand, Dow was a strong believer in the need for industry rationalization. "All the industry participants can see the need to cut back," a Dow manager asserted. "They just have to step in and do it."[6] In this effort, Dow took a leadership role. In the winter of 1982, it sponsored an industrywide meeting in Geneva at which outside experts gave speeches along with some industry executives.

> There was a lot of despondency in Europe, and we were trying to get people together to realize what had to be done. But with exceptions like BP and ICI, they won't do anything until the Saudi product hits and dries up their export markets.[7]

Many in Europe gave Dow credit for stimulating more companies to think seriously about fundamental cutbacks. Dow management, however, while ready to use their strong competitive position in Europe and the United States, was clearly devoting its most creative thought to the problem of inventing a future for the 1990s that was not centrally dependent on commodity petrochemicals.

NOTES

1. "Commodities: Stuck with Low Growth," *Chemical Week,* 26 October 1983, 32.
2. The experience curve conceived by the Boston Consulting Group tracks the decline in average total cost per unit with increases in cumulative volume. For many products each doubling of cumulative volume is associated with a 15–30 percent decline in unit cost.
3. Interviews with Dow manager, fall 1982.
4. Interview with Dow planner, fall 1982.
5. Interviews with Dow manager, fall 1982.
6. Ibid.
7. Ibid.

6
Other Forces in the Market: Oil Companies and the United States Government

Introduction

It is generally true in economic affairs, that the U.S. government's activities have a substantial influence on what goes on, but they can seldom be attributed to a clearly prepared strategy. In petrochemicals, this is particularly true. Inaction would appear to be the policy of the day.

In fact, the lack of specific action masks a great deal of activity among the public and private players that, taken together, results in what we call policy. Despite the prospect of substantial loss of exports and the inroads of some material from hydrocarbon-rich countries, the petrochemical manufacturers have stayed calm.

The Department of Commerce's increasingly sophisticated apparatus has prepared a competitive assessment of the industry and projections for its future.[1] The department's August 1982 report provides a good summary of the aggregate aspects of the situation.

It noted that significant shifts in structure were already under way in the industry around the world; that they would continue over the next decades as hydrocarbon-rich countries built facilities to use their natural gas and priced their production so as to gain markets; and that this strategy would be successful since fuel and feedstock cost were such a high percentage of commodity petrochemical production costs. It suggested, that although the decline in U.S. competitiveness would be gradual without severe crises, it was likely that there would be some calls for government assistance of some form. Without going so far as to say that the calls from the weak should not be heeded, the report called attention to the need for focus on opportunities in downstream specialty chemicals, as well as in high-performance materials where competition among Europe, Japan, and the United States was increasing.

For obvious reasons, the Department of Commerce did not make clear distinctions among the several kinds of companies in the industry—chemical and oil, domestic and multinational—nor among the portfolios of the individual companies. Nor did the report discuss the difference between the impact of restructuring on the companies and on the country. But to understand the position of the United States government, it is critical to remember that most of the important multinational oil companies live here.

Chemical Companies vs. Oil Companies

We have already seen in chapter 5's descriptions of Union Carbide and Dow that there are dramatic differences to the meaning of restructuring. These differences are clearly important to the companies, but they are doubly important to the evolution of United States policy. In our marvelously fragmented federal system of "separate institutions sharing power," the individual players have much to say about what should and will happen.

In the instance of petrochemicals, chemical companies such as Carbide and Dow are very important. Their executives have been leaders in building the industry's associations and in their negotiations with the government. But the oil companies are also important petrochemical producers and are extremely powerful players in dealing with government. For a number of reasons, their perspective is different.

The Chemical Companies

The products of the chemical industry have to be invented, they are not found. Commercialization is a series of problems solved through intellectual effort over a long period of time, often in competition with other creative companies. Given the diversity of products, their scale, and rate of growth, technical management is required in depth. As well, resources must be invested selectively according to some economic measure based on fully allocated cost since it has long been impossible to pursue all of the major opportunities available.

For the U.S. chemical manufacturers, then, the issue of restructuring is an old one. The companies themselves achieved size and success before World War II or in the 1950s at the latest. In the

1960s they experienced an attack from chemical groups of oil companies and others for whom raw material was cheap; this attack resembled in structure the current challenge of the Middle East to Europe and Asia. After 1973, studies revealed that in commodity products, the oil companies could—if well run—achieve a fundamental strategic advantage. Strategic analysis also revealed that the long-term potential profitability of these businesses had shifted as potential value added shifted from 60 percent of sales price to 30 percent.

Two basic responses can be distinguished. Some companies chose to become oil companies. Using the leverage of debt with a negative real cost, Dow moved to acquire oil and gas properties in the southwest United States and the Middle East. Most dramatically, Du Pont acquired Conoco. But with the rise in interest rates and the freeing up of feedstock following significant declines in the consumption of energy worldwide, Dow has since turned around and backed out of most of its oil company ventures. Having acquired important domestic reserves at a reasonable price, Du Pont is taking a long-term view. But it has not expanded its commodity plastics position since the mid-1970s.

Others, Union Carbide being a leading example, have taken a very selective approach to the commodity businesses. Following the logic of contemporary strategic thinking, they have focused the limited cash flow available from their current business mix on those where there was an opportunity to experience sustainable, long-term profits and to grow. For all the chemical companies, this has meant (1) an emphasis on new process technology, (2) upgrading of products through alloys, copolymers, and end-use products, and (3) emphasis on new higher-performance synthetics. Where the basic raw material, technology, and/or commercial position has been strong enough (Carbide in low-density polyethylene and ethylene oxide, Dow in vinyl chloride and styrene, Du Pont in paints and fibers, Monsanto in agricultural chemicals), they have stayed to fight for a position in the endgame. But in every instance, it has been a hard and costly fight.

The Oil Companies

In contrast, the major oil companies have developed around the search for petroleum and its exploitation. Their life is a financial gamble that the oil can be found to meet market needs and that markets can be organized so that price does not crumble. Their work involves alliances among companies and negotiation with governments, mostly at the top. In particular, for the majors, competition is one indivisible global battle to be fought out over decades.

For the oil companies, the chemical business has been a fickle mistress, providing few joys in return for what has seemed like major investments. Whereas an expensive dry hole reveals itself with a certain finality, a weak chemicals business shows up slowly over time and provides no natural exit point. The facilities just do not make money.

The problem in general has been that chemical plants are often very difficult to run and chemical products hard to sell. Until the oil companies developed the capability to build and run state-of-the-art plants and to market the product skillfully, their presence was only disruptive. (For example, ARCO was never able to make a new plant for ethylene oxide work. And a $100 million fertilizer business of Gulf that was a loss for them returned a handsome profit for the Williams Company only months after taking it off Gulf's hands.) Even where they have mastered the businesses, they faced tough competition from chemical companies that yielded market share grudgingly. As well, the same tough markets and difficult economies plagued the oil companies' chemical subsidiaries.

Their ability to respond to the challenge from the Middle East is also different. While Union Carbide can sell LLDPE technology to the Saudis, Exxon, Mobil, and Shell are in a position to help build and manage the plants. An example of an oil major's global view of chemical activity is provided by Exxon.

Exxon Chemical

By 1984 Exxon was the world's largest oil company. Its chemical activity started in 1920 when the company was the first to produce commercial quantities of isopropyl alcohol. As chemical companies began to make large amounts of ethylene from oil and gas feedstocks in the 1930s and 1940s, Exxon became one of their major suppliers of raw materials. Exxon started moving downstream in the petrochemical industry after World War II when it began to produce butyl rubber, which it had invented. In the 1960s, Exxon Chemical Company was set up as a division of Exxon Corporation, beginning a period of rapid expansion into ethylene and commodity plastics.

Although accounting for less than one-tenth of Exxon Corporation's revenues in the early 1980s, Exxon Chemical was, nevertheless, one of the largest chemical companies in the world, with sales exceeding $8 billion. As the company was still expanding ethylene and plastics production, its sales had increased in 1979–82, but earnings had fallen dramatically, both in the United States and abroad (see chart 6.1).

Exxon Chemical's portfolio contained some profitable specialties, such as butyl rubbers and petroleum additives, and many less profitable, high-volume commodities (aside from solvents and agrochemicals, ethylene and plastics) primarily low-density polyethylene (LDPE) and polypropylene (PP). The company began to

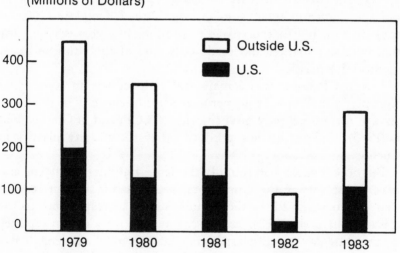

Reprinted from Exxon ChemReport, 1983.

Chart 6.1
Segment Earnings at Exxon Chemical, 1979–1983

make polyethylene in 1968, and initially was a supplier of bulk plastics to the merchant market. It later began to differentiate its products and find special market niches. As one Exxon Chemical executive described the process:

> As a raw material supplier to relatively few big customers, you keep asking yourself: Should I integrate downstream? It looks attractive, but it causes you to compete with your customers. Also, we used to think that the market would set prices such that each stage in the chain of production would receive a satisfactory return.
>
> Over time, we saw that we could become an effective derivatives producer. And we realized that, in practice, market prices did not provide a viable return to producers at each stage. So we began to integrate downstream and to find special market niches for our products. There is a place for us there, but our pace was slowed by our history in raw material production.[2]

By 1980, Exxon Chemical was one of the largest ethylene producers in Europe (see table 6.1). It had a dominating presence in ethylene in Sweden (350,000 tons per year tpy), a major complex at Cologne, West Germany (450,000 tpy), and significant operations in France (300,000 tpy) and the United Kingdom (100,000 tpy). In Europe, Exxon strove to produce low-cost ethylene for the merchant market and made only one of the ethylene-based commodity plastics.

Exxon Chemical was a major LDPE producer in continental Europe, with 490,000 tons per year (tpy) of capacity in Belgium. Except for a small polyvinyl chloride (PVC) plant in Greece (sold in 1983), Exxon did not produce other commodity plastics in Europe.

Exxon Chemical had roughly the same amount of ethylene and plastics capacity in the United States as it had in Europe, except that it also made PP in the United States. In responding to the crisis of the early 1980s, Exxon cut its U.S. production capacity by some 100,000 tpy of plastics and 450,000 tpy of ethylene. It also planned to modernize its U.S. facilities by upgrading its PP plants and entering the linear low-density polyethylene (LLDPE) field with Union Carbide's new Unipol technology. One top Exxon Chemical executive said about these businesses:

> There is no question but that we are in these commodity petrochemicals for the long term. Our mix, locations, and posture may vary, but

Table 6.1
Exxon Chemical Company
Production Capacity and Capacity Share for Ethlyene, Low-Density
Polyethylene, and Polypropylene

	1973	*1978*	*1983*
Ethylene			
France	250	300	300
W. Germany	120	450	450
Sweden	280	350	350
UK	80	100	100
Greece	20		20
Subtotal	750	1,220	1,220
% of Europe	6	7	8
United States	800	900	1,200
% of U.S.	7	9	8
Low-Density Polyethylene			
Bel/Lux	160	490	490
% of Europe	6	8	7
United States	182	300	300
% of U.S.	6	8	7
Polypropylene			
United States	136	227	250
% of U.S.	14	11	11

Source: Compiled by casewriter from data in Parpinelli Tecnon srl, *IPE Service—1983 Olefins Report,* Milan, 1983, and McKinsey & Co., Chemical Industry Data Base.

we are in to stay. But we will not invest in any new capacity in these areas in the foreseeable future, as none will be needed. We believe the industry will solve its problems.[3]

As part of an effort to build downstream plants in hydrocarbon-rich countries, Exxon Chemical did have projects in Canada (for 135,000 tpy of LLDPE), Saudi Arabia (for 260,000 tpy of LLDPE), and the United Kingdom (for 500,000 tpy of ethylene). The United Kingdom ethylene plant at Mossmoran, a fifty-fifty joint venture with Shell, was to use North Sea ethane as a feedstock and promised to be one of the most efficient plants in Europe. One Exxon Chemical executive, who was involved in planning the Mossmoran project said, "We think it will be a very competitive plant, but we wish there were more derivative plants nearby. Shell will take its share, and the rest will go to the continent."[4]

One problem that Exxon Chemical planners admitted as still unresolved was the position of their large ethylene complex at Cologne. When the Mossmoran cracker came on stream in 1985, the ethylene it would sell in continental Europe would compete directly with Exxon's output in Germany. According to one Exxon Chemical planner:

> Cologne is a difficult problem for us. In Europe, everybody's naphtha cracker is in trouble. We and others have downstream customers, such as polyethylene producers, which are directly linked up to our ethylene plants. In such situations, it may be impossible to just shut one cracker down because that increases the costs of the whole complex. That, in turn, may trigger the shutdown of the next marginal unit, and so on. Our problem at Cologne is really a microcosm of the industry's problem.[5]

The problem of Cologne in another sense is the consequence of Exxon's global strategy or, one might say, of "oil company" global strategy. The competition from the facilities built to use North Sea and Middle East natural gas undermined the strategy of an ethylene supplier based on naphtha from imported crude located in the middle of Europe. Cologne is just one of what will be several casualties.[6]

In this sense Cologne is a specially vulnerable example of the problem facing commodity producers in the United States. They may be more effectively forward integrated, but the challenge of low-cost supply is no less real. The peculiar challenge for Exxon management is to think through the problem, given that they are the new competition.

This idea is clear if one considers, for example, the ownership of the projects operating and planned in Saudi Arabia. They are more or less typical of the structures in other hydrocarbon-rich nations of the world. The projects may pose problems as far as U.S. exporters are concerned, but they certainly look like important ventures for U.S. companies (see table 6.2). In 1986, all eight projects had been completed. For the country, the results are likely to be positive.[7] There may be crackers shut down in the United States, but if resources are managed effectively, the consequence should be cheaper commodities and a stronger position in higher-performance, higher value-added chemicals and materials.

The exception to this pattern of strategic adjustment by chemi-

Table 6.2

Major Petrochemical Projects of Saudi Arabia and its Foreign Affiliates

Saudi Company & Partner	Products	Estimated Cost
Saudi Petrochemical Co. & Shell (U.S.)	Ethylene, Styrene Ethanol, Caustic Soda, Ethylene Dichloride	$3 billion
Al-Jubail Petrochem Co. & Exxon (U.S.)	LDPE	$1.3 billion
Saudi Yanbu Petrochem Co. & Mobil (U.S.)	LDPE, HDPE, Ethylene Glycol	$2.0 billion
Arabian Petrochemical Co. & Dow (U.S.)★	Ethylene, LDPE & HDPE	$1.5 billion
Saudi Methanol Co. & Mitsubishi Consort. (Japan)	Chemical grade Methanol	$300 million
Eastern Petrochem Co. & Mitsubishi Consort. (Japan)	LDPE & Ethylene Glycol	$1.7 billion
National Methanol Co. & Celanese (U.S.)★★	Chemical grade Methanol	$500 million
Al-Jubail Fertilizer Co. & Taiwan Fertilizer Co. (Taiwan)	Urea	$400 million

Source: U.S. Department of Commerce, Office of Competitive Assessment, Assistant Secretary for Productivity, Technology, and Innovation, Technical Appendix to "The Medium- to Long-Range International Competitiveness of the United States Petrochemical Industry, A Competitive Assessment" (Washington, D.C.: Government Printing Office, 1982), sec. IV, 12, table 3.

★Dow Chemical withdrew from this project, November 30, 1982.

★★Also Texas Eastern (U.S.).

cal and oil companies may be the undiversified domestic fertilizer manufacturers. After years of arguing that U.S. regulation of natural gas prices was not a subsidy, some fertilizer manufacturers charged that Mexico's energy and economic development programs constitute a counteravailable subsidy. The fertilizer problem seems to be similar to that in steel: certain companies were late to see the competitive threat, and their market position gives them no place to go. They are not the high value-added producers. Their 1982 suit before the International Trade Commission (ITC) was quite serious. The petrochemical producers were concerned that a successful suit could interrupt trade patterns in a wide range of products.

The United States Government: A New Move to Protection?

The U.S. chemical industry has had a long, close working relationship with the government, interrupted by periodic battles. The industry was encouraged to grow in numerous ways. After the First World War, a tariff wall was erected to protect the infant dye industry from European competition, especially English and German. The American Selling Price system (ASP) that was adopted then guaranteed that imports could not sell lower than 8 percent above the average American selling price. The system remained in place until traded away during GATT (General Agreement on Trade and Tariff) negotiations in the Tokyo Round (1978 and 1979).

During the Second World War the development of synthetic rubber and Plexiglas were important contributions as were numerous advances in solvents, lubricants, gases, and weapons, such as napalm. Under the Eisenhower administration, studies were made of the nation's resources. When growth in synthetic fertilizers was identified as a priority, accelerated depreciation was made available under the Korean War Defense Production Act to all producers except Du Pont and Allied, who were then the dominant producers.

In fact, until environmental concerns became widespread, the industry was regarded as a benevolent example of bounteous high tech in the same way that computers are today. Accordingly, despite the fury of the Europeans, the ASP was retained during the Kennedy Round of GATT negotiations (1964) after eleventh-hour efforts by the industry restored the provisions.

The experience of the Kennedy Round provided a lesson for the industry. In the period leading up to the final negotiation, the Manufacturing Chemists Association (MCA, later changed to CMA) and the Synthetic Organics Chemical Manufacturers Association (SOCMA) had neutralized each other politically. The smaller dye manufacturers seeking protection had different interests from large commodity chemical and plastics producers.

In 1973, key company managers who had been involved in what was regarded as the narrowly avoided disaster of the Kennedy Round came up with the idea of creating an umbrella organization to put together a single industry position. The rationale for creating the Organization of Chemical Industry Trade Associations (OCITA) was the upcoming Tokyo Round. OCITA was founded in 1974 to bring together the Society of Plastics Industries (SPI), the Dye Chemical Manufacturers (DCMA), the Fertilizer Institute (FI), SOCMA, and MCA.

OCITA's leadership was in place just in time to take part in the industry sector advisory committees (ISACs) called for by the Trade Act of 1975. It turned out to be particularly useful since the U.S. Trade Representative (USTR) had divided the industry into three groups: chemicals and allied products (inorganics, organics, and fertilizers), rubber and plastics (including the polyolefins), and paints and coatings that cut across the membership of the trade associations as well as the product lines of the major companies.

The chemicals ISAC met twenty-five times a year for three years working hard and seriously to find a limited list of products deserving protection on which very heterogeneous companies could agree. (The average ISAC met four to six times a year.) Some bitter fights took place between the ISAC and USTR, especially when the group in Geneva recommended that the industry receive no exceptions to the overall cuts recommended. In the end, in a deal cut with Alonzo McDonald and Robert Strauss, exceptions were negotiated for sixty to seventy products that constitute 70 percent of U.S. productive capacity. The ASP disappeared in the process, traded away for other concessions when it appeared that there was no longer any American-owned dye manufacturing capacity.[8]

Since that time OCITA has successfully taken part in a series of peacefully resolved negotiations with the European Commission (under pressure from the European companies to "do something" in the face of overcapacity and countertrade deals with Comecon countries). In the summer and fall of 1983 U.S. manufacturers asked OCITA to deal with the problems of ammonia.

The ITC Suit

On 28 October 1982, W. R. Grace, First Mississippi Corp., Mississippi Chemical Corp., and Olin Corp., representing 8 percent of U.S. anhydrous ammonia capacity, petitioned for countervailing duties under the Tariff Act of 1930, charging that Mexicans were subsidizing exports both directly and indirectly—especially with a two-tier natural gas price. As evidence, they pointed to the

Mexican Industrial Development Plan which set forth a series of subsidies and incentives designed to promote economic development and exports. The petition cited Amoco, Phillips Petroleum, Du Pont, and Texasgulf, among others, as importers of ammonia.

Still other interested parties were the major multinational commodity petrochemical producers with interests in Canada, Indonesia, the Middle East, the North Sea, and other places where nations have constructed industrial policy based on cheap hydrocarbon reserves. They thought the precedent posed by the Grace suit unfortunate. Executives involved in the discussions thought it unlikely that OCITA would support the petitioners.

On the other hand, Representative Gillis Long (D, Louisiana) had risen to the defense of one of his state's major industries. Six and one-half million tons, 33.7 percent of U.S. capacity, were located in his state. A new participant in the government's discussions concerning the chemical industry, he had stayed on the sidelines during the Tokyo Round. He now spoke out vociferously. In introducing legislation to amend the United States trade laws, Long attacked governments that

> are conferring an unfair competitive advantage by providing natural gas and petroleum feedstocks to their own petrochemical producers at artificial, government-set low prices, but will only sell the same feedstocks to U.S. producers at the much higher equivalent world price of oil.
>
> This system protects their producers from any competition and at the same time provides an international and contrived unfair advantage for their monopoly or government-controlled producers to sell their products in U.S. and world markets. This is a blatant unfair trade practice by anyone's definition of fair trade.
>
> American petrochemical producers are the most efficient in the world, but they cannot compete with less efficient foreign government monopolies and state-controlled enterprises, because, and only because, of these flagrant and unfair price discrimination practices. This legislation will simply put U.S. petrochemical producers, including producers of ammonia and carbon black, on an equal footing with these governments.[9]

Congressman Long emphasized that

> These proposed amendments have been carefully drawn to avoid acting against any country's comparative advantage in these energy and natural resources, such as some Middle Eastern countries, where

the governments involved permit equal access to any producer and attempt to let market forces set prices for the production inputs.[10]

The ITC Report

The ITC itself had published an extensive report, *The Probable Impact on the U.S. Petrochemical Industry of the Expanding Petrochemical Industries in the Conventional-Energy-Rich Nations*, based on a study instituted in February 1982 on its own motion "for the purpose of gathering and presenting information on . . . the effects of such expansion on the U.S. petrochemical industry." The conclusion that the U.S. trade position in commodity petrochemicals is likely to decrease substantially is not very different from the Commerce Department study already cited, but some of the tables are instructive.

The report highlights first the raw material price advantage of the energy-rich nations, noting that in almost all cases the prices are set by governments or government-owned producers (see table 6.3).

They go on to estimate the consequent impact of feedstock prices expected in the 1985–90 period on the production cost of the three basic primary petrochemicals in a world-scale plant (see table 6.4).

Table 6.3
Raw Material Prices of Energy-Rich and Consumer Nations Compared

Area	Price per Metric Ton in Dollars		
	Ethane	Naphtha	Methane
Energy-Rich			
Canada	80–100		50– 90
Mexico	45– 65		20– 30
Persian Gulf	20– 30		0– 30
Indonesia	20– 30		0– 30
Consumers			
U.S.	205–225	275–285	205–230
Western Europe		320–330	215–230
Japan		340–350	310–320

Source: United States International Trade Commission, Office of the Secretary, U.S.I.T.C. Publication 1370, *The Probable Impact on the U.S. Petrochemical Industry of the Expanding Petrochemical Industries in the Conventional-Energy-Rich Nations* (Washington, D.C.: Government Printing Office, 1983), 29.

Table 6.4

Basic Chemical Prices of Energy-Rich and Consumer Nations Compared

	Price per Metric Ton in Dollars		
Area	*Ethylene*	*Methanol*	*Ammonia*
Energy-Rich			
Canada	250–350	100–150	130–180
Mexico	230–270	100–140	125–165
Persian Gulf	300–340	100–150	140–180
Indonesian Gulf	355–395	125–165	170–210
Consumers			
U.S.	540–580	325–375	315–360
Western Europe	835–875★	380–420	400–440★★
Japan	825–865★	355–395	355–470★★

Source: United States International Trade Commission, Office of the Secretary, U.S.I.T.C. Publication 1370, *The Probable Impact on the U.S. Petrochemical Industry of the Expanding Petrochemical Industries in the Conventional-Energy-Rich Nations* (Washington, D.C.: Government Printing Office, 1983), 32.
★Naphtha feedstock.
★★Methane to naphtha feedstock range.

The report continues, noting that for reasons of national development, the new producers are likely to enter world markets faster than would be expected if they practiced something the ITC chose to call "traditional entry." Traditional entry is growth solely in response to an "increase in the demand for that item." Apparently demand is not thought to be a function of price and tradition nothing to do with history.

In fact, the report notes that the new producers are likely to "depend upon advantages." These include lower cost, linkage of petrochemical sales to access to petroleum reserves, cartels, and countertrade (especially prevalent in Comecon deals). Finally the fact that most new production will be managed by state-owned enterprises is also noted.

The impact of these developments is expected to vary from one product to another. Ethylene and its derivatives ought to be less affected because the one is hard to transport and the other more complex to market. But the bottom line is an end to exports (see table 6.5).

In a brief note, the report does indicate that lower price petrochemical intermediates could help the U.S. exports of final products.

Table 6.5
Estimated Impact in 1990 on U.S. Trade of
Energy-Rich Nation Exports

	U.S. Trade Position *(in millions of tons)*
Ethylene and derivatives	1.3 to −2.0 tons
Ammonia	−3.7 to −5.8
Methanol	−0.12 to −4.8 M tons
Net dollar impact (1982$)	from −$140 M to −$3.8 B

Source: United States International Trade Commission, Office of the Secretary, U.S.I.T.C. Publication 1370, *The Probable Impact on the U.S. Petrochemical Industry of the Expanding Petrochemical Industries in the Conventional-Energy-Rich Nations* (Washington, D.C.: Government Printing Office, 1983), 177–78.
*A negative new trade position indicates a net import status.

As of 1986, the ITC suit had failed, and the protectionist legislation lay dormant in committees, while attention focused on more sensitive manufactures such as autos and electronics.

It looked very much as if the industry would continue to evolve under private managements with negligible government involvement. But the lower relative oil prices of 1985 have lessened the pressure on the weak manufacturers to exit. Managers spoke wistfully of the value of industrywide discussion of the overcapacity problem, but none expected anything except the spread of the disease to new areas. There were too many competitors. The situation in the United States was relatively healthy, however, when compared with the problem in Europe where there were too many nations.

NOTES

1. U.S. Department of Commerce, Office of Competitive Assessment, Assistant Secretary for Productivity, Technology, and Innovation, "The Medium- to Long-Range International Competitiveness of the United States Petrochemical Industry: A Competitive Assessment" (Washington, D.C.: Government Printing Office, 1982).
2. Interviews with Exxon Chemical management, fall 1982.
3. Ibid.
4. Ibid.
5. Ibid.

6. In August of 1985, Exxon finally announced it would shut Cologne.
7. Even in 1986 the impact is unclear. The Europeans have blocked entry of some Saudi product. In addition, the changed price of oil and volume of Saudi production have altered the economics of Sabic's projects.
8. The industry was worried that their interests would be traded away. One key industry negotiator remarked that "originally our concern was that they'd cut our protection 55 percent as a trade-off for textiles and steel. We thought they'd taken the position that 'U.S. chemicals are strong so we'll give you that.' But our fundamental concern was the future. We were worried that hydrocarbon-rich countries would flood the market and there had to be some basis for maintaining a tariff structure. Plus the Europeans were getting very tough. Plus the raw material price swings led to some dumping."
9. HR 3801, "The Unfair Trade Practices Act of 1983," was co-sponsored by Messrs. Whitten, Jones, Hightower, and Mollochan, a formidable group.
10. From the office of Congressman Gillis Long, news release, 4 August 1983.

7

The Restructuring of British Petroleum and Imperial Chemical Industries

In 1984, the structure of the chemical industry in Britain was the result of five major developments.

1. The building of Imperial Chemical Industries (ICI), followed by the decline of its competitive position in the 1960s and 1970s.
2. The development of Shell's chemical activity.
3. The development by Union Carbide and Distillers Ltd. of a chemical business and its acquisition by British Petroleum (BP).
4. The decision of Essochem to build a major olefin facility based on North Sea gas at Mossmoran, Scotland in a joint venture with Shell.
5. The BP and ICI swap.

From the perspective of this study with its focus on commodity plastics, the United Kingdom provides the most notable example of major restructuring of the industry undertaken by private companies. From 1980 to 1983 industry capacity was transformed dramatically (see table 7.1). The story is to be found in the actions of the companies.

British Petroleum

British Petroleum is a seventy-thirty private/public corporation originally organized to control Britain's Middle Eastern exploration and production activities. Its first chemical venture was a fifty-fifty joint venture with Distillers begun in 1956. From the BP perspective this seems to have been more of an investment than diversification because management in the first years came from

Table 7.1
UK Productive Capacity for Commodity Petrochemicals (in thousands of tons)

	1980				1983			
	BP	*ICI*	*SHELL*	*Other*	*BP*	*ICI*	*SHELL*	*Other*
Ethylene	925	975	235	140	720	520	145	110
LD	100	175	155	50	170	—	—	—
HD	140	—	—	—	140	—	—	—
PS	40	0	25	110	—	—	25	135
PVC	230	330	—	150	—	375	—	120
PP	0	160	100	—	—	200	—	—

Source: Company data.

Distillers, and BP exercised little control over Distillers' commercially aggressive management. In 1967, as petrochemicals emerged as a major growth area requiring much capital, Distillers decided to back out and BP took over the remaining 50 percent. For many reasons (including personnel and the coincidental acquisition of Sohio), the chemicals division remained through 1976 largely in the control of a series of ex-Distillers' managers.

The last of these managements bought Union Carbide's European commodity chemicals activities in 1978 for BP. Carbide had been buying ethylene from a BP cracker. (BP acquired certain Monsanto facilities in the same year.) When Carbide announced that it was withdrawing, it seemed to put the cracker at risk. Moreover, owning Carbide would provide an opening to the Continent and re-entry into specialty products for BP.

Robert Horton, BP's corporate planner, had opposed the Carbide investment. As it transpired, he was moved to BP chemicals in 1979 and was made managing director in the late fall. Horton, an engineer with an MIT Sloan School MBA, then proceeded with a series of studies, a reorganization, and some consolidation that reduced manpower from 18,000 to 11,000. In 1982, it became clear that more radical change was needed. In Horton's words:

> We had a very valuable asset, North Sea-based ethane; we had a very big problem in South Wales, we were too small in PVC—we had to exit. We were strong in polyethylene, especially since we were in wire and cable and we had our own LLDPE process.[1]

Out of this came the ICI deal. It was better to swap than scrap.

ICI

Imperial Chemical Industries Ltd. was formed in 1926 by the merger of British Dyestuffs Corporation; Brunner, Mond & Co. Ltd.; Nobel Industries Ltd.; and United Alkali Co. Ltd., largely in response to the aggressive competition of the newly merged I. G. Farben group in Germany. With its line of explosives, dyes, fertilizers, and pharmaceuticals, ICI closely resembled the rival German company. Cartel arrangements enabled ICI to concentrate its activities on the United Kingdom, the Commonwealth, and to an extent, South America; Du Pont and its U.S. rivals held the U.S. market, while I.G. Farben and Solvay dominated the Continent.

ICI always had a very broad product line relative to its rivals and exploited research to develop new products aggressively—polyethylene and Plexiglas (trademarked Perspex).

With the breakup of the cartels after the war, ICI broadened its focus from the Commonwealth toward Europe and from coal-based ammonia to oil as a feedstock. The first naphtha cracker was built in 1951.

In 1983 the company had remained profitable over the entire previous decade but profit, before interest and taxation as a percentage of average assets employed, declined dramatically from 18 percent in 1973 to 7.4 percent in 1982. The decline in profitability reflected weakness in particular businesses more than in the general economic condition, with losses in 1981 of £444 million in fibers, £30 million in dyestuffs and specialties, and £54 million in petrochemicals and plastics.

It was to deal with this decline that the board of ICI reached down in the organization to elect John Harvey-Jones chairman in April 1982. His approach included a dramatic shake-up and trimming of top management and corporate overhead as well as plans to move from ICI's palatial headquarters on the Millbank in London.

For a company whose divisions were still known by the original company name (explosives were made in the "Nobel division" and soda and chlorine in the "Mond division"), the internal restructuring was painful. In 1980 a committee was established to consider the possible benefit of a change in organization. It consisted of the then-deputy chairman, John Harvey-Jones, the Main Board directors responsible for the Mond, petrochemicals, and plastics divisions, and the three division chairmen. For the first time in company history operating management was involved in such a study.

The committee decided to bring the market orientation of the plastics division managers to bear on the production-oriented petrochemical people through a merger of the two groups. The goal was better integration of the plastics and petrochemicals businesses, better strategy, and massive economies. Division headquarters was to be reduced 80 percent as all technical activity was moved back to the plants. Overall, staffing was reduced from 20,300 in early 1981 to 14,000 in the spring of 1983.

Once this merger was accomplished, a small board of executives without profit responsibility was formed. They set about reorganizing the division into a large, integrated core and a set of stand-alone specialty businesses. Five layers of management were reduced to three.

With this reorganization accomplished, it was possible to examine the pieces. The fundamental shift in the commodity plastics was recognized. The era of growth was over and the market glutted. During the slowly growing markets of the 1970s, government companies such as Dutch State Mines (DSM) and CdF Chimie kept building. In PVC, ICI had paused during a period when vinyl chloride toxicity posed unknown problems but the Germans, French, and Solvay kept building. ICI spurted to catch up and built a new facility at Wilhelmshaven.

The studies revealed that ICI possessed fundamental strengths in PVC but weakness in polyethylene. Thomas Hutchison, managing director of ICI's Chemicals Group, recalled "We had a LLDPE process of sorts but concluded that we could only sell the product in the 72 percent of the market that was cheap and that there was new product in those markets coming from the Middle East."[2]

Division management reasoned that if they could exit polyethylene in the United Kingdom, they could reduce their need for ethylene. At the time ICI had two large modern crackers at Wilton, on the northeast coast of the United Kingdom. One unit could provide 450,000 tons, and the half of the other unit (which was shared with BP) provided 325,000. If 325,000 was less than ICI would need, the 775,000 total was too much. The small cracker could be shut down if ICI could get more of the large cracker's output. Higher operating rates in a more efficient unit would then help all the other businesses dependent on the large cracker (polypropylene, vinyl chloride monomer, polyvinyl chloride, and ethylene oxide and derivatives). ICI approached BP and "found them doing their thinking. They were weak in PVC, strong in polyethylene in the United Kingdom, and they had a good LLDPE process. We did a deal."

At the same time, ICI was pushing further in PVC with the acquisition of the business of the Swiss firm, Lonza. In 1983 ICI purchased the dyestuffs business of Pechiney Chemie-Uhlman Kuhlmann (PCUK). Not yet reflecting the effort at restructuring, the petrochemicals and plastics interests lost £139 million in 1982. The annual report attributed the results to extensive overcapacity throughout the world, the impact of a strengthening of the U.S. dollar and deutsche mark against sterling on raw material costs, and inflation in other costs.

Mr. T. O. Hutchison, chairman of the division, commented on the way management changed under these circumstances:

> In the good old days, the CEO's job was to find opportunities for growth, etc. You looked at R&D, technology, the learning curve. What I've had to work on with my board is a closing in of the environment. It's a problem of which we are a part. What can we do for ourselves. (The press always wants to know "who won" in relation to the BP deal.) We both believe that we have strengthened our companies.
>
> We have to think about (1) what we can do to help ourselves, and (2) what we can do to help the industry fix itself by working bilaterally, with governments, and with the EC.
>
> People management is very much more difficult now. Shedding [people] and keeping [them] motivated without strikes is very hard. You have to keep cutting costs, sharpening the system, and so on. And where there is opportunity, pushing forward, for example, PP copolymers with engineering plastics.
>
> Separability is important. We still have to grow and don't want to suppress those businesses that have a chance. For us the spectrum of activity is great, from oil to specialty polymers.
>
> Yes, there are shrinkers and growers. But we try to bring generalists to the top. We are flat now. Five, twelve, and sixty managers in the top three layers.
>
> Our real concerns are France and Italy. France put up Fr 450 billion for their chemical industry. Italy is making huge grants. As long as that sort of subsidy is around, it raises questions as to whether there is

a commercial solution. The question of the depth of your purse arises. Why fight if the government is there? The French decision to devalue and freeze prices has hurt our ability to work on getting prices up.[3]

Hutchison also commented on the competitive threat posed by the new cracker at Mossmoran, Scotland. The issue of Mossmoran was serious because the ethane entering the giant new Essochem/Shell cracker was to be nearly exempted from the United Kingdom's 70-percent energy tax. Moreover, Esso and Shell benefited from subsidies for inward investment. BP tried successfully to have the act providing these benefits for Mossmoran amended so that their ethane at Grangemouth was treated equally. But ICI's naphtha-based cracker at Wilton would become very vulnerable to product based on lower-cost feedstock. ICI was unable to block the bill in Parliament and began suing the U.K. government in the European court for an unfair subsidy.[4]

Sir Peter Carey, permanent secretary of the Department of Industry, commented on the paradox of a tax scheme "that made it impossible for England's most efficient complex to compete with a U.S. oil company induced to enter Scotland."[5]

It is important in learning from the U.K. experience to delve a little more deeply into the unique swap of capacity between BP and ICI. The approach of the two managements is instructive.

The BP/ICI Swap

The importance of company behavior is highlighted by the reductions of capacity evident in table 7.1 at the beginning of this section. But the most dramatic aspect of the reduction was the exit of BP from PVC and ICI from polyethylene. Not only was capacity reduced, the number of competitors was reduced.

The reader will have already noted that both BP and ICI had changed their top management team and structure before they were able to conduct the strategic studies that led to this radical move. (More is said of this later.) But at that point in the development of the picture facing management, the relations of the two companies to each other and to the U.K. government are of particular interest.

One early development was a suggestion that swaps of capacity ("portfolio exchanges") might make sense floated in a January 16,

1982 article "Rationalization: An ICI View" in *Chemistry and Industry*. In a sense, this was the first communication between the two companies that a swap might make sense.

Action began to take place, however, when Horton and Hutchison approached each other in November of 1981. The shape of the deal had been broadly defined by March 1982, the government was approached in April, and an August 1 completion date was announced in mid-June. After the deal was conceived by Horton and Hutchison, it was worked out by the others without staff. On the BP side, the BP Chemicals chairman, Robert Horton, two directors of BP Chemicals, three business general managers and two works managers that would be affected, and the U.K. personnel director were involved. On the ICI side, an equally small group worked the issues under Hutchison's direction.

Speed was essential. Horton noted that "if we'd diddled, the divisions would have found that they needed another month on this or that." Externally it was important to present a clear, worked-out package to the U.K. government bodies and the European Commission.

BP and ICI each approached the Office of Fair Trading and presented their case. As one manager put it, "We both went to the government and said, 'We have done our strategic planning, chosen to emphasize this business and exit that one. It is more economic and socially satisfactory if we trade our facilities than if we shut down.' " The deal was approved by the office, reportedly after cabinet-level discussion.

Sir Peter Carey, Permanent Secretary of Industry, in a speech given at Stanfield in July 1982 said, in effect, that it was a commercial decision, and the best way for industry to restructure is for government to keep itself out of it. Department of Industry staff suggested that the BP/ICI swap was an easier issue to respond to because of the good relations the companies kept with the department and the cabinet.

At the European Commission (EC), the competition directorate (DG IV) reviewed the deal. Although F. Andreisson, DG IV commissioner, in a speech to European executives on EEC antitrust policy, used the BP/ICI swap as an example of imaginative restructuring that was acceptable under EEC Articles 85 and 86, the precedent-setting nature of the deal was such that it was challenged by DG IV and in summer 1983 was reviewed for its potentially anticompetitive effects. Only in January 1984 did the Commission finally publish its favorable ruling, and it was spring before final clearance was given.

In discussing the deal, both managements called attention to the efforts they had made to get their own houses in order. The intercompany swap emerged as a sensible option only after steps were taken to improve management of the chemical business.

The executive groups at BP and ICI were clear on this point. BP's Robert Horton described (by way of example of the problem) a trip he had made during the seventies to one of the large U.K. plastics facilities. A plant engineer had proudly showed him a wonderful new polymerization unit. Horton was duly impressed but asked whether the cost of the conversion was greater or less than the difference between the price of the polymer and the price of the feedstock. The engineer did not know.

Much of the management in the chemical industry embraced a similar product-and-process orientation. Top management at BP might have had a different view, but during the 1970s they were distracted by strategic moves that dwarfed the chemicals operation. There was first the acquisition of Sohio, second the development of the North Slope and the North Sea, and third the management of the 1973 and 1979 oil shocks. Against the background of these multibillion-dollar problems, a four-hundred-million dollar opportunity to improve the company's chemical business could not have loomed too large.

After the acquisition of the Union Carbide facilities BP faced the problem of integrating two management cultures into a third, the ex-Distillers managers representing a fine chemicals orientation, the Carbide men having a commodities perspective, and BP taking an oil company's approach. Both Carbide and Distillers shared the typical chemical industry approach: the best way to solve a problem is to spend money on new equipment. It was only the crisis of mounting annual losses beginning in 1979 that provided the impetus for a radical look at the business.

With the arrival of Horton, in effect an outsider from the corporate financial group with a mandate to clean things up, a process of analysis and review was initiated. As he described it, "We did thorough competitive studies and concluded that in several areas we were miles away from the leading edge—because of poor feedstocks or poor technology or we were overmanned. The studies were finished in September–October 1982. On the basis of them we exited a number of businesses. From January 1981 to January 1982 we reduced manpower from 18,000 to 11,000 starting in headquarters at the top." Of nine directors present when Horton arrived, two years later one was left. Of nineteen reporting to them, three were left. "In 1982 we got more radical. We said, OK, we've taken the easy decisions, now let's look at the more difficult ones. The BP/ICI swap came out of that. Working with a team of only nine key managers, the deal was conceived, discussed, and closed with great speed."

As at Union Carbide, the basic problem was to prepare for rationalization by getting an accurate assessment of the economic potential of the company's businesses. With badly overstaffed facilities and inaccurate or inappropriate accounting, it was not immediately possible to assess the strategic strengths and weaknesses of the company's position. Only in 1982, after a great deal of work had been done to improve the efficiency of the assets in hand, was it clear that parts of the portfolio could never be made profitable.

The point is important, for certainly there were analysts that believed that the moves to be made were always clear. Horton himself had recommended against the acquisitions. But there is a great difference between taking a position in a boardroom as part of the staff responsible for arguing the best interests of the company and taking action to reduce employment and close facilities as managing director responsible for a company's chemical business. In the latter situation the audiences that must be persuaded are far more diverse, including as they do unions and government ministers. The strength of the case must be that much greater.

In effect, for the organization and its principal constituencies to agree that radical surgery is required, there must be consensus as to the seriousness of the problem. For there to be consensus, there must be shared understanding as to what goals are not being reached, what damage is being sustained as a result, and what the consequences of inaction might be. Figuratively speaking, it is only when the engineer that showed Horton the plastics facility knew that the unit operated at a loss that the company could develop the actionable plans that were necessary for turning a profit.

This necessity for the organization at large to embrace the objective of profit was made clear in discussions at ICI. Again a small team of executives was picked to run the show. They spent substantial discussion time establishing the principles by which they would operate the company. These were even written down, though not published. Three of the key ideas were that the business would be run for a profit, that layers of management would exist only if they added value, and therefore that general managers of specific businesses should be given extensive business responsibility for their activities.

Again the economic crisis provided impetus for change. One executive involved noted that with the shift from high to low growth, the power of the "technocrats" shifted.

> The general managers could pay more attention to us when they saw red ink all over their bottom line. Once we had given them clear responsibility, then they could say, "Bugger the long term, with results like this, John Harvey-Jones might pull the plug on us."
>
> Before the crisis it was difficult to get people to understand what a profit objective was. We were still making money so the problems we saw looked like academic objections. But we are also giving the staff better data.[6]

The difficulty of the task facing top management was compounded by the fact that at the same time that they were transmitting downward the pressure for short-term profit, they had to persuade the ICI board of the wisdom of maintaining major long-term positions in petrochemicals in the face of the strength of the oil companies and state-owned enterprises. As Hutchison put it,

> When we did our thinking about where we were strong and where we were weak, we were thinking long term. We saw that we could win even if the oil companies and the state-owned companies stayed in businesses where they were weak.
>
> In our core, where we were strong, we had made the medium- and long-term investments. So there is no need to go to the board for long-term money. What we [had to] be able to do [was] invest short-term money to improve the current business.[7]

After the swap, both BP and ICI had work to do. BP still had to decide what to do with facilities at Barrie that were uneconomic; and ICI had to deal with a threat to its competitiveness at Wilton, resulting from the discrepancy in tax treatment of feedstock price between its facilities and the new Exxon/Shell venture at Mossmoran. Moreover, although 1984 and 1985 were black ink years for chemicals, both managements foresaw the possibility of a downturn ahead.

The prospect of softening markets was not pleasing, nor was the prospective arrival of Saudi product in Europe, but in both cases, managements believed that they had understanding of and control over their business.

It is precisely the issue of control that poses problems in the next two countries considered. In France and Italy the governments have posed direct problems of control for company management.

NOTES

1. Interview with Robert Horton, then-managing director, BP Chemicals Ltd., spring 1983.
2. Interview with T. O. Hutchison, managing director, Chemicals Group, ICI Ltd., spring 1983.
3. Ibid.
4. In the spring of 1985, ICI received some satisfaction. While holding that the grants received at Mossmoran by Exxon and Shell were not illegal subsidies, the judge indicated that the price at which ethane was to be transferred to Mossmoran was perhaps a third below the market. Andrew Arends, "ICI Appeals over Gas Tax," *Financial Times* (London), 1 May 1985, 8; Raymond Hughes, "ICI and Revenue Both Claim Victory," *Financial Times* (London), 28 January 1985, 38.
5. Interview with Sir Peter Carey, spring 1983.
6. Interview at ICI, spring 1983.
7. Interview with T. O. Hutchison, spring 1983.

8
The Restructuring of French Chemical Production

History

The evolution of the French petrochemical industry reflects geographic, historic, and political factors in addition to economics. To begin with, the French industry developed around gas and coal deposits spread out over the country—in the north and east for coal, in the southwest for gas, in the south and along the Rhone for harbors. In particular, the production of chlorine developed where brine and cheap electricity existed, while ethylene production was centered first near the coal and later near the harbors. This spread of facilities posed problems when the development of modern technology favored integrated complexes of great scale.

Additionally, the French industry was very much in the shadow of the Belgian Solvay and the German giants (BASF, Bayer, and Hoechst) strung out along the Rhone. The major French producer of dyes, Rhône-Poulenc, was in fact part of the cartel dominated by I. G. Farben and ICI. Rhône-Poulenc was organized in the 1920s to control textiles (not chemicals) and to enter pharmaceuticals. It was always small in comparison with the Belgian, German, or British companies.

Consequently France entered the 1950s without a major chemical producer—Rhône-Poulenc (R-P) and Kuhlmann made some organic chemicals but R-P's focus was on textiles. Pechiney was focused on aluminum although it made inorganic chemicals (Pechiney Chimie and Kuhlmann joined Uhlman in the giant PCUK); and St. Gobain was focused on glass. Ato Chimie was founded by Elf in 1956 to see if there was something to be done in petrochemicals but was for a long time an appendage to a growing oil business. And Charbonnage du France (CdF) Chimie was founded in 1968 as an appendage to a coal company organized to rationalize a fragmented family-owned industry.

In fact the earliest French plastics projects were often joint ventures. Naphtha-Chimie was founded in 1947 by Pechiney, Kuhlmann, and British Petroleum to exploit the new petrochemistry. Kuhlmann was also in a joint venture with Chimique de Dieuze. Société Normande des Matières Plastique was a joint venture among CdF Chimie, Air Liquide, Pechiney, and Hoechst. The only stand-alone French capacity was Solvay's.

French observers of their industry assert that the industry has never really recovered from its splintered origins. Although there are strong units, the industry is poorly positioned to compete. Table 8.1 below reveals that no French producer had a number one or two position in the commodity plastics, while Esso, Shell, BP, and Solvay all had important positions in France. Nonetheless, nearly half of France's output of plastics is exported, two-thirds of that staying in Europe.

The French Government

The weakness of the industry and the preoccupation with other businesses of the French participants are important to keep in mind when considering the role played by the French government. At first, French governments left chemicals alone except for the influence of regional policy. As one manager remarked:

The development of the chemical industry was guided from the 'grand écoles' none of which has a "corps" in chemistry. In the Fourth Plan, the chemical industry did not exist. Under Giscard, chemicals was not one of the seven key industries." The focus instead was on steel which was perceived to be a core sector, autos that are important to employment and trade, and computers seemed to be the new wave of high technology. Nonetheless, French government efforts to induce the geographic diversification of industry were important since they led to the construction at the Lacq gas fields in the southwest, the Carling complex in the southeast, and the new large cracker at Dunkirk in the northeast. The last was particularly unfortunate since it was the only greenfield facility built since 1973. Its location further fragmented the French industry.[1] The development of the chemical industry was only considered at the national level. The European market did not exist. The central problem was that France only had a strategy of

Table 8.1
1982 Production Capacity in France
in metric tons

	Ethylene	LDPE	LLDPE	HDPE	PVC
French Producers					
Ato/Chem					
Balan		120			125
Feyzin	280				
Lacq	100				
Mon		80			
Gronfreville	375	150	30	80	
St. Auban					135
St. Fons					183
Cdf					
Carling	220	220			
	220				
Lillebonne	220	100	55		
Dunkirk	270	170			
w/Qatar					
PCUK					
Brignoud					100
EMC					
Mazingarbe					170
30% DSM					
Ex-French Owned					
Solvay					
Feyzin	200				
Sarrable				125	
Taveaux					235
Esso					
Port Jerome	300				
BP/Ato					
Lavera	490		250	80	
Wingles					150
Shell					
Berre	350				100
BASF/Shell					
Berre		50			

Source: Derived from Chem Systems, Ltd, "Restructuring the European Petrochemical Industry," London, 1983, and Parpinelli Tecnon, 1984.

production: we had the new materials but we had no idea of market share. Then we shifted from coal toward oil in the 1960s and the government pushed chemicals toward oil. But the oil companies had no chemistry. We did just the opposite of Germany.

More recently, however, as French industrial policy has become more "dirigiste," or top-down, attention in the Ministry of Industry focused on the chemical industry. The first major step in restructuring was the sale of Rhône-Poulenc's petrochemical business to a combination of the state-owned Elf Aquitaine and state-controlled Total just prior to the 1979 crisis. R-P's chairman, Jean Gandois, had become general manager of the company in 1976. By that time it was clear that the effort to turn R-P into a giant chemical-fiber-pharmaceutical complex would not succeed. The 1973 oil crisis had changed the economics and the competition was too great. There were heavy losses in fibers. Because fibers was a core business, the decision was taken by Gandois to attempt to sell petrochemicals. Reinforcing this logic of the portfolio was the fact that $500 million were needed just to replace obsolete equipment. Given that overcapacity already existed in petrochemicals, the investment looked like a poor one. Moreover, oil companies were entering the business, making competition even more severe.

On the other hand, Rhône-Poulenc's conversations with the government revealed that a foreign buyer was out of the question. France's President Giscard d'Estaing indicated that the future of the country was to have large French petrochemical groups. Gandois initiated conversations with Albin Chalandon, chairman of Elf, who was seeking "debouches" [resting places] for oil and diversification to use his cash flow. They made a deal in 1980 just before the Iranian crisis.

The subsequent escalation of oil prices was devastating to the French petrochemical industry. The only independent manufacturer, PCUK, was virtually bankrupt and staggering from further gigantic losses in aluminum as well as chemicals. They were anxiously looking for a buyer. The answer seemed to be Occidental Petroleum's (OXXY) chemical group. Led by Zoltan Merzei, who had risen to the presidency of Dow Chemical on the record of his accomplishments in building Dow Europe, OXXY seemed to be Merzei's second effort at building a multinational chemical company. OXXY had concluded a merger agreement with the chemical activities of the Italian state company, Enichemica, and the proposal to acquire PCUK seemed a logical second step. Giscard d'Estaing turned down the proposal before the 1981 elections. Ministry of Industry officials and industry executives suggested that he would have blocked the acquisition after the election as well.

If France was to have a modern chemical industry when most of its participants were weak, government investments were required. Because by the early 1980s all the French players were government-related, nationalization was a more logical step here than elsewhere in French enterprise. In any event, many point to the virtual nationalization of steel under Giscard d'Estaing and say that his successor President Mitterrand has made only a minor difference to what would have happened to the chemical industry. The commitment to strong French-owned industry permeates the technocracy and crosses party lines.

Company managements disagreed strongly, however, pointing to their loss of autonomy under Mitterrand. First Gandois and later Chalandon resigned around issues having to do with their ability to pursue profit as independent managers.

In the summer of 1983, the French-owned petrochemical industry was fully nationalized. The government acquired PCUK and its parts were divided among R-P and Atochem (Elf's chemical division). Rhône-Poulenc produced fine chemicals, pharmaceuticals, and fibers while Atochem produced the commodity plastics and other bulk chemicals. CdF Chimie continued to produce polyethylene and to experience losses. There was talk of combining CdF Chimie with Atochem.[2]

The statistics summarizing French production capacity in the studied commodities reflect the extensive restructuring of the industry under the tutelage of the government. Table 8.2 shows, as well, the extensive investment of public funds.

What the numbers do not show is the extensive politicization of the industry. In contrast to the situation in Italy, the French-owned companies moved very slowly to rationalize capacity. The reasons have to do with history, the structure and attitudes of the French technocracy, as well as with the commercial history of the French industry described above. When the oil shock hit, the French companies, like the Italian, were poorly capitalized and awkwardly structured. Sensible mergers and necessary restructur-

Table 8.2
Government Aid to Industry, 1983
(In Millions of Dollars)

Newly Nationalized Companies		Other State-owned Companies	
Usinor/Sacilor	815.8	Renault	210.3
Pechiney Ugine	305.9	CdF Chimie	127.5
Kuhlmann		Snecma	38.2
Rhône-Poulenc	229.4	Entreprise Minière	31.9
Thomson	204.0	et Chimique	
CII-Honeywell-Bull	191.2	Others	210.3
Compagnie Générale	110.9		
d'Electricité			
Saint-Gobain	95.6	Total	2,549.4

Source: "French Socialism Stubs Its Toe," *The New York Times,* 31 July 1983, sec. F.

ing had been delayed by controlling family owners and government offices (such as the bureaucracy tied to the coal company, Charbonnage du France). When the crisis hit, there had been no rationalization.

In turn, when the French government recognized the crisis, they did so against a background of increasing government control of industry which had begun at least as early as 1945 and was grounded in the ideological heritage of Napoleon's technocrats. The Hanoun Report of 1980, published by the French Ministry of Industry, revealed that the then-private Thompson-CSF received direct and indirect government aid greater than their cash flow and that the private Peugeot paid the state in taxes four times the dividends of the publicly owned Renault, who had twice the sales.

The French central bureaucracy has been strong, so that its wishes have considerable influence in the management decision-making process. Moreover, the failures of the managements and owners, while the companies were private, weakened the credibility of their successors in fights with their technocratic and political masters.

This last point is important, for there is evidence from other studies of French state-owned industry that where the managers of the company in question were regarded as technically and commercially competent, for example the state railway, SNCF, they have been able to resist ministry and ministerial demands.[3] In the case of petrochemicals, however, the commercial problems were so severe that government involvement was inevitable. According to some managers, while Giscard d'Estaing was in power, working with the government was fairly efficient—top managers could negotiate their terms of reference and strategy with six or eight key people. But once Mitterrand arrived, and especially after Chevenement was appointed Minister of Industry, the top managers faced an endless array of bureaucrats and ministers with whom they had to bargain. The executive interviewed who named the five men in addition to Giscard with whom he would discuss his plans spoke contemptuously of the "eighty" with whom he had to fight for his company's programs.

Perhaps just as important a factor for management was that the French legal structure gave bureaucrats and politicians extensive access to the operations of the companies. The mechanism for this was the Conseil de Surveillance, composed of representatives of the government and unions. The Commissaire du Gouvernement—who is designated by the responsible ministry (industry in the case of chemicals)—participates in all the discussions of the Conseil de Surveillance. The Commissaire is informed of all major strategic-planning activity and he has veto power. One ministry official interviewed stated that "the government interferes with companies' strategy but not with management."[4] One strategic planner indicated that substantial efforts were made to keep such representatives ignorant of what was going on.

In such a setting, the training and perspective of the bureaucrats becomes important. The lack of emphasis on chemical engineering in the French "grandes écoles" thus contributes to the problem. For with the economic crisis of the early 1980s and the massive losses in the companies there was every incentive to "do something." One executive remarked that, "When Chevenement arrived he wanted to do everything. After three months he understood the complexity of the problem. In the meantime it was a very difficult period of discussion and delay."

Still another complicating factor needs to be introduced. In a sense it is also a mitigating factor. The parties to the final restructuring of the French petrochemical industry included both public and private shareowners. The allocation of the loss-making activities of PCUK and the establishment of prices at which assets were to be transferred involved, therefore, questions as to which private parties would be compensated and which would bear the cost of the loss-making activities. By French law a losing partner cannot be imposed on a private company because it means in effect taking money from a shareholder.

Finally, the extensive involvement of the government owner meant that the legitimizing process of bankruptcy was not available to French companies. As one executive put it, "When you have a nationalized company, you cannot say that 'the state is bankrupt.' " While the need for cutbacks was recognized, it was deemed politically difficult to lay off workers at the same time that *billions* of French francs were being invested in modernization so that there would be a French-owned industry. This kind of logic meant that when CdF Chimie and Atochem/Solvay were arguing whether one or the other should shut down excess capacity at Carling or Feyzin respectively, the answer was a classical reverse of Solomon's decision. Each cut back some, thus satisfying the politicians and penalizing the French economy.[5] Cutting the baby in half is the clearest example of politicization.[6]

It was to this problem that my respondents referred again and again. "We don't want the involvement of government technocrats in our affairs. The way to protect ourselves against interference is to play one ministry off against another from the groups of labor, finance, and environment that we have to deal with. We are trained that we are not in an easy business. We know how to defend ourselves. We are good negotiators." Another manager took a less sanguine view. "To compete with countries that do not have socialism is very hard. As a French company, if you need the cooperation of the government, it is difficult to avoid tutelage. If heavy labor costs are involved, it will be impossible to compete."

The position of the union affected more than cost. "The unions are saying that monomers are strategic for France. I disagree. We must specialize in order to compete. I will make one product, someone else can do the other. The government doesn't like this, but they can replace me if that is what they want.

Am I the head of an industry like steel, or is it an economic enterprise? If it is like steel, though I like my minister and colleagues in the industry, I wouldn't take this job."

The result has been that the restructuring of the French petrochemical industry was accomplished through nationalization and specialization but without any specific planning, carried out by the government as to how the industry should look or how much would have to be invested. (Company management, of course, had plans.) At the time of my study there was an attempt in the Ministry of Industry to draw a global restructuring plan for the chemicals group. In 1982, it was decided to invest Fr 8 billion ($1.2 billion) in the industry, but questions remained as to how the money would be used. To assist, the Ministry of Industry asked the Boston Consulting Group to propose "a technico-economic and strategic approach in order to define the appropriate competitive industrial structure to be set up at the state level."[7]

The Boston Consulting Group report hypothesized that with the proper industry structure in France, there could be serious improvement in financial results and competitiveness. The report surveyed the entire industry in France (including non-French owned), focusing on the production "platforms" (too many), the market prospects (weak), the lack of plant competitiveness, the separation of plant sites from their markets or sources of feedstock, and the stakes of the players at the several sites.

The spirit of the report is captured in the following summary of a section in the chapter on European integration.

In Europe, French petrochemical firms are among the weak. In the short term, their participation in European ventures might lead to their absorption in mergers by stronger firms. One should remember that a balanced agreement with a European partner is conceivable only if the French producer's activities are economically viable and appealing enough in terms of market proximity and share. Therefore, French organizations first need to be reinforced by making them solid enough to be true partners. In the medium-term, French and foreign producers could enter some agreements in order to rationalize production facilities and reduce overcapacity.[8]

The Ministry of Industry asserted that

Whatever happens, France will have an important base in petrochemistry, although France will become a net importer. It is a political decision. Whether the government should agree on having foreign partners, it will approve them so far as they remain a minority control.

What has been done does not come from the ideology of a political party. There is definitely consensus among the French people to reduce our dependence on the outside. This policy is part of a coherent line tightly connected to our national defense policy.

At that time France had shut down fewer of its units than any of the other major producing countries. Problems with the work force were given as the main reason. Under these circumstances one could sympathize with managements of private firms based in other European countries that were skeptical of the advantages to be gained from European agreements in petrochemicals that included the French.

Remarkably, the story was different in Italy. Given its reputation for self-serving expansion of its industry, the prospect of petrochemicals in Italy had improved substantially.

NOTES

1. One French manager noted that since five of the six points on the French geographic "star" had a cracker, it was inevitable that the sixth point should have one.
2. Ato Chimie was a division of Elf Aquitaine. It merged with the Chloe division of Rhône-Poulenc that produced commodity products and for a while was called Ato-Chloe. Then after further restructuring was completed, the name was changed to Atochem. For simplicity, the latter name is used in all three situations.
3. See, for example, Taieb Hafsi, "The Strategic Decision-Making Process in State-Owned Enterprises" (Ph.D. diss., Harvard University, School of Business Administration, 1981).
4. Interview with M. Yolin, minister of industry of France, spring 1983.
5. "Feyzin Closure Confirmed," *European Chemical News,* 2 May 1983, 6.
6. See Joseph Bower's discussion of politicization of this sort in *The Two Faces of Management* (Boston: Houghton Mifflin, 1983), 114–165.
7. Boston Consulting Group, *Analyse Strategique et Organization de la Chimie Organique Lourde Française,* A report prepared for the French Ministry of Industry, Paris, France, April 1982, 3.
8. Boston Consulting Group, op. cit., 95, 96.

9

The Restructuring of Montedison

The situation in the Italian chemical industry in the spring of 1983 was critical for the participants, the country, and for Europe.[1] Notoriously the "bad boy" of Europe, its chemical producers expanding rapidly and dumping product, the industry had been restructured into two parts—a giant, publicly owned, bulk chemical and fiber company, Enichemica (ENI); and a giant, privately owned specialty, fine chemical, fertilizer, and fiber firm, Montedison.

As is clear from table 9.1, between the two giants, Italy had formidable positions in all the major commodity plastics. If costs could be contained, profitability might be in prospect and Italy could for once contribute to the stability of European chemical markets. Costs, however, were high because of excess labor costs, low productivity, high interest expense, and major logistic penalties from moving intermediates among remote sites. New managements at Enichemica and Montedison faced formidable challenges as they tried to revitalize management cadres, lay off workers, and fight for major influx of equity investments from a government under perpetual pressure from strong unions.

History

The chemical industry in Italy developed under the tutelage of the Germans. Montecatini, a mining company founded in 1886, entered fertilizers in 1913, synthesized ammonia (in 1925) and dyes in a joint venture with I. G. Farben and paints with Du Pont. In the thirties it also entered fibers in association with Rhône-Poulenc and pharmaceuticals through acquisition. It was a strong and pervasive company.

Another force in the industry was Edison. A hydroelectricity company, it diversified into chemicals and fibers in the 1950s. The

Table 9.1
Market Share of Italy's Competitors

		Europe's Leader % as of 12/31/82	ENI %	Montedison %
			as of 6/1/83	
LDPE & LLDPE	BASF	11%	13	
HDPE	Hoechst	25	10	
PP	Montedison	15		19
PS	BASF	24		17
PVC	Solvay	15	16	

Source: Italian company documents.

two companies were merged as Montedison in 1966 and reorganized along product lines in the early 1970s. The other major players in Italy in the 1950s were Esso, Shell, Mobil, Gulf, BP, and ENI. By the 1970s only Solvay, ENI, Exxon, and a minor Mobil interest remained. Control from the state and aggressive expansion by Montedison and government-supported efforts of Italian companies drove the foreigners from the scene.

"The basic philosophy," said one Italian manager, "was scale economy, market share, and build ahead of demand and the competitors. Using ENI money, Montedison money, and government money everyone rushed ahead to invest. Since none had a chemical background except Montedison, they purchased technology. The state increasingly used its role to try to take over the industry. The government even bought a 16-percent interest in Montedison."

The competitors that remained were all Italian—Montedison, ENI, ANIC, and Liquichemica. In the early 1970s, however, another Italian company, SIR, emerged as an important competitor, building new capacity in Sardinia with government regional subsidies and vastly enriching its owners and certain politicians.[2] One observer noted that "the capacity was uncompetitive technically when it started up."

When the oil crisis hit, Italy's industry was fragmented and uneconomic. Until 1975 all Italian petrochemical activity was based on naphtha. Capacity was built near refineries in the south.

As a consequence, there were twelve to fifteen petrochemical centers, all small and poorly integrated, resulting in costly transfer of intermediates. When oil prices rose the companies were in trouble. Raw material costs rose from $3 per barrel to $30. As products matured, plastic prices rose only from IL 7 to IL 35. Meanwhile, the dollar rose against the lira.

Despite the situation, companies continued investments. The philosophy of ENI's chief executive, Eugenio Chefes, was "find good projects and I will find the money." The result was the awesome indebtedness of Montedison and its Italian-owned competitors.

To comprehend this pattern, the political wars between Christian Democrats and Socialists as well as the role of the banks must be understood. Put briefly, a five-minister council approves state investments. While Socialists may favor the distribution of patronage in state-financed projects, Christian Democrat bankers can also appreciate the advantages of government contributions to indebted companies. In the late 1970s the Socialists grew in power until in 1980 they formed a coalition with the Christian Democrats. As part of that "concordat," they gained the Ministry of Finance (responsible for taxation and fiscal matters but not the Treasury or the Budget) and the Ministry of State Participation.

As the new government took over, SIR had collapsed; Montedison was exposed with increasing capacity in all lines; and ANIC and Liquichemica had the same product lines. Debt for the companies was extremely high and the proportion of interest to sales was over 10 percent.

Restructuring was an obvious necessity. A complex series of events followed during which (1) Enichemica was established to hold ENI Chemical, ANIC, SIR, and Liquichemica, (2) the leadership of ENI changed four times, (3) ENI, under the leadership of Alberto Grandi, and Occidental founded a joint venture ENOXY to own and manage the restructured Enichemica, (4) ENOXY and Montedison sought each other out to rearrange capacity in order to permit further rationalization of derivative production which, in turn, implied rationalization of ethylene cracker capacity, (5) the ENOXY-Montedison deal, approved by the Socialist Minister of State Participation, Gianni de Micheles (an ex-professor of chemistry), and opposed on price by the CDU president of ENI, Umberto Columbo, foundered in December 1982, (6) an ENI-Montedison deal proceeded despite the ENOXY divorce, and (7) Colombo was fired and replaced by the Socialist Reviglio. In the process some 1,700 workers were suspended with state-subsidized pay (450 were to be offered early retirement).

Gianni de Michelis stated publicly that the overstaffing of the plants had to be reduced, and, with what seemed to be fingers crossed and breath held, the managements of ENI and Montedison proceeded with their cutbacks: ethylene was to be cut from 1.8 million tons to 1.2 million, and the derivatives similarly.

In the spring of 1983 plans for the two companies became clearer at the same time that losses reported for 1982 were the worst in history—ENI lost $1.2 billion, approximately $500 million in chemicals; and Montedison $509 million (chemicals were not broken out). Montedison pruned its portfolio (e.g., quitting nylon fibers), strengthened its acrylic fibers business, and formed joint ventures to exploit a new polypropylene process and pharmaceuticals with Hercules. Overall Montedison was predicting that its results for the second half of 1983 would be profitable.

Meanwhile, ENI reported that it needed some $3 billion from the state in order to survive. Chemical losses over the 1983–87 period were estimated at $200 million. Whether cutbacks would be continued or accelerated under these conditions would depend in part on the new Socialist government's approach to the industry. Perhaps more important was whether ENI's leader, Dr. Lorenzo Necci, could transform his diverse inheritance into an efficient chemical company. When asked what were his most significant strategic problems, he responded, "people; too many people serving time and too few seeking profit."[3]

Whether Italy's approach to restructuring petrochemicals was to be more successful than that of France would depend in part on the success of the Montedison strategy, and in part on the ability of ENI's management to turn around a very uncomfortable mix of facilities, products, and people. This, in turn, would depend on the government's willingness to fund interim losses as well as investments in modernization and rationalization. Questioned as to why it was appropriate to struggle on in so difficult a business, one ENI executive said, "Italy's ratio of exports to consumption is lower than the other major producers, we don't even satisfy our own needs. Why shouldn't we have our share?"

A New Montedison

The restructuring of Montedison, managed by Mario Schimberni, was one of the most dramatic restructurings of any contemporary company. He inherited a financial disaster with too many product lines, poor organization, and weak management. In addition, "the huge, diversified company was little more than a bloated political football, run by political appointees and dedicated more to the furtherance of state social policies than to profitable operations."[4]

In May 1980 when Gianni de Michelis became Minister of State Participation, he recognized that a fresh approach was needed to deal with Italy's industrial crisis. After months of study by a high-level, blue-ribbon commission, his ministry published a white paper setting forth a new industrial policy. The report paid special attention to the problems of state-owned enterprises and traced their origins directly to the influence of politics on company management. The comprehensive plan he proposed emphasized a more rational and consistent approach to state intervention and called for efforts to

encourage private shareholders to provide risk capital to substitute for state participation;

increase the influence of market forces;

increase the international scope of Italian businesses through agreements, joint ventures, and acquisitions;

reorient unions and workers toward efficiency and productivity goals; and

improve the quality of managers and especially to replace their current production orientation with a new market orientation[5]

Although the government owned only 17 percent of Montedison's shares, it was the largest shareholder. Also, the state's financial holding company, Instituto per La Reconstruzione Industriale (IRI), controlled many of the banks which held Montedison's debt. The government's effective control over Montedison was unchallenged in board meetings and its multiple stakes in the future of the company were widely recognized.

Once in charge, President Schimberni tackled Montedison's deep-seated problems in rapid succession with substantial support from the government. The state's shares were first sold to private entrepreneurs, fresh equity and long-term debt were raised, operating companies were spun off, the organizational structure was revamped, new people were brought in at all levels, and major capacity rationalization deals were struck with ENI, Monsanto, and Hercules.[6]

Schimberni noted that compared to previous Montedison presidents, he lacked one notable attribute—he was not a political man.

> I made it clear from the beginning that I would manage the company without political goals. In discussions with the government, it was useful that I did not belong to any party; I stood at equal distance from all of them. Although I was born in Rome, as was my father, I do not have extensive family connections to one faction or another.
>
> After I realized that privatization was an essential first step in restructuring Montedison, I arranged for some private families to be willing to make a high-risk investment in the company. Then I took the proposal to the government.
>
> Since World War II, there had been a steady move toward greater public ownership of industry; but, by the end of the 1970s, government leaders began to realize that privatization might be good in some sectors. They now recognized that making Montedison private again would serve to demonstrate these intentions. It also became clear that the state could not support the financial burden much longer and that a private Montedison could raise additional funds on the market. I convinced them that if Montedison were to become 100 percent state-owned, it would fail and the whole Italian chemical industry would go down with it.[7]

The privatization of the company coincided with Schimberni's assumption of the presidency. Immediately after that, he began massive reorganization of the company. By year's end the largest operating divisions were split off to form seven autonomous operating companies, and Montedison S.p.A. became a holding company. The new companies in the group and their products are shown in table 9.2.

There were several reasons, according to Schimberni, for the spin-off of these businesses.

> It was primarily a move to a better way of managing the different businesses. They could now be managed separately and more professionally. Italian managers are good at dealing in innovative ways with small- and medium-sized enterprises, but not with large ones. The new organization also allowed greater flexibility in the structure and

Table 9.2
1980 Montedison Sales by Subsidiary

Company	Products	
Montedipe	basic petrochemicals	$2,289 million
Montepolimeri	plastics	1,908 million
Ausimont	specialty chemicals	380 million
Resem	resins and emulsions	229 million
Acna	dyes and pigments	403 million
Fertimont	fertilizers	545 million
Farmoplant	pesticides	82 million
Montefibre★	synthetic fibers	928 million
Farmitalia/ Carlo Erba★	pharmaceuticals	821 million

Source: Annual Report 1980.
★These had been independent companies before 1980.

culture of each business, and the businesses were pushed closer to the market.[8]

While the same people continued in most cases to head the businesses, their jobs changed markedly. They had previously been loosely responsible for contribution margins, which often did not include working capital costs. After the reorganization, the results of their operations became much easier to identify, and they became responsible for managing working capital, personnel, and other fixed costs. Although they now had to plan their own investments, expenses, and sales, major financial decisions were still taken at the holding company level. Staff units at the holding company were also responsible for supporting their counterparts in the operating companies and for designing the overall strategy of the group.

As the new group considered how to reduce costs, they were met by a crisis with the unions over a decision not to rebuild a cracker destroyed in an explosion. After a very difficult negotiation, the unions "decided to help save the chemical industry in Italy. They have been very realistic."[9]

In 1979, Schimberni had hired Giorgio Porta away from Phillips Petroleum and put him in charge of strategic planning. Montedison's planning staff had about seventy people, most of them econometricians and technical specialists who were not used to doing the kind of business analysis that Porta wanted. He recalled the situation he had faced.

They had an overly analytical mentality. They were well qualified in their fields, but there was always one part missing from their reports . . . the action plan.

Because of the urgency of the situation, I did not have the twelve or fifteen months that it would take to produce a detailed strategic plan. So I simply identified four or five people who knew Montedison's businesses and who could help me understand them. In a month I put out a strategy document.[10]

Porta's 1981 strategic plan for Montedison took into account government policies in each business. These had been formulated by Minister of State Participation de Michelis in his 1981 plan for the chemical industry. That plan was an outgrowth of the celebrated negotiations between the unions, the government, and Montedison and elaborated some of the ideas first set out in de Michelis's 1980 white paper.

The de Michelis plan called first for "polarization" of the industry by creating two national monopolies, one in primary chemicals and another in specialties. Montedison was to be the specialty company and ENI, the commodity producer. "Rationalization," a second stage, would follow with swapping and closing plants so that each national champion could become competitive in Europe. In a third phase, called "internationalization," joint ventures would be set up with strong firms abroad to help the Italians improve their managerial and technological expertise as well as their overseas market access. Government and industry officials greeted this plan with great optimism, calling it "la volta buona," a turn for the good.

An Agreement with ENI

The negotiations leading to an ENI-Montedison capacity swap began in late 1980 and continued until March 1983. During this time ENI changed leadership three times, but Montedison's strategy remained constant. According to Schimberni:

The negotiations required much determination. We knew what we wanted and thus could define the terms of the rationalization. Our job was to convince ENI and the government that our proposal was the best for Italy. We became the national leader in the restructuring effort.

We also made clear what our restructuring timetable was. We said that we would shut down here, lay off people there, on such and such a date. These were the alternative moves if no agreement could be reached on joint actions.[11]

Basic agreements were reached early in 1981 and laid down in de Michelis's plan and, a few months later, in a letter of intent between the heads of Montedison and ENI. "The discussions with ENI precipitated an internal debate in Montedison on the size and the composition of the deal," recalled Howard Harris, who had become director of strategic coordination in February of 1982. Schimberni asked Harris to forecast what Montedipe's and Montepolimeri's businesses would look like in 1990 under different assumptions about divestments. Harris's group concluded that these businesses would show a positive cash flow in 1990 but that huge amounts of cash would be needed up to 1987. "This analysis," Harris said later, "made us realize that we had to be more aggressive in selling assets from our heavy chemicals businesses."

Montedison presented a detailed proposal for industry rationalization in April 1981. A second letter of intent was signed in the summer. Then, as Umberto Colombo took over as ENI president that first week of November, *European Chemical News* reported that apparently "last-minute intervention from the Italian government coaxed a signature [for the final agreement] out of outgoing ENI interim president Enrico Gandolfi."[12] The agreement was almost identical to Montedison's proposal in April. When Occidental dropped out of the joint venture with ENI at the last minute, the money for buying Montedison's plants had to come entirely from the government. ENI's purchases amounted to $319 million and Montedison's to $11 million.

The final agreement left ENI the Italian leader in ethylene, LDPE, HDPE, PVC, ABS, and synthetic rubbers, while Montedison led in all forms of PP and PS. This meant that both companies now had strong positions in the European market for commodity plastics.

New People and a New Culture

Following the privatization of Montedison, some of its senior executives left. Others left during Schimberni's first two years as president. By mid-1982, about two-thirds of the holding company's top staff, as well as many in the operating companies, were new recruits.

The turnover of top staff made it easier to change the organizational structure of the company, an essential part of Schimberni's privatization plan. He explained the importance of such changes. "Governments in many countries are declaring that they want to privatize state-owned enterprises. But saying so, or even selling shares, is not enough; it is important to institute management which is profit oriented and professional, rather than political." Schimberni described how he went about changing attitudes:

> I entered the company alone, without a team, and only afterwards built a team by taking some good managers from inside the company and adding some from outside.
>
> I had several criteria for the new people I hired. First, they had to have a profit orientation, not a political one. Second, they had to be eager to accept a challenge. And third, they had to have the professional skills required in their new jobs. At the same time, I also sought to internationalize the orientation of management.[13]

Several of Schimberni's major executive appointees were foreigners, especially Americans (e.g., Howard Harris). He also hired some English, Dutch, and German managers and some Italians with international experience (e.g., Giorgio Porta). The American candidates were generally "more profit oriented than Europeans," noted Schimberni, "and more competitive. They love a challenge." Schimberni managed the cultural mix of his company quite consciously, putting "Americans at the holding level or in staff and Germans at the operating levels, because these two cultures did not work well together and Americans worked better with Italians." In the negotiations with ENI and the government, he used mostly Italians.

For lower levels of management, many graduates of the Boconi University business school in Milan were recruited. Schimberni believed that

> these people had the same culture and information system and were highly competent. Their personal motivation was very important; we got their commitment by convincing them that there was a mission to be accomplished. They had to demonstrate that a big company could be restructured and turned around. I made it clear that it was an emergency: we had to recover from failure in three years, otherwise the private entrepreneurs would lose interest in us.[14]

A New Structure for a New Strategy

In the early 1980s, there was hardly an important chemical company anywhere in Europe, Japan, or the United States that was not trying to shift out of commodities toward specialities. But when Schimberni became president of Montedison, explained Alfredo Ambrosetti, a Milanese management consultant who helped in the reorganization:

> There was no focus for fine chemicals; all operations fell under one managing director at the holding company. Through the deal with ENI and other moves, Schimberni was trying to move Montedison away from chemical commodities and toward specialties. In February of 1982, he created a new position with a lot of power in the fine chemicals area. It was clear that one general manager below Schimberni was too little, but more than two positions were not yet identifiable.[15]

Schimberni promoted Giorgio Porta to managing director of the basic chemicals group and hired Jack Sweeney to head the fine chemicals group. Sweeney had been a vice president at Celanese and president of Drew Chemical, a specialty chemicals producer in the United States.

Schimberni also began to emphasize nonchemical activities. Montedison had always been involved in sectors such as energy and services but still thought of itself as a chemical company. Ironically, the nonchemical activities performed better than chemicals and provided cash which was used by other businesses (see financial results of major groups in table 9.3). By 1984, improvements in the petrochemicals business would change the relationship. In 1983, all service activities were grouped together in Iniziativa Montedison Terziario Avanzato (Iniziativa ME.T.A.) and listed on the Milan stock exchange.

An important element in Schimberni's plans for Montedison was greater involvement in international markets. The first international moves which Schimberni made, while he was still vice president, were the divestment of operations in Spain, Holland, and the United States to raise cash. After he became president, he recruited managers with international experience. Then, as the burden of loss-making commodity chemical businesses was being transferred to ENI, Montedison's new strategists began thinking

Table 9.3
Changes in Montedison's Portfolio (1982–1984)
(% Composition)

	1982			1984 Estimated		
	Sales	Gross Margin	Net	Sales	Gross Margin	Net
Basic Chemicals	43	3	47	36	34	37
Health Care	8	25	4	10	19	6
Other Fine Chemicals	7	4	6	7	8	6
Sub-total chem.	57	32	57	53	61	49
Energy	29	54	37	27	29	45
Tertiary [services]	14	14	6	20	10	6
	100	100	100	100	100	100

Source: Montedison document presented to financial analysts, September 18, 1984.

hard about their company's international advantages. The same strategic principles which had guided their domestic planning were now applied to global operations and to the search for "international alliances." Harris said they looked for "places where Montedison had good technology and decent business positions, and where it needed to grow but couldn't do so alone."

Montedison proceeded to move quickly. In fibers, a series of deals with Monsanto and Bayer saw them exit nylon and emerge as the leading producer of acrylic fiber in Europe with plants in the United Kingdom, Spain, and Italy. In polyolefins, their technological leadership and market position in Europe provided the basis for a dramatic deal with Hercules.

Montedison had been a leader in the early development of polypropylene technology. Its technology began to lag behind those of other major competitors when a second-generation process was introduced by Solvay and Mitsui in the mid-1970s. In response, Montedison soon developed its own second-generation process and joined forces with Mitsui to work on a third-generation one. In 1982, with two hundred eighty research people working on PP, Montedison spent $10 million on research and development for this product alone. Montedison and Mitsui unveiled a third-generation process in 1983 that promised important savings in capital and energy costs.

Aside from its technological advantage, Montedison also enjoyed a dominant market position in the European market for PP. After absorbing ENI's plants, it held about 20 percent of European capacity, followed by Hoechst, Shell, and ICI. This gave it some power to influence prices and to keep its plants running at high rates.

This leadership position augured well for Montedison since, according to Harris, "polypropylene looks like the only thermoplastic with some growth left in it." The demand for PP was moving up.

Montedison's position, however, was not without its problems. The company was relatively weak upstream at the raw materials end of the production chain, having sold all but one of its naphtha crackers to ENI. This was not yet a problem in the early 1980s, but most analyses of the propylene market forecasted increasing raw materials prices and tighter supply for later in the decade. Because propylene was a by-product of naphtha cracking, supplies declined as crackers shifted to lighter feeds, such as liquid petroleum gas (LPG) and ethane. Montedison projected the propylene supply/demand balance in Western Europe would shift from a surplus of 160,000 tons per year in 1980 to a deficit of 900,000 tons per year in 1990.

Entry into the U.S. market was usually a top priority for European companies looking to become international. Montedison was a good case in point. It had entered the U.S. market for polypropylene in the early 1970s with a greenfield plant but underestimated the costs of penetrating the market. As Mario Mauri, financial director of Montedison, later explained:

> We had about 4 percent of the market, but needed at least 10 percent to survive. The U.S. company needed continued investment to make it; it needed to grow or it would die. We did not have the cash at that time and, had we invited in another partner, we would only have ended up with a minority position in a small and difficult-to-manage joint venture. As it happened, we sold the plant to U.S. Steel in 1979, and for a good price too.[16]

By 1982, Montedison was again eyeing the U.S. market; this time it planned to enter the right way. It had already decided that its unique strength lay in polypropylene, especially now that the Spheripol process provided a fresh competitive edge. Montedison commissioned Arthur D. Little, the Cambridge, Massachusetts consulting firm, to assess the PP business in the United States, survey the strengths and weaknesses of the major competitors, and evaluate various entry strategies.

Arthur D. Little concluded that the U.S. market offered good opportunities for growth and that Montedison's new technology would provide it with a vital cost advantage, especially because it could use lower grade propylene. The consultants argued that a major penetration of the U.S. market would best be achieved by acquiring Hercules International's extensive PP business in the United States. Alternatively, buying one or two older plants for conversion to the new process and focusing on a niche in the copolymer business could produce modest but profitable results. Entry via construction of a new plant was not recommended.

At the time, Montedison already had a fifty-fifty U.S. joint venture in pharmaceuticals with Hercules. The venture, launched in 1979 and called Adria Labs, sold Farmitalia/Carlo Erba's products in the United States and Canada and had only minor finishing operations. Adria sold over $80 million in 1981, mostly adriamycin, while several other products were being evaluated by the Federal Food and Drug Administration for release on the U.S. market.

But the Montedison–Hercules joint venture was not without problems. According to Schimberni, "there was an imbalance in the type of inputs that the partners brought to the venture. We contributed our products and technology, while Hercules only contributed finance."[17] The two partners also had different objectives for Adria Labs. Montedison wanted to use Adria as the U.S. sales arm of its global pharmaceuticals business, while Hercules wanted to make Adria the core of a new, self-sufficient company capable of developing and manufacturing its own products.

Negotiations about a possible joint venture in polypropylene started in the fall of 1982. Working groups from both companies met to draw up a preliminary business plan and estimated total tangible savings of a joint venture (as compared to two separate ventures) at about $50 million annually. Most of these savings came from the increased efficiency the Hercules plants would experience after conversion to Montedison's new technology. The preliminary business plan projected sales of over $800 million from 1984 onward, with a positive cash flow of $10 million in 1984, rising to over $100 million by 1987 (investments of $88 million would be spread out over 1983–85). As a result of these projections, the groups recommended the creation of a "freestanding company capable of attracting financing in the public and private markets, primarily in the United States."[18]

Detailed negotiations on the valuations of each company's contribution followed. From the beginning, it was clear that Hercules' PP business was larger and more profitable than Montedison's, so that Montedison would have to pay Hercules in cash if a fifty-fifty venture were to be created. Originally, both companies planned to put all their PP business in the venture, including film, fiber, and international operations. But, to balance the contributions and minimize the Montedison cash payment, the two CEOs agreed in February of 1983 to exclude both firms' PP film plants and Hercules' joint ventures in Taiwan and Brazil. Under this arrangement, Montedison would need to contribute about $50 to $60 million in cash.

The remaining points to be negotiated were the management control of the new venture, the form of the cash payment, and the structure of the related deal in the health care business. Hercules wanted clear management control, 50.1 percent ownership, and one additional member on the board. It also wanted more money up front and a larger share of the new health care venture, Erbamont.

As part of the deal, the companies' relationship in the health care field was also changed. Hercules gave up control of the Adria venture and a new company was formed to integrate all of Montedison's related businesses. Erbamont came to hold Farmitalia/Carlo Erba (assets at $62 million) and Kallestad Labs ($15 million), another U.S. operation. Hercules sold its 50 percent share in Adria for a 13.5 percent share of Erbamont, valued at $87.5 million. In 1983 this seemed a high price for half of Adria, but the value of Adria to Montedison lay in the future, when scores of new products were slated for introduction in the United States.

When the final agreement was signed in April 1983, both parents had equal ownership and neither had full control. But the headquarters of the new venture, called Himont Inc. was in Wilmington, Delaware, close to Hercules' headquarters, and the first president was from Hercules. Montedison paid Hercules $20 million in cash upon signature, $15 million in the form of a three-year note, and $20 million in a note convertible to shares in Erbamont.

According to a Montedison document, Himont offered as strategic advantages: (1) market power based on its being the undisputed worldwide leader in the business; (2) immediate worldwide application of Montedison's new technology; (3) fusion of Montedison's process technology and European business with Hercules' marketing capability and U.S. business; (4) an attractive vehicle for partial or full divestment of the business by selling shares to third parties, including to U.S. investors.

Schimberni's dramatic restructuring of Montedison's business was already paying off in 1983. Losses had been cut in half, and business conditions for Montedison's remaining activities were picking up. Schimberni continued to forecast break-even, or close to that, for 1984. (In fact, profits were achieved.)

There would be many difficult problems to face in the future, but at least Montedison had a potential as a commercial enterprise. As Schimberni put it, "The biggest problems are in the past. Montedison has a new structure. We have selected our business portfolio; we have clear strategic goals. We know who we are. We are a diversified company, with strengths in primary chemicals, specialty chemicals, energy, and services. We know where we want to go. We want to grow in some areas, shrink in others; we want to become more international. Our management is now innovative, flexible, open-minded, and accepts the challenge of change."[19]

NOTES

1. This chapter draws heavily from "Montedison, S.p.A. (A)," a case study (385-065) prepared by Benjamin Gomes-Casseres, under the supervision of Professors Joseph L. Bower and Francis J. Aguilar. Boston: Harvard Business School, 1984.
2. ANIC, Liquichemica and SIR were independent companies as were Sarda Polimieri and Rumianca. Eventually all were "rescued" and merged into ENI. In most of the tables in this book they are treated as part of ENI. An exception is chart 1.5 that attempts to display the pattern of restructuring.
3. Interview with Dr. Lorenzo Necci, president, Enichemica, spring 1983.
4. George Bickerstaffe, "Montedison's Recovery Plan: Taking on the World," *International Management Europe* 39 (January 1984), 12.
5. These are freely translated excerpts from Ministerio delle Partecipazioni Statali, *Rapporto Sulle Partecipazioni Statali,* 1980.
6. In 1985, Mario Schimberni moved to weaken the power of the private entre-

preneurs holding large blocks of his company's stock. He thereby weakened the influence of the "families."

7. Interview with Mario Schimberni, spring 1984.
8. Ibid.
9. *International Management Europe* 39 (January 1984).
10. Interview with Dr. Giorgio Porta, spring 1983.
11. Interview with Mario Schimberni, spring 1984.
12. "ENI, Montedison Sign Interim Deal on Plastics Restructuring," *European Chemical News* 8 November 1982, 6.
13. Interview with Mario Schimberni, spring 1984.
14. Ibid.
15. Interview with Dr. Alfredo Ambrosetti, president of Studio Ambrosetti, spring 1983.
16. Interview with Mario Mauri, financial director, Montedison, spring 1984.
17. Interview with Mario Schimberni, spring 1984.
18. Company document.
19. Mario Schimberni, op. cit. 17.

10

The Restructuring of Europe's
Petrochemical Industry

Introduction

A glance at table 10.1 reveals the unhappy state of European petrochemicals in 1984. Chart 10.1 reveals the same point graphically. While the number of producers of ethylene had declined, there were still more than two dozen and capacity had not been cut while demand had fallen.

The basic problem is that there are twelve petrochemical-producing nations among the fourteen nations of Western Europe and even twelve is too many competitors. In the preceding chapters we have described important examples of corporate and national response to the problems of Europe. Generally, it has been easier for companies to exit than for government.

There are further lessons to learn, however, and for this purpose it is important to have a view of how the German companies and Shell have behaved for they are among the most important producers in Europe. The efforts of regional bodies to deal with the problems are also revealing.

Germany

The German chemical industry is unique, owing to the presence (in an economy one-third the size of the United States) of three of the largest chemical companies in the world—Badische Anilin & Soda Fabrik (BASF), Hoechst, and Bayer. The descendants and predecessors of I. G. Farbenwerk, they represent tremendous commercial power. A fourth large German company, Huels, is the chemical group of a partially government-controlled, diversified energy group, Veba AG.

Table 10.1
Summary of Ethylene Production in Europe

	1978	1984
Number of producers	29	26
Total capacity (millions of tons)	14,000	15,245
Total shipments (millions of tons)	10,902	10,140

Source: Data base of Parpinelli Tecnon, Milan, Italy.

The origins of the industry are important for they explain its structure. Chemistry and chemical engineering have their roots in Germany. Hoechst, BASF, and Bayer invented and developed various parts of the basic and applied science of chlorine, ammonia, synthetic dyes, pharmaceuticals, explosives, coatings, rubber, and fibers. When the same problems of economic structure emerged that plague the industry today, the companies first allied themselves and then merged to form the giant I. G. Farbenwerk.

According to the memoirs of Kurt Lanz, one of Hoechst's leaders in the postwar growth of the company, attempts were made to rationalize the group by eliminating competing activities. Lanz suggests that these efforts were only partly successful.[1]

The creation of this German cartel catalyzed the English interests of Nobel and Mond to put aside their battles and form ICI, and working agreements could then be made among I. G. Farben, ICI, Solvay, and the Swedish Nobel group.[2] Du Pont was regarded with somewhat the same mixture of respect and hostility that contemporary Americans reserve for their Japanese competition.

In the 1930s and 1940s I. G. Farben management, purged of its Jewish scientists and executives, incorporated into the Nazi war machine. Later, some of Farben's leaders would be tried at Nuremberg. During the Occupation, the Allies broke up I. G. Farben, but even in the immediate aftermath of the war, its constituent parts (BASF, Bayer, and Hoechst) were too large for purchase by any interests other than the U.K. or U.S. chemical giants. As they emerged from their alliance and the war and rebuilt their facilities, the ex-partners returned to their earlier interests and strengths. By 1983 they were very different companies.

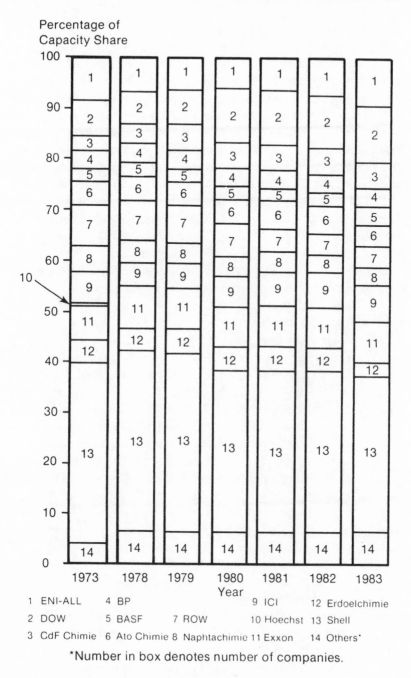

Chart 10.1
Ethylene Capacity Share Western Europe, 1973–1983

BASF

Badische Anilin & Soda Fabrik (BASF) was founded in 1865 to produce coal tar dyes, for which it received the first patent in Germany. In the twentieth century, the company grew through internal development as its researchers discovered new processes for synthesizing ammonia (1913) and methanol (1920). BASF's discoveries in coal and oil hydrogenation contributed to the early growth of the petrochemical industry. Following its merger with the other major German chemical firms to form the I. G. Farben trust (1925), the company's researchers discovered polystyrene (PS) and polyvinyl chloride (PVC) and produced the world's first magnetic tape (1930s). During World War II, with Germany cut off from its traditional raw material supplies, the company emphasized production of synthetic rubber and fibers. Throughout its early history, BASF had remained a producer of basic chemicals, leaving final product development to its customers or to other members of the trust.

BASF became an independent company again when the I. G. Farben trust was broken up by the Allies in 1951. As the company had now lost its captive market for basic raw materials, it started to integrate forward through new product development and acquisitions. In the 1950s and 1960s BASF introduced several new plastics, such as expandable PS and acrylonitrile-butadiene-styrene (ABS). The company entered the paints and pharmaceuticals businesses through acquisitions in the late 1960s and the 1970s, long after its principal German rivals, Bayer and Hoechst.

In addition to forward integration, BASF's postwar strategy included a shift from coal raw materials to oil feedstocks. In 1953, BASF joined with Shell in a fifty-fifty venture at Wesseling to produce ethylene and low- and high-density polyethylene (LDPE and HDPE) in the Rheinische Olefinwerke (ROW), which became one of Germany's major petrochemical complexes. But Germany's (and the world's) largest chemical complex was at BASF's original location across the Rhine in Ludwigshafen, where, by 1983, 50,000 people worked in 300 chemical factories. Only during the 1950s did BASF expand at other sites in Germany and abroad. BASF entered the U.S. market through a joint venture with Dow Chemical in 1958, and later bought out its partner. In the 1960s and 1970s, the company also expanded in Europe, with

Table 10.2
Production Capacity at ROW in 1980
(Tons per Year)

Ethylene	970,000
LDPE	640,000
HDPE	210,000
PVC	0
PP	75,000
PS	0

Source: Parpinelli Tecnon, 1983.

plants in Belgium, Spain, and France. BASF integrated backward into oil and gas production and refining when it bought Wintershall, a small German oil company, in 1969. Because of BASF's concentration on basic chemicals, the crisis in petrochemicals seriously affected its overall performance, especially in 1975 and 1980 to 1982.

In 1983, 21 percent of BASF's sales were in oil, gas, and other raw materials, 20 percent in base chemicals and petrochemicals, 15 percent in agrochemicals, and 15 percent in plastics. BASF's heavy commitment in commodity plastics gave it a prominent position. It was the European leader in PS, with about 28 percent of the market; its plants at three European locations had a total capacity of 825,000 tons per year in 1980. The company was weak in PVC, but strong in LDPE because of the huge LDPE capacity of ROW. The bulk of BASF's capacity in HDPE, PP, and ethylene was also at ROW (see table 10.2).

Because of the concentration of BASF's ethylene and plastics production in this one joint-venture complex, the company's strategic moves depended on the plans of its partner, Shell.

The Economist described how BASF's reliance on commodity products hurt the company:

> BASF, the largest German producer of bulk chemicals, has been left even further behind than its big rivals, Hoechst and Bayer, by the collapse of prices and profits in bulk chemicals. It is losing money in plastics, artificial fibers, fertilisers and refining, which accounted for over half its group sales [of $13 billion in 1982].[3]

Judging from the actual cutbacks achieved, these disputes had been resolved for BASF succeeded in cutting back one-third of its

LDPE capacity between 1980 and 1983 (including cutbacks in Belgium) and shut down two of ROW's crackers. In 1980, the company decided to scrap a proposed linear-low-density polyethylene (LLDPE) plant because it expected an oversupply of this product in the future. In addition, BASF shut down some PVC capacity and 75,000 tons per year of PS capacity at Ludwigshafen and in Belgium. BASF also pulled out of LDPE joint ventures in France and Austria. Gernot Winter, managing director of polyolefins and PVC at BASF, said in February 1983, "So far the strategic measures taken at ROW have had the full concurrence of Shell. Of course, there are disputes as to how to do it but not on whether it should be done."[4]

BASF executives asserted that they saw the crisis in petrochemicals coming and that they dealt with it routinely. They maintained that BASF was the first company in Europe that made drastic capacity cutbacks. Winter said, "We have not changed our strategy; we concluded early on that the extraordinary growth was over and that there was no sense in keeping excess capacity." But he felt that BASF's exit barriers were significant.

> We have to ask ourselves: Can we afford to quit? The exit barriers for an oil company are lower than for a chemical producer. In Shell, for example, the chemical business is a small part of the whole. With us, if you cut off petrochemicals, you lose a major part of the company.
>
> Yes, integration makes it more complicated to cut back capacity. But it also makes us more flexible in trying to optimize our operations. When you only have one operation and one product, there is just one way to cut back. But when you are as integrated as we are, there are several ways of accomplishing the same thing. Moreover, large complexes like ours can absorb people more easily. We cannot just lay off 3,000 people—that's politically risky in Germany today."[5]

BASF, like Bayer and Hoechst, did not look to their government for aid in dealing with the crisis. There was no government relations office in BASF, and each line and staff manager dealt with the government as necessary. The company's political lobbying was all done through the existing industry associations. Winter said, "There is not much cooperation with the government. We run day-to-day operations independently of the government, although there are many regulations, such as pollution controls." Like Bayer and Hoechst, BASF went out of its way to publicize their compliance with pollution controls and their commitment to environmentally safe operations.

BASF executives, like Winter, did not see governments playing a constructive role in the restructuring of the industry.

> Wherever the government gets involved, it goes wrong. In PVC, for instance, ICI invested in new capacity in northern Germany because it got a subsidy from the Lower Saxony government. The result is an increase in overcapacity.
>
> The study that Messrs. Gatti and Grenier are preparing for discussion with the EEC authorities is only for political purposes. We know there is overcapacity. But maybe the governments need more proof.
>
> Also, people are now saying, "Let's wait until the study is ready." The study and the activity of the EEC's Competition Directorate may thus actually delay action.[6]

The one type of government involvement that BASF executives were careful not to criticize were the actions of the Kartellamt, the German government's antitrust division in Berlin. Even though the German companies felt that they could solve their industry's problem through private actions alone, the Kartellamt, functioning as an independent ministry, had to approve all domestic and external deals. The minister of economic affairs, who could override the decisions of the Kartellamt, reportedly understood the need for companies to make profits better than the antitrust lawyers did.

Hoechst

The Hoechst company's predecessor, Meister, Lucius & Co., was founded in Hoechst (near Frankfurt) in 1863 and initially manufactured dyestuffs. Through a combination of internal development and acquisitions, Hoechst expanded into vaccines and analgesics in the 1890s and into organic chemicals and fertilizers, beginning around 1910. In 1925, Hoechst became part of I. G. Farben.

After World War II, Hoechst expanded into fibers, plant engineering, paints, cosmetics, industrial gases, and plastics. Hoechst also established subsidiaries in other European countries, in the United States, and elsewhere. The company's largest foreign subsidiaries, such as American Hoechst Co., grew through local acquisitions to duplicate most of the parent company's product lines.

Because Hoechst had less than 15 percent of total sales in commodity petrochemicals, the company continued to show a profit all through the 1970s and early 1980s. But their commodity petrochemical operations did lose money heavily, especially in 1975, 1977, and 1980 to 1982. This contributed to a decline in Hoechst's return on equity from 13 percent in 1974 to 4.4 percent in 1982. Some of the reasons behind Hoechst's poor performance in 1982 were described in *European Chemical News*.

> [In 1982], a marked decline was suffered in the sales of organic chemicals and plastics. . . Capacity utilization is said to average 66% to 47% for low-density polyethylene (LDPE), 59% for high-density polyethylene (HDPE), 62% for polystyrene (PS), 76% for polyvinyl chloride (PVC), and 85% for polypropylene (PP).[7]

Hoechst like BASF was a major producer of commodity plastics in Europe. Hoechst, with its share in Wacker Chemie and Ruhrchemie, was the largest European producer of HDPE; its five plants had 500,000 tons per year of capacity in 1980. In PVC production, Hoechst itself had a minor position, but including Wacker Chemie, the group ranked fourth in Europe, as it did in production of PP. Hoechst was a relatively small producer of LDPE, but it had good technology in the new LLDPE which was replacing conventional LDPE in many applications. In Europe, Hoechst was fourth or fifth in production of PS, but in the United States, with about 12 percent of the market, it was one of the top three producers.

Unlike other petrochemical companies with sizable operations in commodity plastics, Hoechst did not have its own supply of ethylene. It was Europe's largest merchant buyer of this basic raw material, depending on five companies for its supplies— Erdolchemie (Bayer/BP), Veba, Marathon, Caltex, and URBK at Wesseling. (In 1984, Hoechst sold the 25 percent share it had in URBK Wesseling.) Three of the crackers of these companies had been built especially to serve Hoechst's needs.

Hoechst cut back its plastics capacity heavily in the crisis of the early 1980s. By its own account, it cut its capacity in HDPE by 22 percent, PP by 25 percent, and PS by 28 percent between 1980 and 1983. In addition, there were rumors in the industry press that the company was considering exiting from selected parts of the business, if not from the whole industry.

European Chemical News reported that

> The most likely candidate to be jettisoned by the West German major is LDPE . . . . After this, PVC or PS could be the next most likely candidates. At the moment, though, no one is saying anything. Hoechst's only official comment is "Hoechst has no plans to close down PVC or LDPE production. . ."
>
> Hoechst and other German firms would undoubtedly like to rationalize their operations, but they have felt inhibited by the watchful eye of the cartel office.[8]

In the summer of 1984, *European Chemical News* reported that ENI had reached an agreement with Hoechst, under which the Italian state-owned company would lease all of Hoechst's LDPE facilities in Germany and take over its marketing operations for that product. But, "neither company would comment on the agreement. It is understood that government and union approvals still need to be secured before an official announcement can be made."[9] The deal was finally concluded in late 1984.

With another product, PP, Hoechst seemed to be poised for expansion, not retrenchment. Early in 1984 it acquired a nonexclusive license to use Montedison's new PP process, which resulted in much lower manufacturing costs than other existing processes.[10]

Bayer and Veba AG

Of the three major German companies, Bayer is the least involved in petrochemicals. It manufactures ethylene and LDPE in a fifty-fifty joint venture at Cologne with BP called Erdolchemie. The venture has operated near breakeven. Bayer's only real significance to petrochemicals comes from the fact that Erdolchemie serves as an important source of propylene and other hydrocarbons used by Bayer in its other chemical businesses. These are predominantly dyes, pharmaceuticals, photographic products, agricultural chemicals, and bulk and specialty chemicals and plastics. Because these businesses have been profitable, there is a problem shutting down the ethylene and polyethylene activities.

Veba AG is Germany's largest industrial enterprise and

diversified group. It is 44 percent owned by the government. Chemische Werke Huels AG is owned 88 percent by Veba. Huels has significant positions in HDPE, PP, and PVC but in none of them does its product mix, technology, or cost position give it a position of leadership. Despite the poor performance of its chemical group, Huels is thought to be sufficiently strong financially to wait out the present crisis without exiting any of its positions.

These four companies—BASF, Hoechst, Bayer, Veba AG—and their subsidiaries are located along the Rhine and its tributaries from Cologne to Ludwigshafen. The ethylene producers of the upper Rhine are linked with each other and the North Sea ports in a pipeline network. In the south, there are connections among those on the lower Rhine. In Bavaria as well there are freestanding complexes at Munchsmunster and Gendorf (Hoechst) and Burghausen (Wacker).

As the largest market in Europe, Germany is a strong base for the leading exporters. Typically, more than half of the German production of BASF, Hoechst, and Bayer is exported. Historically, Germany has penetrated the EEC and other countries, but exports are a lower percentage of sales than, for example, the Dutch or Belgians whose industries were built primarily for export. In 1983, however, production, sales, and exports were down while imports—especially from the Eastern bloc—increased 5 percent.

The Germans have been leaders in the battle to cut capacity in commodity plastics without state aid for reasons that are ideological, political, and commercial. To begin, the three big companies are all privately held and are leaders of the conservative business community. They do not believe in state support. Second, while they are leaders of the German chemical industry association (VKE) as well as the Association of Plastics Manufacturers in Europe (APME), the company managements are very sensitive to the surveillance of the cartel office in Berlin. In a Europe rife with meetings in 1982 and 1983, there were no stories of discussions among the Germans. Finally, as a practical commercial matter, the Germans thought state aid and cartels would help their competitors stay in business. As noted, BASF executives were leading exponents of the view that government interventions were counterproductive. Creating a study group under the Council of

European Industrial Chemical Federations (CEFIC) with the European Commission's blessing would "only delay action."

This point of view was also reflected in the reluctance of the German companies to meet with Viscount Davignon, and their unwillingness to sponsor the Chem Systems study. (They later bought it.)

In May, just before a CEFIC meeting to discuss the Gatti-Grenier report on collective restructuring,[11] BASF announced capacity cutbacks in polystyrene. It reasserted the view that unilateral measures were the only way to approach a rationalization of the European industry. On the other hand, in May of 1983, Professor Dr. Rolf Sammet, the chairman of Hoechst, spoke out in support of the CEFIC study. His position apparently reflected a view that Brussels could have a positive effect on the French politicians and could support the steps underway in Italy.

Shell

There is a certain arbitrariness to discussing Shell with Europe, since Shell is one of the most multinational of companies and since its United States chemical activities are extensive. One could just as easily put Shell in a supra-European category. Nonetheless, one of Shell's two centers is in London, the other is in the Hague, and its jointly owned facilities with BASF at Wesseling are enormous. Legal structure aside, the general management of Shell's chemical business sector is in London.

Shell was the oil company most deeply involved in chemicals. Having entered olefins prior to World War II, it built olefin facilities in conjunction with refineries, exploiting good feedstock situations provided by its producing and trading parent. It is regarded as very strongly positioned.

On the basis of this sound position in olefins, Shell has constructed essentially a commodity business with a portfolio of higher value-added business. Within commodities, they are more balanced toward propylene and its derivatives than other competitors, especially the other oil companies.

Until the purchase of U.S. Shell is complete, Shell's relations with its sister company are those of a friendly minority shareholder and are governed by the U.S. antitrust laws. There is complete exchange of technology in areas where both are interested.

There is no cooperation in others. And, said one executive, "There are circumstances where we could be very competitive."

Initially, during the 1950s, Shell saw chemicals as a useful growth business synergistic with oil. To pursue the business, chemists and chemical engineers were hired. There were statements of company objectives that said, "The Shell Group will have two pies (oil and chemicals) by 1990 that will be equal in size." "From then on," said one executive, "growth was self-perpetuating. It was a me-too exercise; everyone did what everyone else was doing. But you must not underestimate the sex appeal of the industry, its sophistication, substitution, and huge growth."[12]

The driving force that led Shell to crack ethylene was the need to find a home for the naphtha being produced at its major refineries in the United Kingdom, Holland, France, and Germany. Interestingly, there is a cautious note to Shell's development for they entered the United Kingdom at an acquired site, perhaps to avoid ICI head on, and joint ventured with BASF in Germany, clearly to avoid direct confrontation. There was a short-lived joint venture in Italy. The cracker they had in France came quite late. In Japan, where it was required by law, Shell joint ventured with Mitsubishi Petrochemical, and in Australia, Shell sold its ethylene to ICI.

Shell's pace of development was affected by its possession of licenses to the Ziegler process for polypropylene that favored the construction of smaller ethylene crackers than what might have been built to compete in polyethylene.

By the late 1970s, the disappearance of the basic factors that drove the expansion of chemicals was finally noticed and Shell began to put its house in order. Shell believed that it would lose volume for structural reasons. As the market dropped in 1980 it became increasingly clear that not only would there be no growth but that horrendous losses could continue (1982 losses were £65 million). The result was a major consolidation with old crackers closed at Berre (France), Carrington (United Kingdom), and Pernes (Holland) for a total of 320,000 tons. Shell experienced some frustration as its partnership with BASF at ROW slowed the cutbacks in Germany.

By the mid-1980s, Shell was positioned in three places to compete based on its newly completed Mediterranean capacity (Berre), its crackers on the Rhine (ROW across from Ludwigshafen), and its share of the giant ethane-based cracker at Mossmoran. The problem taxing chemical group management was that a coordinated "three-legged" strategy required a centralized management with product divisions such as the Germans or Dow had; Shell was accustomed to operating with a highly decentralized structure, built to manage a multinational oil business.

With such extensive interests in ethylene and commodity plastics, Shell actively supported restructuring efforts in the industry. Between 1979 and 1983, Shell shut down one million tons per year of its worldwide ethylene capacity. By 1983 small profits had been earned. Its top executives, such as J. H. Choufoer, encouraged others to follow suit. In a 1982 speech on petrochemical restructuring, focusing on ethylene, Choufoer argued for restructuring.

> The basic objective must be to ensure that European producers, who must continue to meet the major part of European demand, can thrive in the future. The prevailing pressure to oversupply the market and reduce prices to unacceptably low levels must be eliminated. The process will be hard, as it will involve major reductions in capacity, but it will lead to lower unit costs by improved plant utilization rates and increases in efficiency. The resultant industry will be smaller, of course, but would then have regained an acceptable level of profitability and should be competitive in the domestic markets as well as in some, but fewer, export markets . . .
>
> The petrochemical industry is highly complex and cracker loadings result from interdependent feedstock supplies to the derivative plants; i.e., any closure of a derivative plant affects loadings on the upstream cracker and thus the economics of the total complex. The rationalization measures undertaken so far, and there have been a number, have so far been on sites where more than one cracker existed. The more difficult problems relate to petrochemical manufacturing sites with only one cracker. In such a case, if the logistics of feedstock supplies to economically viable derivative plants are complex or too costly, closure of a complete site must be contemplated. Alternative arrangements would then have to be made with another producer for product supplies to allow continuation of marketing. Such arrangements might then run up against legal difficulties and constraints with the national and international competition authorities . . .
>
> It is my conviction that it is in the consumer's interest, as well as the industry's, that rationalization take place; surplus capacity is an unnecessary extra cost, and is a major factor in making the European petrochemical companies incompetitive internationally.
>
> This is a challenge facing every company in the industry, and one

which only those companies can face. Direct official intervention by national or international authorities is not needed, and cartelisation would simply prevent the basic problem being addressed and is, of course, not in line with the principles of free competition.[13]

Shell's vision then was that efficient producers would replace inefficient ones at the same time that overall capacity was reduced. Shell could take such a position because its crackers were among the most efficient in Europe. Striving to maintain this position, Shell also had plans to expand its ethylene capacity by building modern plants worldwide. The Mossmoran project was one example of this strategy. Another was Shell Chemical USA's $3 billion joint venture in Saudi Arabia to build a 650,000-tons-per-year ethane cracker. In Choufoer's words, "It makes economic sense for gas (ethane) produced in these regions, which would otherwise be flared, and for which no other, more economic, use is available, to be used as chemical feedstock." Shell Chemical USA was also studying the possibility of participating in a consortium to make petrochemicals from Alaskan petroleum gases.

Aside from striving to be a low-cost ethylene producer, Shell also tried to focus on building a good derivatives portfolio. This meant cutting back capacity in products where Shell had no special advantages and expanding in others. In this vein, Shell Chemical USA shut down 320,000 tons per year of vinyl chloride monomer (VCM) in 1983 and made plans to expand in synthetic ethylene-based detergents, a business in which the group had strong proprietary processes. Shell Chemical USA also worked with Union Carbide to develop a new process to make polypropylene, the group's other area of strength. According to the companies' descriptions of the new process announced in 1983, it enabled plants to switch back and forth between PP and LLDPE. In addition, the plants were cheaper to build and operate than conventional ones.

In the same vein Jan Slechte, head of petrochemicals for Shell International Chemical Co., commented on the need for greater financial sense in pricing and investment in the European industry.

With twenty-six heterogeneous managements it is unrealistic to speak of pricing discipline. The problem must first be faced by the individual firms. If each company looked at its balance sheet carefully, then its board could say "thou shalt not sell below variable cost plus direct fixed cost plus working capital cost." Then after that we could go into inflation, maintenance, R&D, and headquarters cost. There would be very little problem remaining if the companies all made their pricing decisions based on sound economics.

Shell is taking part in the CEFIC discussions because we are doing everything we can to influence thinking of company managements. It is paradoxical, but it is less important to try to influence governments because it is so very difficult. They must deal with their politics. We talk to them, but the impact is influenced by what happens this afternoon.[14]

Nonetheless, for Shell, relations with governments were key; Shell was one of those multinational corporations that seemed to defy a national affiliation. From the beginning, it was as much a Dutch company as a British one, and the "national champion" in neither country. In the 1980s, its operations in the United States were so extensive that it might have been considered a U.S. company. The Shell group's major operations in Germany, France, and, in the future, Saudi Arabia, added to the impression that the company was truly supranational.

Shell's individual national operating companies, of course, had to deal with national governments. In the United Kingdom, for instance, Shell UK had succeeded with Exxon in getting important concessions from the tax authorities on the pricing of ethane used in their Mossmoran cracker. A 70 percent tax was due on usage of petroleum feedstocks, but since natural gas was not traded on the open market, the transfer price used for tax purposes had to be set by agreement. The price agreed upon was relatively low and helped give Mossmoran an edge over its competitors using naphtha as feedstock. British Petroleum (BP), which was converting its Grangemouth cracker to ethane, subsequently fought for and received similar tax concessions. But Imperial Chemical Industries (ICI), which only had naphtha crackers, was left to complain loudly about the "hidden government subsidies" its competitors were getting.

Consistent with Shell's supranational position, its executives were deeply concerned with the positions that the regional authorities took in the restructuring process. Shell's top executives called for a clear and constructive role for the EEC's political authorities. J. H. Choufoer argued that there were at least three things the authorities could do: (1) provide workable competition guidelines to indicate what types of private bilateral arrangements would be allowed; (2) help reduce financial and social hardships caused by plant closings; and (3) adopt a novel suggestion patterned on what was done five years earlier in the refining industry, which Choufoer described.

> At that time, when the underutilization of primary distillation capacity was reaching alarming proportions, the Commission initiated a meaningful dialogue with individual refining companies in order to broaden knowledge about capacities, investments, and throughput rates . . . The information so gathered was published and made available to the industry by the Commission in aggregated form . . . this role of the Commission was of a purely monitoring nature, but the experience has shown that, without actual involvement in business decisions, the Commission may indirectly assist in the restructuring process by providing to a highly complex industry a reasonable degree of transparency not previously available.[15]

The Role of CEFIC and the European Commission

As Choufoer noted, there is an old tradition of collective action in Europe. It is often expressed in a desire to set up cartels and is occasionally successful in consummating that desire. In the history of the industry are the relationships of I. G. Farben, Solvay, and the Nobel interests. At the same time, the great private companies know that they are in a virtual war to stay independent and to beat back the tide of socialism in Europe. There is also the reality that some of the companies that wish to set up cartels are state owned. And at least one of the states has a remarkable record of breaking agreements when it appears to be in the national interest to do so. Consequently, while there is an obvious usefulness to collective action to deal with the situation of overcapacity in Europe, there is a reluctance to take part among the British and German companies, the only two groups of financially strong and legally independent companies among the EEC states.

It is against this background that the Council of European Industrial Chemical Federations (CEFIC) and the European Commission should be considered. In the latter, the two principal forces are Viscount Etienne Davignon of the Industry Directorate and DG IV, the Commission's antitrust arm.

CEFIC is the European council of national associations of chemical manufacturers. It meets regularly as does the Association of Plastics Manufacturers in Europe (APME), a subgroup of plastics manufacturers. For many reasons, the U.S. companies operating in Europe cannot take part in the discussions for fear of violating U.S. antitrust laws.

In the fall of 1981 the heads of two of the more troubled groups—Jacques Solvay of Solvay and René Malla of Rhône-Poulenc—approached Davignon and asked if he would organize in petrochemicals a capacity reduction of the sort arranged in fibers. Davignon said he would support the sort of effort they were seeking but demurred at using the offices of the Commission. Instead, a group of nine CEFIC members, "the nine," met with Davignon to discuss the problems.[16] BASF and BP were not present, nor were Dow, Exxon, or any U.S. company.

Apparently there was some embarrassment at the meeting due to the lack of consensus as to whether any need existed to have such an agreement. In the end, Sammet and Harvey-Jones (Hoechst and ICI) proposed that a study be carried out to document the problem and suggest useful solutions. Pierre Grenier (ex-Rhône-Poulenc) and Piergorgio Gatti (Montedison) were asked to do the work.

Many at the meeting thought this unnecessary for, by remarkable happenstance, the private U.K. consulting firm, Chem Systems, had just completed a study of ethylene and its principal plastic derivatives as an act of private entrepreneurship. They had sold the idea of the study to a large number of European producers and had just published their findings prior to the meeting.

Particularly dramatic was the graphic presentation of the relative positions of manufacturers. Chem Systems identified that the costs of leading plastic manufacturers varied by as much as 30 percent and consequently that margins were often negative for several years (see chart I.1).[17] For ethylene, LDPE, HDPE, PS, and PVC Chem Systems displayed the commercial position of *all the units* in Europe on what they called a "survival matrix" (see chart 10.2). Individual subscribers knew their position on the chart and thus it was readily apparent that many high-cost or poorly located units should be shut down.

Still, many of those who thought that Gatti and Grenier would merely replicate the work just completed by Chem Systems regarded even the effort as a step forward, if the Germans would acknowledge the accuracy of the findings. BASF in particular was

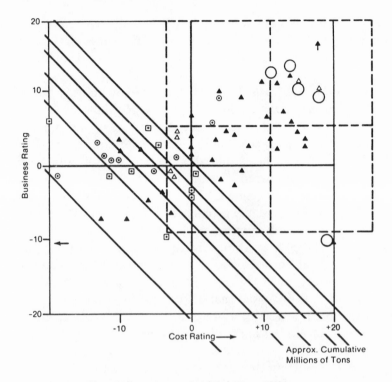

Source: Chem Systems International Ltd., June 1983.

*Each entry on the survival matrix represents a production facility, in this case, a steam cracker. Each triangle or circle was identified by a number. Only the subscribers were given the key. Position along the horizontal axis reflects relative cost. Position on the vertical axis reflects commercial strength as a function of product mix and geographic location. Both assessments are the judgment of Chem Systems based on their accumulated expertise and on-site visits.

Chart 10.2
Steam Cracker Survival Matrix

known to be suspicious of the findings of the Chem Systems group, reputedly charging that it was a Shell-sponsored project.

The Gatti-Grenier report was written in April 1983. When it circulated, the British and Germans objected strongly to findings that proposed a cutback in activity proportionate with volume rather than in accordance with efficiency or some market-driven measure. Moreover, they questioned whether the proposals were practical and legal. Were they merely an invitation to delay? The draft version discussed at another meeting of "the nine" at the end of May was characterized as "washed out." As evidenced by the excerpts below, the characterization is apt.

Actions

There is a consensus amongst companies operating in the EEC that a major restructuring of the industry is required if the industry is to return to economic health. The process of restructuring needs to embrace a reduction of capacity and the creation of larger unsubsidized and more efficient groupings capable of competing profitably both in a European and world context.

The Working Group which prepared this Report will contact all producers to ensure that the scale of required reductions in capacity are clear to them. This should lay the foundations for the companies to take decisions which will lead not only to reductions in capacity, but probably also to a reduction in the number of producers of any one product.

The available courses of action for the companies appear to be:

Autonomous decisions: such as the closure or putting on stand-by of some plants.

Bilateral arrangements: such as those already reached in the United Kingdom and in Italy.

Multilateral arrangements: where the solution of particularly complex problems requires three or more companies to reach simultaneous bilateral agreements.

These actions taken together should foster the closure (or putting on stand-by) of the least efficient plants, thus reinforcing the competitiveness of the West European industry.

To assist the companies to achieve these goals, the Commission should support the concept and facilitate the applications of bilateral and multilateral actions. Moreover the Petrochemicals Industry seeks support from the Commission for the following procedures:

Compensation: that could be given to an individual company which was prepared totally to withdraw from a business, by those other European firms remaining in that business.

Definition: of a common rule to define the circumstances whereby stand-by capacity could be brought back into operation.[18]

In addition, in the event of any major disruption of the EEC market by substantial imports from, for example, countries with ready access

to cheap raw materials, the companies would look to the Commission
to safeguard the industry by revision of GSP criteria and by rapid
application of GATT rules (e.g., antidumping procedure).

The meeting of "the nine" with Davignon to discuss the report
ended in something of a shambles, with no consensus reached as
to what should happen. In fact only seven attended.[19] Not surpris-
ingly, further consultation was recommended and agreed to.

Meanwhile the European Commission's antitrust arm, DG IV,
proceeded with its inquiry into the BP/ICI swap.

The Commission

DG IV is the directorate of the European Commission responsible for the enforcement of Articles 85 and 86 of the Treaty of
Rome—the Common Market's antitrust laws. Compared to U.S.
law the provisions are quite lax as far as conversation and agreements among competitors—so that discussions of joint capacity
cutbacks in the face of disastrous markets are legal. But they
also quite clearly prohibit conspiring to raise price or injure
competitors.

As Fritz Andreisson, director general, presented the case, competition was a way of "avoiding the artificial protection of old
structures" and helping to "keep our borders open" while "serving the interests of our consumers." Nonetheless, he recognized
that there were conditions where "crisis cartels" were appropriate
because "structural overcapacity" existed. His comments, too,
give a flavor of DG IV's approach.

> Structural overcapacity exists where, over a prolonged period, the
> undertakings concerned have experienced a significant reduction in
> their rate of capacity utilization, a drop in output, and substantial
> operating losses and there appears to be no prospect of improvement
> in the medium term.
>
> Structural overcapacity may result from entry onto the market of
> new products or from erroneous demand-trend forecasts which give
> rise to excessive investment.

In the appropriate circumstances, the Commission would approve
a coordinated attempt to reduce overcapacity.

A sectoral agreement providing for a coordinated reduction of over-capacity in an entire industry can be regarded as compatible with the rules of competition where:

(i) its only objective is to reduce structural overcapacity without serving at the same time to fix or control quantities produced, quantities delivered, or prices;

(ii) its duration is restricted. Certainly that their agreement will come to an end in the near future makes the undertakings concerned take account of the fact that in due course they will once again become full-blown competitors.

(iii) it provides for no protectionist measures *vis-à-vis* outside competition, notably, imports from third countries;

(iv) it contains, for each production unit, a detailed, binding plan of closures guaranteeing that the overcapacity will not merely be mothballed, but irreversibly dismantled;

(v) it guarantees that, during its application no new capacity will be created beyond that provided for in the restructuring plan as replacement capacity;

(vi) it provides, if necessary, for a system of sanctions to ensure compliance with the dismantling plan, under the responsibility of the undertakings concerned.[20]

Andreissen added that it was not always necessary to approach such problems on an industry-wide basis and that "Bilateral agreement between large undertakings by which each agrees to close down part of its production capacity and obtain its requirements from the other can have the same results and is exemptable under the same condition."[21] In the question and answer period, he cited the BP/ICI swap by way of example.

As noted, the Directorate chose to investigate the actions of BP and ICI despite Andreisson's apparent approval. And in October 1983, the Commission's police raided five manufacturers of polypropylene that were alleged to have conspired together.[22]

At the same time DG III, the Directorate for Industry was working in a different direction as its leader tried to shape a European industrial policy. Until he stepped down in 1985, the Commissioner for Industry, Viscount Davignon, had tried hard to help the states of Europe to deal cooperatively with the problems of industrial competition that are tearing at the fragile bonds of Europe. In one industry after another, companies have been unable to stand up to the ravages of lower demand, increased raw materials and energy costs, social democracy in the work force and the tax system, and efficient competition from overseas—East Asia or the United States. Davignon has tried with some success to reduce chaos in both steel and textiles by means of agreements to cut back capacity. His success has varied because especially in textiles, Italy has posed problems. As noted above, they have actually *increased* capacity in fibers. The "lessons" of the fiber experience affected the willingness of chemical producers to take "the nine" seriously.

In the summer of 1985, such progress as had been made, came from companies working on their own or through deals with national competitors. The "good news" seemed to be confined primarily to western and southern Europe where BP, ICI, Shell, Atochem, Montedison, and, to a considerable degree, BASF had made progress in balancing capacity with demand. Problems existed on the northeastern part of the continent where lack of balance was aggravated by the imminent start-up of Mossmoran. The arrival of Saudi product in Europe was also destabilizing, although it had not as yet posed the cataclysmic upheaval that some were anticipating. There was no doubt that lower oil prices helped a great deal. Still, substantial overcapacity characterized the market for commodities; even the best producers made modest returns in those businesses; and the future offered no prospect of much better. True progress required cross-national solutions and so far, with the dramatic exception of Montedison, these defied the efforts of managements.

It is fascinating that this troubled industrial setting was the school that Japan's Ministry of International Trade and Industry (MITI) used to teach Japanese chemical company managements the need for restructuring. For while that very homogeneous country did not need a supranational commission to deal with excess numbers, the fact was that Japan had too many chemical companies competing for the limited business of the eighties.

NOTES

1. Kurt Lanz, *Around the World with Chemistry* (New York: McGraw-Hill, 1980), passim.
2. W. J. Reader, *The Imperial Chemicals Industries: A History,* 2 vols. (London: Oxford University Press, 1970–74), 2, passim.

3. "BASF: Slow Reactions," *The Economist,* 14 May 1983, 81–82.
4. Interview with Dr. Gernot Winter, managing director of polyolefins and polyvinyl chloride, BASF, spring 1984.
5. Ibid.
6. Ibid.
7. "Hoechst Hopeful for Future but First Quarter Profits Fall," *European Chemical News,* 9 May 1983, 23.
8. "Hoechst Nears Pullback?" *European Chemical News,* 18 April 1983, 6.
9. "Enichem to Lease German LDPE Units as Hoechst Quits Market," *European Chemical News,* 30 July 1984, 6.
10. "Montedison Grants Hoechst Catalyst License," *European Chemical News,* 2/9 January 1984, 18.
11. The Chem Systems and "Gatti-Grenier" reports are discussed later in this chapter. They were both attempts to study Europe's petrochemical capacity problem, but Gatti-Grenier was intended to provide the basis for collective action.
12. Interview with Jan Slechte, Shell International Chemical Co., spring 1983.
13. J. H. Choufoer, "The Problems and Implications of the International Restructuring of the Petrochemicals Industry," paper presented at the annual meeting of the European section of the Society of Chemical Industry, Brussels, Belgium, 18 October 1982, 2–4.
14. Interview with Jan Slechte, spring 1983.
15. J. H. Choufoer, op. cit., 2–3.
16. The nine were Ato-Chloe, Rhône-Poulenc, ENI, Montedison, DSM, Solvay, Shell, Hoechst, and ICI.
17. Chart I.1 contains other data describing the lack of profitability.
18. These two proposals were withdrawn from the final version that was sent to the Commission.
19. "European Plastics Producers Abandon 'Crisis Carter' Idea," *European Chemical News,* 6 June 1983, 6. The managers' lack of enthusiasm is important for several managers in petrochemicals spoke of "the lessons of fibers." By that they meant that even Davignon's heroic efforts would not succeed if governments chose to subsidize losers.
20. Fritz Andreisson, commissioner of the Directorate for Competition of the European Commission. Paper presented at the London School of Economics, February 1983, 3, 17–19.
21. Ibid, 19.
22. In the largest case in history, nine polypropylene producers were fined tens of millions of dollars.

11
The Restructuring of Japan's Petrochemical Industry

History

In the early winter of 1983 there was an odd phenomenon to be seen in Western Europe. The chief executives of twelve of Japan's leading petrochemical manufacturers were traveling en bloc around the continent visiting many of Europe's major manufacturers. Leading the tour and making the arrangements was an official from the Ministry of International Trade and Industry (MITI). As described by one MITI official, "Our industry is in a very difficult situation with much overcapacity and too much competition. We could not get the companies to cooperate. We thought that seeing Europe's condition would persuade them of the structural nature of the crisis and that traveling together might help build cooperative relationships."[1]

The source of the concern was clear. In a country with half the population of the United States, there were just as many large, powerful manufacturers. Ethylene capacity was some 6.5 million tons against a requirement in 1982 of 3.6 million tons. The Industrial Bank of Japan estimated that the combined operating deficit of the petrochemical manufacturers was ¥400 billion (approximately $1.6 billion).

But the source of the crisis was more complex. Why would Japanese companies get into such a Western problem? How was it that the famous MITI had not anticipated and fixed the problem?

In 1981 the chemical industry accounted for 8 percent of the manufacturing's value added, Japan's largest industry. Petrochemicals accounted for 46 percent, up from 7 percent in 1960. Japan's petrochemical industry was the second largest in the world. Ethylene production was 60 percent of the United States, but 33 percent more than Germany's and twice that of France. It was second in synthetic resins and fibers.

The industry's beginnings were in the late 1950s. In line with the overall plan for the rebuilding of heavy industry, chemicals were identified as a key industry to be supported and guided by the government. MITI's measures for fostering the industry included a crude oil allocation system, foreign exchange allocation for the import of petrochemical plants and technology, extra depletion, and loans by the Japan Development Bank. The idea was to establish integrated complexes of crackers and derivatives adjacent to refineries.

Four companies (Sumitomo Chemical, Mitsui Petrochemical, Mitsubishi Petrochemical, and Showa Denko) entered ethylene between 1957 and 1959 at four different sites. All were representatives of major, former zaibatsu groups.[2] Three of the entrants, however, were new companies set up by their groups specifically to enter petrochemicals. In each case the chemical company of the group established a relationship with an oil company. The detailed reasons differed: one may have lacked the capital to make the move, another lacked interest in the new risky field, while another may have lacked the approval of MITI. (Mitsui, for example, wished to take over an old naval site but it was not to be made available to an already existing company.)

Then from 1960 to 1964 one oil refiner after another entered the industry, five altogether. MITI encouraged this development in accordance with its 1959 plans for commercialization of the petrochemical industry.

The Combinatos

The years from 1965 to 1967 represented a third phase during which two of the original entrants, Sumitomo Chemical and Mitsui Petrochemical, built additional facilities of larger scale to support synthetic fibers businesses and other olefin-based products. In this instance, MITI established the Council for Petrochemical Industry Cooperation and a plant construction approval standard to control investment: crackers had to be larger than 100,000 tons per year. One direct consequence of this ruling was the "combinato," a complex in which several companies located in one area to take the output of a single cracker. Chart 11.1 provides a description of

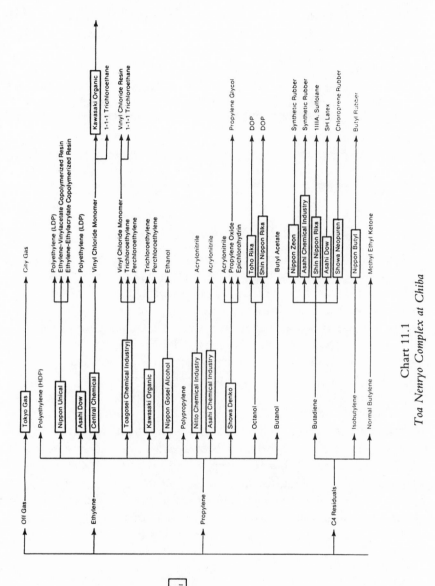

Chart 11.1
Toa Nenryo Complex at Chiba

Toa Nenryo's complex at Chiba. Note the presence within this complex of several companies, such as Nippon Unicar, Asahi Dow, and Showa Denko.

From 1968 to 1972, five new entrants built crackers, as well as Mitsubishi Petrochemical and Mizushima Ethylene. Among these entrants were subsidiaries of Mitsui Toatsu and Mitsubishi Chemical, both of which had decided not to leave this booming field to sister companies and had entered directly. At the start of this period, however, the Council established 300,000 tons per year as the standard in order to strengthen the industry's international competitiveness.

The Naphtha War

A major problem that had emerged over this period of development was the pricing of naphtha. As Japan had no native gas, all feedstock was naphtha cracked from imported oil. During the 1960s a fixed price ruled, but by the early 1970s demand exceeded supply and naphtha was imported directly. After the 1973 oil crisis the imported naphtha was in heavy demand since "domestic naphtha" was priced at its average value in use and this was above the world market. (The primary use was gasoline which had been priced high at this time to discourage consumption.)

For a while, the price of naphtha was set in negotiation by representatives of the petroleum and petrochemical industries. This also entailed a negotiation between MITI's energy agency and its basic industry bureau, each siding with the industry they "guided." Some feeling for the intensity of these discussions may be gained from their being referred to as the "naphtha wars." During this period olefin prices were set at a constant factor of the naphtha price. In 1982 the naphtha price was finally set at market levels.

After 1973, the petrochemical industry entered a long period of depression. Nonetheless, following plans made earlier, Showa Denko (finally opening its own combinato) and Ukishima Petrochemical (a joint venture of Nippon Petrochemical and Mitsui Petrochemical) brought new 300,000-ton crackers on line. It was in this period that the companies first came under pressure as demand stagnated, imports strengthened, and naphtha prices increased.

The second oil crisis in 1978 only heightened the problem, persuading at least some that the industry faced long-lasting structural problems. Exports which had peaked at 20 percent of production in 1977 dropped to 12 percent in 1979 while imports rose from 0.7 percent to 4.3 percent. The deterioration in Japan's basic position can be seen in chart 11.2.

In this dismal situation Japan found itself with thirteen major producers of ethylene and derivatives at eighteen major petrochemical complexes spread out along the southern coast of Honshu and the northern coast of Kyushu and Shikoku. (See the map in chapter 3.) Around each complex was a host of plastic fabricators, some 23,000 altogether, employing 322,000 employees (three percent of all manufacturing). In 1981 pretax profits/sales for the eight largest chemical companies ranged from a high of 1.7 percent to a low of − 1.1 percent. As noted already, losses in commodity plastics were catastrophic.

The situation was even worse than in Europe. Because the combinatos were symmetric, the ownership involved was as complex as the management, and some of the companies were more than 90 percent devoted to petrochemicals (e.g., both Mitsubishi and Mitsui Petrochemical were nearly 100 percent). In 1983 each was expected to shut down a major cracker. On the other hand, Mitsui Petrochemical had specialized in high grades of high-density polyethylene (HDPE) and this would help them survive, while Mitsubishi Petrochemical was strong in polypropylene (PP) but not HDPE. It was thought that each might withdraw from its area of weakness.

MITI Acts

In this critical situation, MITI was able to act. The distinguished Industrial Structure Council set up a special blue-ribbon Petrochemical Industrial Capacity Subcommittee under the standing Chemical Industry Committee (CIC) in order to examine the structure and make plans for the future. The subcommittee made two basic recommendations.

1. Attempts to recover cost competitiveness through energy-saving technology, diversification of raw materials, and disposal of inefficient capacity should be made.
2. Excessive competition should be eliminated.

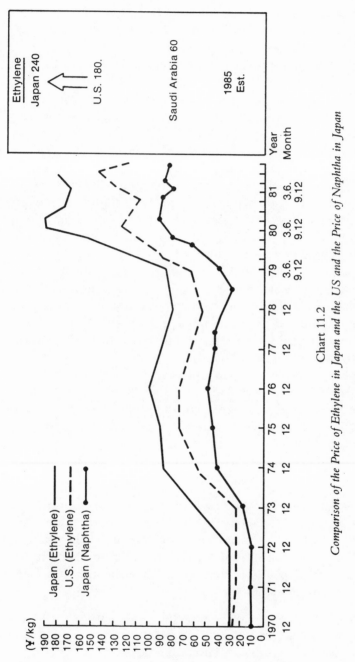

Chart 11.2

Comparison of the Price of Ethylene in Japan and the US and the Price of Naphtha in Japan

Sources: Japanese figures are from the Industrial Bank of Japan. American data are from *European Chemical News*; 1985 estimates are derived from the United States International Trade Commission, Office of the Secretary, USITC Publication 1370, *The Probable Impact on the U.S. Petrochemical Industry of the Expanding Petrochemical Industries in the Conventional-Energy-Rich Nations* (Washington, D.C.: Government Printing Office, 1983), 32; 1985 estimates are converted from $/ton to Y/kg.

MITI took a very strong role here—encouraging the companies to carry on discussions, leading the trip through Europe, and promulgating a very pessimistic view of the situation. (While the CIC called for a reduction of ethylene capacity to 4 million tons, MITI originally sought 2 million tons as a goal—the level based on "domestic naphtha"—but relented when pressed by the companies.) MITI's view was that it would be better for Japan to import basic derivatives at the distressed prices expected for the next decade.

To assist the companies MITI promulgated a new law for the restructuring of depressed industries. It is interesting to quote from the section on retreat and revitalization in a MITI description of the "Philosophy and Ideas of the Temporary Measures Law for the Structural Adjustment of Specific Industries."

> The law is in no way intended to protect the industries from the adjustment forces, including overseas competitors, but to encourage private enterprises to retreat; that is, to dispose of the inefficient and obsolete facilities with no prospect of recovering economic viability. Under this law around 30 percent of present facilities are expected to be curtailed. At the same time, it purports to revitalize the remaining portion through innovative activities of businesses such as fuel conversion, sophistication of the products, R&D, and cooperation or consolidation of business. In this sense, the law embodies the idea of positive adjustment policy.[3]

A manager of the Industrial Structure Division of MITI's Industrial Policy Bureau offered the following explanation of how this philosophy developed.

> We are concerned that we have a number of industries that are fundamentally weak. The affected industries are petrochemicals, electric furnaces, pulp and paper, synthetic fiber, ferro alloys, chemical fertilizer, and aluminum. There were three reasons for the difficulty in these industries:
>
> 1. High energy cost, especially after the second oil shock.
> 2. Demand declined, this was a long-term structural decline. Demand got thinner and thinner.
> 3. There is excessive competition; I like to say "abnormal competition" because people don't know what excessive competition is. As a consequence, performance is poor. The costs are high and prices are low. Within a small market there are many fighting for increased share despite demand growth.

Competition is OK, it is reasonable in most cases. But we can judge the existence of excesses of competition from the outcome and by the structure. For example, in ethylene there are twelve companies and a small demand. Abnormal competition is competition whose outcome is not good. Based on the recommendation of the Industrial Structure Council, we established a petrochemical industry advisory policy.

1. We want to reduce capacity to improve demand supply situation. For example we want to scrap 40 percent of petrochemical capacity in three to four years.
2. In order to do that we have to consult, so we had to exempt consultation and discussions from the antitrust laws. MITI can designate a process to do this.
3. In order to promote fair and reasonable competition MITI will encourage joint ventures and mergers.[4]

A colleague in the Basic Chemicals Division commented:

The route to breakeven is to maintain a better price. Of course there is an international market, but we think plastics can be priced at 10 percent over the market price because of marketing factors. A premium of 5–10 percent can be counted for stable price and technical service. But today because of excessive competition, for example in styrene monomer, the domestic price is way below market.

So we see groupings for joint sales in high-density, low-density, polypropylene and so on. We will make four groupings for marketing and sales.[5]

The first manager continued:

We discussed all this in the Council and MITI took the results to the FTC [Fair Trade Commission]. But the groupings created were a problem. The largest was greater than 25 percent. So we set up a new clause. The company should bring a proposal to MITI and MITI would bring it to the FTC. This was the coordination clause. If the situation changes so that market share relationships are altered the FTC can come to comment to MITI. So for the first time we have coordination of industrial policy and antitrust policy.

For MITI the biggest issue is competition among the groups. We see competition dynamically in an international context. We are not concerned with concentration here in Japan because there is so much international competition.

We have made a clear, explicit, international survey. Japan can survive as a smaller, more efficient industry. We don't seek to be a major exporter. We plan on a stronger role for international competition here in Japan. If European petrochemical industries can survive, Japan can, but we cannot compete with the United States.

This is a painful and long process. The companies must discuss inside their organization and create the right atmosphere. The Japanese petrochemical industry is in so much difficulty so may decide to rationalize very soon.

Employment will be a special problem. This is a very rapid scrapping of capacity, therefore it implies a very rapid cutting of employment in a company. This means transferring workers to other plants in the company or other companies in the group. But if cutting down is implemented there will be a real problem. The Ministry of Labor is considering legislation to promote retraining. (The labor union saw these issues in the Chemical Industry Council, but they also saw that if there was no action the industry would lose.) So in law the labor unions sought import relief. No one else wanted this, however, so the labor union's representative from aluminum said, "Scrap down; it's the second best solution."

Then in discussions the Liberal Democratic Party said yes, the Social Democrats said yes, and the Clean [Environment] Group said yes. The Socialists said no. They wished to have more emphasis on employment. We said this is industrial policy, not employment. They understood. The Communists said no.[6]

As to whether the policy would succeed, there was considerable disagreement. The international press took it for granted that the proposed reductions would take place, 36 percent in high-density, 27 percent in low-density, and so on. But some of the managers were less sure. The companies all intended to survive based on their strengths. Rivalry among the Keiretsu, reluctance of banks to take write-offs, reluctance of companies to lay off workers, and problems posed by relations with plastic converters exacerbated the resulting competitive climate. One key manager expressed his hesitation artfully: "I cannot say that there will not be a reduction in capacity."[7]

There was a consensus, however, that grouping would be necessary if the manufacturers were to survive the circumstances of intensive international competition. Sales groups would form and help firm up prices. The idea was to divide up the manufacturers of each major product (e.g., low-density polyethylene) into four groupings which in turn would negotiate price.

A model for such an approach already existed. In the summer of 1982, fourteen polyvinyl chloride (PVC) manufacturers had succeeded finally in setting themselves up in groupings for sales and in getting FTC approval of those groupings, and prices *were firming*. There were differences certainly. A different set of companies was involved because PVC was dominated by chlorine/ammonia-related companies with different stakes. In particular, leadership in the PVC industry was in the hands of specialists, who faced fewer problems of integration if they cut back. Also different, the industry was guided by the Ministry of Finance through its control of imported salt. Nor was PVC under the purview of MITI's basic chemical desk. Finally, customers tended to be larger and stronger than in polyolefins. Still the precedent of success was viewed as important.

In the spring of 1983 the companies were looking forward to improving prices. The various groupings were sorting themselves out and trying to determine how they would operate. The plan is shown in table 11.1.

Managers in the industry foresaw many difficulties but essential progress. Under the 1983 law, they had five years to reorganize. Rationalization was a prerequisite for international competitiveness. But closures posed problems that would have to be negotiated. Who would shut down? How would the thousands of small converters be helped? How would the companies be compensated for taking care of their workers? And how would the burden on the local communities be handled? Should the surviving companies help or should the government provide assistance?

Table 11.1
Proposed Selling Groups for Polyolefins

Leader	Total	Market Share		
		LD	HD	PP
Mitsubishi	17	21	13	18
Showa Denko	25	26	38	19
Mitsui	22	19	30	22
Sumitomo	32	34	19	40
Imports	4	—	—	—
Total	100	100	100	100

Source: Company interviews, spring 1983.

"Frankly," said one executive, "each company must work to survive. It must apply its own power and energy. Each company has its own strategy. The fact that oil prices are down helps provide time in the short run."[8]

The Prospect

The companies thought they could predict the eventual outcome. Managers expected the product leaders in a field to emerge as the dominant forces: Mitsui Petrochemical and Showa Denko in high-density; Mitsui Chemical, Mitsubishi Chemical, Showa Denko, and Sumitomo in low-density; Nippon Zeon, Kanegafuchi, and Shiantsu in PVC; and so on.

This sense of direction was impressive given the disorder observed in Europe, but it should not be exaggerated. The 1982 losses of Japan's polyolefin manufacturers were as bad as those in Europe—hundreds of millions of dollars at each firm. And MITI did not have the total confidence of the manufacturers. After all it was under their tutelage in the late sixties that the overbuilt combinato system had been constructed, and MITI had been unable to persuade the FTC to accept the original plan for three, not four, sales groups. There was, however, an agreed-upon diagnosis of the situation and some rough goals. Most important, the Industrial Structure Council's deliberations over the course of 1982 and 1983 had been sufficiently publicized that a broad political base existed for action if the parties involved could figure out how to proceed.

The contrast with France was perhaps the greatest. France's government technocrats had imposed structural change without a strategy or a political consensus. Japan had collectively worked out the strategy and built the consensus. It remained for the companies to formulate and negotiate a plan for implementation.

For managers outside Japan the numbers in table 11.1 and the now well-reported formation of company groupings are in some ways much less interesting than are the peculiar history of the industry that contributed to its problems and the unusual repertoire of institutional arrangements and practices that could be drawn upon for their resolution.

And perhaps it will be more interesting to executives in Japan that the special features to be described here are not the differences that Japanese managers thought were the most important when they described themselves in contrast to Europe and the United States. For example, one banker wrote me that

> Your description as to the Japanese petrochemical industry is accurate. But I hope you will extensively discuss considerable differences existing between Japanese business environment and those of United States and Europe . . .

> The Japanese business environment has such unique features as lifetime employment system, familylike management, corporate groups covering small business. So Japanese management, when they make decisions, have to take into account noneconomic considerations in relation to above, in addition to conventional Western rationalities (e.g., profitability of the business).[9]

In fact, managers in the West spoke no less of the problem of workers than those in Japan. The problem of small companies in groups was less an issue because of the fully integrated nature of many of the Western companies. What was different in Japan was the "familylike" management. But even more different was the historical and institutional setting. The combinatos, the keiretsu (or family of companies related to a trading house), the practice/ strategy of building ahead of demand, the habit of conversation among competitors, the deeply ingrained value of consulting with government managers for the greater benefit of Japan, the experience of decades working with the very prestigious Industrial Structure Council of MITI, and the view in government that profitable large companies can help an economy were all central to the problem and its resolution.

The Japanese petrochemical industry developed while the participants were relatively weak. In the initial post-McArthur period of economic development, basic industrial chemicals received high priority. But until the extraordinary usefulness of plastics and synthetic fibers was perceived, petrochemicals were low priority business for MITI and for the major chemical companies.

The combinatos were an answer to the need to assemble new capital and talent. They also appeared to be a very efficient approach to the business since all facilities were in one location around a refinery, units could be sized optimally, and pipeline connections from one complex to another were obviated. That the size of facilities might not match the Japanese market was not an issue either. As one manager put it:

Please note, however, that overcapacity in any part of the economy has been a perennial problem in the postwar Japan. We should say that it was exactly the basic driving force of the miraculous growth of the Japanese national economy up until the first oil crisis. During such a period, the company strategy was geared to continued growth in a growing industry.

Restructuring surfaced as a basic strategic problem only when people realized that there would not be any significant growth potential in that particular industry despite the huge overcapacity and the particular business segment was too big for the company to simply discard.[10]

In other words, it took the Japanese companies longer to deal with the problem because periodic overcapacity had been a central feature of the national industrial policy. Japan's basic manufacturing strategy is to invest steadily ahead of demand in the most modern production equipment, and then run the equipment near 100 percent of capacity to ensure low cost. The investments are financed with debt, often obtained at favored rates from the long-term credit facilities. These highly leveraged facilities are then protected from the vagaries of world business cycles by growth-oriented, domestic macroeconomic policy, and antirecession cartels to allocate local markets and limit price-cutting when domestic demand weakened. At such times extra product would be redirected into foreign markets as part of subsidized export drives. The shift in relative prices in oil, naphtha, and plastics meant that the overcapacity that developed in the 1980s represented fundamental uncompetitiveness rather than temporary decline.

When managements did recognize that conditions had changed, they found that the large complexes—conceived as a way to assemble management and financial resources for unlimited growth on a global scale—were very hard to reorganize for the more centralized task of rationalization. The Japanese needed a government-led effort at restructuring, in part, because the individual companies did not—as did Dow, ICI, Shell, Hoechst, or BASF—control individual vertically integrated complexes with a history of management responding to shifting markets. And because of the rivalry between the original chemical companies and the petrochemical companies at Mitsui and Mitsubishi, these two great keiretsu could not easily resolve problems within their groups.

The experiences of Sumitomo are an exception that proves the rule. At Ehime, they possessed an old but wholly controlled integrated complex. As early as the spring of 1979, they shut down one of their ethylene units and began to conceive a strategy of restructuring that would involve the transfer of all commodities from this older complex to their more modern Chiba complex and the development of higher value-added products at Ehime. It may be that Sumitomo was able to move early precisely because it did not have the sibling rivalry problem. The timing may explain its relative profitability during the crisis period.

As they faced the collapsed markets of 1980, the immediate reaction of the managers was to talk over the situation to see if something could be done. But with more than 33 percent overcapacity, uncompetitive costs, and, therefore, no world markets to absorb product, the shutdowns required posed problems greater than could be handled in the normal antirecession cartel. It was not just a question of temporary gluts that could be dumped outside Japan at a loss. Moreover, MITI was somewhat reluctant to use cartels in a situation where they could generate much resentment. Because of what MITI called "abnormal conditions," Japan would be permanently disadvantaged in competition with ethane-based petrochemicals. Worse still, some of the newest (and lowest cost) facilities had been built by lower status newcomers. One company manager compared the situation in the industry to that of excessive debt in Latin America. "The companies kept going because of rivalry among the zaibatsu groups and the problems of overextended banks."

The position of the companies remained somewhat different in the immediate period following the collapse of the market in 1980. They took the view that losses in petrochemicals were due to the unrealistically high price at which naphtha was transferred from the refineries to the ethylene crackers. Since imported naphtha was cheaper, they took the view that they should be permitted to import it.

In Japan, complex issues of this sort are often raised for discussion in the very prestigious Industrial Structure Council. The Council, consisting of a maximum of 130 persons of learning and experience, is the central forum used by MITI to establish a broad political consensus behind major policy directives. The committee originated in the period during which the laws liberalizing Japanese trade policy seemed to threaten Japan. "Therefore, it would seem that the goal of the ISC [was] to promote the restructuring of Japanese industry to increase Japanese competitiveness."[11]

The ISC is composed of a coordination committee that explores the general direction of Japanese industrial policy and specialized committees such as the ones that were involved with the future of petroleum and petrochemicals. The Chemical Industry Committee of the ISC is made up of representatives of the petroleum and petrochemical industries' members, users, suppliers, workers, as well as academics, and media people. Its chairman was Professor Arisawa, credited by some with the idea of a "priority production system," the basic approach adopted by MITI in the postwar period. In 1981, MITI wanted the CIC to study the naphtha price problem and the restructuring of the petrochemical industry.

By law, anyone wishing to import naphtha was required to register with MITI's Agency for Natural Resources and Energy (ANRE). That agency believed that it would be destabilizing to several aspects of national energy policy to allow the petrochemical companies to import naphtha directly. As well, the Petroleum Council of the ISC opposed imports on the grounds that their bargaining power with sources of hydrocarbon would be weakened and that prices within Japan were low enough anyway as a result of the resolution of a naphtha war in 1962. Since the Basic Industries Bureau (BIB) of MITI looked after petrochemicals, the naphtha war also represented an intramural dispute within MITI. The problem for the petrochemical industry was that within MITI, ANRE allegedly had higher status and power than BIB.

The settlement of the naphtha war came in April 1982 when the recommendation entitled "A Proposal for Policy Measures on Petrochemical Feedstock Naphtha" was jointly issued by the Chemical Industry Council and the Petroleum Council. The main points of the policy were as follows:

—Prices of domestic naphtha will be determined on a quarterly basis in such a way that they reflect prices of imported naphtha.

—Petrochemical companies will be assured of free import of naphtha through an agreement between the oil and petrochemical companies. The naphtha-importing company belonging to the seven oil companies became the major naphtha importing agent.[12]

The settlement of the war set the stage for an attempt to solve more fundamental problems of the industry. Even with market prices for naphtha, it was clear that the industry would lack competitiveness. The problem is evident from chart 11.2. Even if the combinatos were very efficient, they could not make up for the raw material cost disadvantage. MITI's problem became evident when less than half the industry would cooperate with a rationalization on the scale required by long-term strategic considerations. Basically, those newcomers with the new facilities and the lowest costs refused to accommodate their economic position to the political power of the established players.

To work on the issue, and to indicate its gravity, a Petrochemical Industry System Subcommittee was set up in July 1982 with a prestigious professor as its chairman. The formation of this group appears to have precipitated the trip to Europe by the leaders of the twelve ethylene producers. MITI officials found them so recalcitrant that it seemed useful to show them how sick their industry was, while at the same time providing the opportunity for bitter rivals to form friendships that might become a basis for cooperation. Here one branch of the government, while explicitly recognizing the principles of competition underlying the efforts of a sister agency, the FTC, made radical efforts to help the companies "collude" in order to define and solve the industry's problems.

Some final remarks are worth making from the perspective of 1985. The solution devised after the trip—four polymer sales companies—seems to be working. Prices are firming and capacity is being shut down. One manager suggested, however, that the relationship between the action taken and the new law for restructuring depressed industries are more indirect than one might expect.

The point, he notes, is that the real changes in the industry are more complex and situational than the committee plans and neat numbers would suggest. Prices are firming, but for all sorts of reasons. To begin, growth in world gross national product has meant that supply and demand are closer to balancing. Another factor is the announced position of the government. Said one manager, "There is no law to police price-cutting. But we are a cohesive, closely built society (familylike). If a company really broke the line on price it would be difficult for it to do business."[13] Another company suggested that the position of MITI and the new law made the necessity and legitimacy of the cutbacks easier to understand for the many small user companies that would be hurt.

In effect, the processes of discussion, the passage of the law, the formation of groups, and the negotiation of plans were the mechanisms by which that famous Japanese consensus was established. The actual process of cutbacks will not necessarily take the form suggested in the speeches that are being given or the press releases. One typical example is in HDPE. Mitsubishi Petrochemical will scrap its entire capacity (36,000 metric tons) despite the fact that under the new law it would theoretically be allowed to produce 30,000 metric tons. Mitsubishi Petrochemical will buy the HDPE they need from Mitsubishi Chemical, Showa Denko, and Asahi Chemical and will sell to those three companies LLDPE, ethylene vinyl acetate, and PP in almost equal volume. (Showa Denko and Asahi are not in the Mitsubishi polymer group). By such carefully bargained swaps, a rationalization will be accomplished that looks much more like the ad hoc bargaining of Europe than the neat planning of MITI, but it is the environment created by MITI's leadership that has made it possible and legitimate.

The spirit of the change underway is captured by the response of one manager to an inquiry as to whether there had been any reports on what was happening. He said, "To our best knowledge there is no report. We think that comprehensive papers may be compiled some time after March, 1985, when excessive capacities are fully curtailed as provided in the restructuring program."[14]

NOTES

1. Interviews at the Ministry of International Trade and Industry, Tokyo, Japan, spring 1983.
2. The zaibatsu were giant, privately owned and often family-controlled industrial groups surrounding a bank.
3. "Philosophy and Ideas of the Temporary Measures Law for the Structural Adjustment of Specific Industries," English translation of a MITI discussion paper, spring 1983.
4. Interviews at MITI, spring 1983.
5. Ibid.
6. Ibid.
7. Interview with Japanese manager, spring 1983.
8. Ibid.
9. Personal communication from Japanese banker who reviewed an early draft of this chapter.

10. Interview with Japanese chemical company manager, spring 1985.
11. Reiko Sakuma, "The Role of Advisory Committee for Revitalization of Declining Industry—Japanese Model," unpublished study, John F. Kennedy School of Government, Harvard University, June 1984, No. 10.
12. The description of the "naphtha war" that follows draws heavily on Sakuma's study.
13. Interview with Japanese manager, spring 1983.
14. Ibid.

12
A Restructuring Agenda for Managers

Introduction

Today in the petrochemical industry, as in most global businesses, good strategic analysis reveals that the long-term prospect for the core, high-volume businesses is more competition, more capacity, and low profits or losses. During the last decade, return on investment in manufacturing has seldom provided shareowners their real cost of capital, and the prospects for the future remain poor as long as the same structure prevails. As long as certain governments and Japanese savers have been willing to provide capital at lower than world market rates, the prices for goods reflect those lower costs of capital rather than the "target rates of return."

I have argued in chapters 2 and 3 that the only options for the individual firm operating with private funds are exit or participation in a collective restructuring of the market. There is no successful strategy that an individual firm can use to compete because all firms are drawn to the same strategy. If the long term matters, cooperate or exit. But for company managements to cooperate in the restructuring of industry, public policy in the form of antitrust laws must be modified along lines suggested in chapter 4.

This leaves a dilemma for the management that has to continue to do business "tomorrow morning" before some undetermined future when policymakers will have fixed the industrial environment so that normal competition produces healthy results. It will take considerable time for policymakers to move because, when they ask the economists, their "experts" will argue that "no problem exists." The traumas described in chapters 5–11 are simply "transition costs." As one economist who read an early draft of this book put it, "At least from the viewpoint of business planning, if governments do these things [make 'dumb' investments or protect jobs], rational strategies must recognize that governments 'move first' and make the best possible adaptation to the fact [later]."

What I have shown in chapter 3 is that in a politicized environment, there is no "rational strategy" as the economists would define it. Too many ongoing games are affected by the same moves. To maximize long-term profit can very easily mean to liquidate. To let the government move first may easily involve sinking more funds in a dying business.

What lessons, then, can be drawn from the experiences in petrochemicals that have *immediate* import for managers? There are three main lessons, and they correspond to the three phases of the restructuring process cited in chapter 3.

Three Tasks for Management

1. Preparation. It is vital to do the work of preparation as early as possible. In order to participate effectively in the competitive battle during restructuring, it is absolutely mandatory to have the information, controls, and management that can run the firm on the basis of its economics. The task here could be called *creating a profit capability*.

2. Concentration. It is essential to structure the company so that each piece of the business can be treated according to its prospects. Otherwise during the phase of concentration, one may well be creating a kind of Penn-Central amalgamation of dying enterprise. This work I call *organizing for turmoil*. An important warning is that the stage of preparation should precede concentration. Otherwise what lawyers and financiers put together may have no economic viability.

3. Rationalization. It is important to recognize that restructuring is not just an economic game. Because major changes are involved, the political dimensions are of great significance. A business manager must deal with politicians; his moves, taken for entirely private reasons, have major public consequences. Like it or not, businessmen engaged in restructuring are playing politics. Managers must aquire the legitimacy necessary to deal with politically sensitive issues. This task I call *building legitimacy*.

These three tasks constitute the pressing agenda for top management of major firms who must deal with the difficult circumstances of the last part of this century. They are dealt with in turn.

Creating a Profit Capability: Preparation

It may seem peculiar that in a study of so complex a topic as restructuring markets, the first short-term recommendation is so obvious—firms should have the capability to make a profit.

In fact, as we have seen, many firms have not been profitable. Much of the work of top management in this last decade has consisted of taking over large organizations that grew up in the benevolent growth markets of the 1960s and transforming them into leaner, tougher enterprises, capable of competing in the turbulent 1980s. Before managements came to understand that they also had to deal with politics, this turnaround work was considered among the most basic but most difficult in all of management.

The task has two dimensions, one administrative and the other strategic.

The Administrative Task.   When top managements turn to their organization for help in developing plans to deal with crisis circumstances, they usually find that the lower levels of managers are not persuaded that the problem exists. Usually a division's response to a request for an exit plan is a proposal to spend new money. The consequence is that when top management seeks to do the work of portfolio analysis described in chapter 2, they often have to rely on consultants to do the analytic work. Their own staffs have neither the predisposition nor the talent.

In other words, while crisis plays a role in driving change, the first step for top management is to call attention to the economic consequences of what is happening. It is easy for middle-level and functional managers in a large organization to lose sight of the profit objective. Such managers almost always understand their job in much more immediate terms, such as running the plant safely with low costs or introducing a new product or increasing sales. Profit is the objective, of course, but the information available to the manager may not include profit, or if it does, it is likely to be calculated after subtracting all sorts of allocated overhead and corporate costs for which most managers do not feel responsible.

In addition to these internal or organizational forces, there are external pressures. Many managers see themselves in professional terms. They are competing with other managers as engineers, salesmen, innovators, cost reducers, or whatever. Especially in Europe, the technically trained employees are likely to put their profession above profit.[1] There are political pressures as well. Simple nationalism is a powerful force that distracts managers from pursuit of economic objectives. Much of the European work force is unionized, and many of the unions have a socialist or communist orientation. In the extreme situation faced by some Italian managers in the early 1980s, the decision to close a plant was tantamount to putting one's life in mortal danger.[2]

Japanese managers face a special problem: Most important companies are members of a keiretsu or family of companies related to a trading house. The rivalry among these groups is intense, so that relative standing in market share is usually a far more important objective than profit.

To these omnipresent pressures to ignore profit, the chemical industry adds its own special set of forces. Most of the managers are engineers, and the facilities are hard to design, hard to build, and hard to run efficiently. It is possible to be a very happy engineer just getting a major facility to operate well without blowing up. Chemical engineers love their plants.[3]

In order to control these facilities, to keep them safe and efficient, the plant management team exercises powerful functional control. Good plant managers are virtual czars of their facilities. Even in the best of times, running a chemical company is a constant battle between these czars concerned with the vigorous health of their facilities and the economic planners and marketers at headquarters concerned with profit and the long-term prospects of the businesses based on those facilities.

Chemical businesses are also extensively interdependent so that it is very hard, in a totally unambiguous way, to measure performance of one from among the hundreds of products produced by a chemical company. Until recently, there were many firms that did not provide profit information to middle-level managers. Some did not calculate profit by product.

Pricing is also a problem. The most obvious costs to a producer are the direct ones. But since so many of these are fixed, there is a tendency when demand is soft to price so as to cover variable cost. Even when demand is strong relative to capacity, it is easy for managers to ignore, in their pricing, costs for which they are not responsible, such as R&D, working capital, and corporate overheads. In chemicals, allocated fixed costs can run to 25 percent of sales so that their omission is quite serious.

Under these circumstances, it is not surprising that crisis is required to get the troops' attention focused on profit. Nor should it be surprising that when top management works on building a corporate strategy it often requires consultants to do the work. Had the management cadre understood what were the economics of their portfolio of businesses, it is unlikely that they would have dug themselves into quite so deep a hole.

The Strategic Task.   There is such a familiar ring to the phrase "corporate strategy" that we popularly assume that the activity is regularly carried out. The familiarity of the word belies the difficulty of the task. Most managers do not think strategically, in the sense that they question the very premises of the business they are in. They fight for market share in steel rather than wonder whether steel will be used in the same ways or needed in the same quantities. They take for granted knowledge about how steel is made that may be out of date. It was Alfred North Whitehead who wrote, "routine is the god of every social system."[4] The manager who would follow a different muse undertakes, in effect, a religious conversion of his organization.

It is for this reason that top managements so often reach out to consultants. The analytic capability required to gather, organize, and interpret data of the sort required for a useful portfolio analysis is rarely present in the ranks of major companies. But especially difficult is the task of marrying the technical and commercial expertise of one's own organization with the point of view, techniques, and personnel of the consultant.

The horror stories of megadollar consulting projects that proved useless often have their origins in two aspects of this human equation. If the consultants have been unable to draw on the knowledge of the engineers and marketers from the operating divisions, their studies and proposals may be substantially flawed. But the same lack of communication with the line organizations almost guarantees their rejection of an approach to the business that challenges the premises of routine activity. Precisely because it takes time to help the operating units to learn why changed commercial and technological conditions require a different approach by the company, years are involved in rethinking strategic change. This same requirement for the involvement of operating managers is one reason "corporate culture" has become such a hot topic.

Strategy consultants discovered that a new strategy was not like a floppy disk that could be inserted in some sort of executive disk drive and "booted up" but instead required a retooling of the organization's entire operating systems. In contrast, well-managed companies have always known that their strategy, structure, and systems are interdependent, and they invest regularly in their renewal.

While executive development, selective recruiting, reorganizations, and other conventional measures can be used to upgrade a management team, years are required before significant change can be accomplished. Even if consultants do an imperfect job, and even if they bruise organization sensibilities in ways that take time to heal, a top management trying to deal with the sorts of crisis circumstances I have described reaches quite sensibly for any reasonable map that will help them plot direction in the short term.

A clear example of this process is provided by the turnaround at Montedison where the consultants were used extensively to help Schimberni's team as they redirected their organization and negotiated with ENI and the government. While it was a somewhat different process, the MITI-organized trip to Europe catalyzed the Japanese companies into a series of planning and negotiating exercises aimed at restructuring. In an odd way, MITI served as the consultant/change agent.

Where outsiders are not used, top management usually creates their equivalent in the form of a small, high-powered task force such as the ones created at ICI and BP in order to negotiate the swap. Still other approaches are off-line strategic planning exercises, such as those used at Union Carbide during the early 1970s or the work in the late 1970s led by Gandois at Rhône-Poulenc. In each case, special circumstances require nonroutine procedure for response. A team must be created that can seek the underlying economic reality, unswayed by the powerful biases inherent in membership in divisional or functional organizations.

In the search, an inevitable first problem is the lack of good information. Not only are the middle levels of management likely to be biased, but also they rarely have good cost information to work with. Building new information systems is a regular requirement of the turnaround process. Without it, the crisis remains external and corporate. It is not until managers at lower levels see hard evidence that their own unit is bleeding that they can accept the need for action.

Organizing for Turmoil: Concentration

The administrtive and strategic work just described represents two-thirds of the preparation phase of restructuring. In order to take part in concentration, there must also be a process of reorganizing to deal with brutally competitive but constantly changing market circumstances. The management consultant, Henry Strage, has summarized the changes that he has seen (and that I also observed in petrochemicals) in four words, "Alfred Sloan is dead."[5] That classic corporate center with static planning systems; parallel administrative relationships between line and staff; common levels of authority and responsibility; identical processes among divisions for reporting, monitoring, and control; all united by a single, uniform approach to management development, compensation, and career planning is obsolete.

Instead we find divisions set up in whatever form seems to reflect strategic need, reporting to a small, flexible, elite corporate center that plays a variety of roles—coach, sponsor, surgeon, and architect are Strage's four categories. Examples of attempts to create this kind of new corporate center are evident in this study. Schimberni's small corporate group holding variously structured subsidiaries and joint ventures is prototypical. ICI's announced intention (not yet fulfilled in 1986) to close its palatial headquarters at Millbank is symbolic, and the move by Hutchison of a small top management group out of London to a plant site is exemplary. Dow has always tried to maintain a small center, and Exxon Chemical's is self-consciously tiny, located in Connecticut far from its magnificent parent. It remains to be seen whether BASF, Carbide, and Shell (which remain large relatively integrated giants) can avoid further changes. The fall 1985 cutback of 4,000 employees at Carbide suggests not. More to the point, the attempt of GAF to gain control of Carbide is premised on the notion that the company is worth more in pieces.[6]

Again, the Japanese represent a different situation. The members of a keiretsu operate in a network of relationships that are not corporate. The corporate center as a building with associated overhead costs does not exist. Instead, there is a meeting, and changes in leadership are followed by changes in the portfolio rather than by radical changes in structure.

The challenge in rebuilding a management structure is considerable. Not only is there restructuring to deal with new sources of supply and new materials costs; but ahead lie further earthquaking changes. Industry leaders, such as Robert Malpus of BP, predict that a new chemistry for commodities based on methanol rather than ethylene lies just over the commercial horizon in the 1990s and beyond that a shift from the use of heat and pressure in the manipulation of molecules to the use of microbes. Whether or not their vision is accurate, the corporate center that would deal with such challenges needs to be knowledgeable about commercial and technological changes and fast on its feet. It must understand where it must withdraw in the face of overwhelming power in the hands of oil companies or hydrocarbon-rich countries and where it can stand to fight based upon innovative capability that provides value to well-understood markets. While the chemical companies make their money as chemists, marketers, and traders, the oil companies and oil-producing countries must carefully manage the timing and technology of their investments.

Building Legitimacy: Rationalization

The process of managing the restoration of a company to competitive health resembles closely the treatment of a human patient with a mortal disease. Doctors can be very callous in their delierations even when they are deeply concerned with the survival of the patient. In the same way, managers and consultants can sound quite brutal as they discuss the necessity for cuts in cost that imply direct cuts in employment.

In this instance appearances may be deceiving. In all my interviews, top managers expressed considerable concern for their work force, both because it was part of the human fabric of their company and because they were concerned about the political and administrative consequences of a disgruntled labor force. This concern was reflected by top managers' desire to respond to the crisis of overcapacity and losses in a way that would be regarded as legitimate by the employees. The restructuring policies of many of the companies already considered provide examples.

One manager involved in restructuring spoke of the care he took
to apply to his own operation the draconian measures he was
enforcing. He cut his own staff and made a point of a spartan
headquarters.

Horton at BP made sure that the first purges were in headquarters,
and extensive communication about product profitability (or
the lack of it) was taken all the way to the factory floor.

ICI management gave emphasis in their work to the principles
used to plan the restructuring. These had been discussed at
length among the senior working party and were written down.

Schimberni emphasized the extent to which Montedison could be
a model of a professionally run company and drew young men
from Boconi business school for his new cadre.

It was the absence of a commitment to the legitimacy of an independent pursuit of economic profit on the part of their government bosses that drove Gandois to leave his post at the head of
Rhône-Poulenc, and Chalandon to leave Elf Aquitaine.

The extensive work of the Petrochemical Industry Subcommittee
of MITI's ISC made it acceptable for the companies to collabo-
rate on so anti-Japanese an activity as shutting down capacity.

Finally, it was the absence of an issue on this point made the non-
U.S. managers so jealous of their American counterparts.

The point is a subtle one, but hard to overemphasize. The process of restructuring industry is a form of economic surgery.
Pieces of companies are sold off or destroyed. The feelings of
those involved are somewhat like a friend of mine who remarked
after a kidney operation, "In order to get at the problems they
sawed off a perfectly good rib and threw it away!" He accepted
what might otherwise have seemed frivolous or sadistic because of
his understanding of the necessity. The same is true in a company.
There is a powerful contract between organization and members
that implies that the company will be there to provide employment, that accomplishments of a career will not be cast aside
without reason, and that leadership will protect the interests of
followers. These are the things that led Enichemica's president to
respond passionately that his chief problem was "people!"

Relative prices, new technology, and foreign competition are
often very abstract and distant forces in the minds of operating
managers and workers. They may never believe that cuts in em-

ployment, the exit from businesses, or the sale of facilities make sense. For them, the more immediate question is "How are the costs being shared?" "Are my stakes being recognized?" Where the answers provided by the actions of management are positive, then active commitment to the long-term health of the company is more likely.

No management that I interviewed was unconcerned about this issue. They dealt with it in different ways, but none thought that labor was merely a "factor of production." What made life difficult was that poor prior management or macroeconomic forces resulted in conditions that created the need for change. It was the present managers, however, who had to confront their colleagues and workers with the unhappy consequences. That was why they were so careful to emphasize the professional care used in coming to the decision. To make the changes in employment acceptable, they had to be accomplished legitimately, that is, both the substance and process had to seem reasonable. If taken as a definitive finding of this research, the unqualified assertion in the preceding sentence is either too strong or tautological. But as a description of management sentiment it points to a revolution in management thinking. Managers revealed *considerable concern* for the impact of planned restructuring on their work force.

In France and Italy, there was concern that unneeded facilities not be kept open by pressure from unions or political parties. Management knew that worker expectations were conventional and that they had to be skillful and resolute. While brutality had no place, a symbolic riot might help politicians see the issue clearly. In Germany and the United Kingdom, the concern was that the cutbacks be managed so that further relations with the unionized workers in other plants not be jeopardized. Petrochemical facilities are not run well by lackadaisical crews.

Companies in the United States were no different. Cutbacks were viewed as managerial defeats to be handled as humanely as possible. The problem was mitigated somewhat by the physical structure of the U.S. industry where many plants are located near each other, and feedstock and product pipeline connections constitute a virtual web of steel along the Gulf Coast. Labor is mobile relative to Europe. There, the employment consequences of shutting down a stand-alone complex, such as the one in Cologne, cannot be worked out with intercompany swaps and moving German technicians to the new plant in nearby Scotland. But in the life of U.S. workers, moving to another state is not an unusual event.

In Japan the problem posed by cuts in employment represented a true barrier to exit. The perceived obligation of company to workers and customers was very strong. The geographical configuration of the combinatos left strings of facilities and derivative manufacturers dependent on one or two crackers. Numerous interviews made clear that managements believed they had the responsibility to plan for the well-being of their workers. The difference in degree of concern might be considered a difference in kind. The Japanese certainly thought that they were less free to cut labor than their European and U.S. counterparts.

No matter where plants were located, however, a key first step in establishing the legitimacy of surgery was the diagnostic determination that there was a serious economic crisis that was not going to disappear with the next uptick in the business cycle. Because both operating managers and workers tended to be suspicious of top managements' motives, the process of making a credible determination had considerable political overtones both inside and outside the company. In achieving credibility, outsiders played a central role.

The Need for Outsiders to Deal with Politics

For the managers of the firms studied, the issues discussed here were of enormous import. None were unaware that they led some of the most important companies in the world. The firm's history often paralleled the industrial history of their country. For the old soda companies, it paralleled diplomatic history as well for they were the producers of explosives. Also synthetic dyes, paints, solvents, coatings, and lubricants are at the heart of a modern, automated, and mobile society. The managers' club at Hoechst is in a thirteenth-century castle in the center of the city of Knapsack near the plant complex that employs 30,000. Wilmington has grown up with Du Pont just as Midland has with Dow. And Showa Denko's origins date to the post-Meiji surge of industrialization in Japan.

As a group, managers in the chemical industry are well educated, more like the cadres in today's high-tech electronic firms than the typical basic manufacturing executives. Especially since the late 1960s, most have an international perspective, have trained or operated in the United States, and know their markets to be global. Their business involves them in committing hundreds of millions of dollars to investments in technology, plant, and product that will be coming to market four to five years after the decision in what they know will be competitive circumstances. While some might say that they are responsible for assets, they know they have power at the center of their country's economy.

Solvay isn't just a chemical company, it is one of Belgium's strongest economic enterprises. Montedison is one of Italy's oldest groups. Should a joint venture with Hercules be considered entrepreneurship or U.S. colonization? The petrochemical producers contributed $8 billion in 1984 to a beleaguered U.S. balance of payments. That can be thought of as a return on the tariffs that have helped the U.S. industry.

In other words, the essential strategic decisions taken by these firms are likely to be politically salient. Only a fool would ignore the likely public reverberations. The managers interviewed in this study all spoke of the need to deal with the politics of their decisions. For some, speed was important. A decision made good sense for the company and the nation, but the injured might mobilize political sentiment; therefore, present the government with a fait accompli. For others, such action was unimaginable until public sentiment was prepared by the government.

For all, the great necessity was to persuade those outside the company—in the unions, the government, and the press—that the decisions being taken made sense, not only for the company but also for the country.

Mario Schimberni noted that despite the prominent role of Americans in Montedison's management, only Italians were present for the negotiations with ENI and the Italian government. The American staff work and the Chem Systems report provided ammunition, but only Italians could argue credibly what was best for Italy.

It is in this delicate negotiation and positioning that the role of objective outsiders is so critical. The Chem Systems study was important within companies to persuade reluctant directors that heirloom businesses had to be sold. But it was also critical outside the companies in persuading ministries of industry or state-owned competitors that they had to cut back. (The author could not help noticing a copy of the Chem System study on the credenza of a French Ministry of Industry official.)

As noted earlier, it was over exactly this sort of issue that Hoechst and BASF divided on the Gatti-Grenier Report—Zaefelder of BASF taking the view that the study would be used by weak companies to delay action and Sammet of Hoechst arguing that it would be useful to the state-owned companies in France and Italy when dealing with their governments.

In the United States, the political issue was somewhat different. The major U.S. producers deployed their assets effectively to exploit opportunities in the changing industry. Dow, Du Pont, Exxon, and Carbide all made major shifts in their portfolios. After study, they either found very strong positions based on technology and/or raw material or they exited. Their political problem was posed by the less nimble companies who found themselves weakly positioned in commodity products squarely in the path of surging imports from hydrocarbon-rich countries. These weak players, especially in fertilizer, led the political charge for protection.

The problem for the U.S. winners was that the studies made by the Department of Commerce and the International Trade Commission showed a loss of world share for the U.S.-produced commodities without showing the increases expected in newer, more specialized products. More complicated still, the studies did not deal with the extent to which the U.S. companies stood to benefit greatly from the activities of those hydrocarbon-rich countries. There certainly was no forum in which the interests of the United States could be discussed, nor would the companies be interested in taking part in such an event.

A related issue was posed by the absence of a report for the United States like that of Chem Systems for Europe. Without a thoroughly documented picture of the industry's condition, only the strong made the studies that showed the structural weaknesses. (Interestingly, there appeared to be very few copies of the European study in the U.S. companies.) As one executive of a major company pointed out in the fall of 1983, "It would help this industry a great deal if the recession would continue for another year. As it is, with the recovery, a number of companies that should drop out will hang in for another round." The remaining competitors could only count on the consultants and the stock market to persuade the inefficient that the time had come to withdraw.

In contrast, as usual, was Japan. There, MITI, in its complex role of leader, custodian, protector, and regulator of Japanese industry, found itself in an awkward situation. The combinato sytem had evolved in unanticipated ways. Rather than producing a limited number of world-class facilities, it had led to the construction of too much capacity; a good deal was not modern and was situated in managerially and financially complicated structures that were inflexible. They had, therefore, to urge and lead the repair of a system that they had shaped with their own hands.

Nonetheless, their approach made the work of the companies a good deal easier. Led by the Basic Industry Bureau, MITI sought first to clean up the raw material pricing problem. Then, they prepared the ground for collective action, using the mechanism of the Industrial Structure Council. Concurrently, discussions were carried on with the producing companies. Finally, the trip to Europe provided the basis for consensus among the companies. In short, very extensive political work was carried out by MITI which simplified the political situation of the companies.

One final observation should be made at this point. It is by no means obvious that the initiative for all this activity came from MITI. At least some of those interviewed suggested that one or more of the company leaders played a key role in stimulating and guiding MITI. From the perspective of this discussion, the critical point to observe is that in structure and practice MITI and its Industrial Structure Council provided a forum that managers found useful in handling the political aspects of their restructuring problem. The subsidies and tax benefits associated with the new law were also attractive.

The Japanese companies believe that it is helpful to have organizations such as MITI that use the best intelligence possible to provide a view of the industrial situation and powerful bureaucrats to negotiate with other ministries and the Diet. The bureaucrats at MITI believe that it is essential to have strong, independent private companies to develop and implement strategic plans. These beliefs contribute to the basis for a consensus-building process in which the companies accept an interference from, or a dependence on, the government that German, United Kingdom, and United States companies would find unacceptable. That would seem to leave the task of depoliticizing the restructuring of European and American industry to ad hoc arrangements.

Given the ideological foundations of politics in the West, in particular given the challenge from communist ideology, ad hocracy may be exactly the right position for the companies to take. The easiest way to avoid government interference is to solve the problem privately. But it leaves managers with a very difficult set of challenges.

I believe that it would be extremely helpful in both the United States and Europe if industry associations were asked to produce long-term forecasts of supply/demand balance. It would also help if they were to sponsor on a regular basis projects such as the Chem Systems study that revealed reasonably clearly to those concerned their competitive situation measured by production cost and market position. One of the virtues of a well-run monopoly is that its management can determine which of its productive capacities serves the market most efficiently. In the confused market circumstances exemplified by petrochemicals in the 1980s, it might help a great deal if managers and those with whom they had to negotiate at least had a sound idea of their competitive position. Since it is often the weak who are least informed and whose thrashing about most destabilizes the market, it is especially in the interest of the strong to support such studies.

This argument for better information may strike managers as incredibly optimistic, particularly in the light of the somewhat pessimistic description of a politicized environment already given. That may well be. But my optimism is based on an observation made to me in 1964 in a conversation with Herbert Simon, the Nobel Prize-winning student of administration. His conclusion, he said, was that when presented with facts that they could understand, all but the sickest organizations used them in a reasonable way. We can imagine that many instances exist where it would help the competitors figure out what made sense if they just had credible information.

In Europe, the Industry Directorate of the European Commission would be a natural home for such work. But rather than create a staff of generalists, they might well want to contract out specific studies to consulting groups in industry or the universities. In the United States, the Department of Commerce and the United States Trade Representative (U.S.T.R.) both have developed analytic capability, as has the Congress. Again, however, it might be better if they contracted out their studies so that industry expertise could be brought to bear directly. The marriage of government legitimacy with business expertise is a consummation devoutly to be wished.

The Work of a Leader

The implications of the foregoing analysis is that none of the tasks that faced major corporations in less-politicized environments can be ignored and that a new set of demands must be met. Not only must strategy be based on a clear appreciation of conditions in the company's market and an accurate assessment of its own competence relative to competitors, but also there must be a comprehensive understanding of how the range of options facing the firm are regarded politically by those governments that take an interest in the company's activities and have the legal or physical power to make their interest influential.

Even well-run companies, or perhaps especially well-run companies, have problems taking the political dimension into account when devising and executing strategy. Intelligent, dedicated managements trying to succeed economically in today's competitive battle often find it perverse to take seriously the demands made by public officials. They perceive their government counterparts to be far less informed on the substance of issues, such as where a petrochemical unit should be located; and their motives are regarded as suspect—either ideologically tainted with socialist thoughts or warped by the need to pander to the electorate.

The emotions are understandable but highly dysfunctional. A strategy that serves the needs of the company but not the community is vulnerable to political attack. When management chooses to ignore the community under the ideological protection of the free market, it creates a political vacuum which those not represented in the strategy formulation process may choose to fill. They may seek government help to reflect their unrepresented views.

Companies involved in restructuring need the government to

give their strategies legitimacy and to make sure that political forces do not lead authority to be used to sidetrack a program. But this dual objective is not easily accomplished. Many managements interviewed for this study acknowledged the validity of the first half of the preceding sentence. "Of course government has a near-monopoly of legitimacy." But they denied the possibility of having government intervention without government interference and preferred to cope as best they could on their own.[7]

The problem is that restructuring by major corporations technically involves power shifts that governments regard as part of their domain. Their interest is unavoidable, just as the work of divisions of a corporation unavoidably catches the interest of corporate management. What can be achieved, sometimes, is for business to manage the appearance as well as the substance of its strategy so that its objectives and programs can be perceived as meeting the community's need as well as the company's.

This was Schimberni's triumph at Montedison. While fighting for the interest of his company, he was able to present his program as serving the interests of Italy.

This is what ICI was unable to do in presenting their case for treatment equal to BP, Exxon, and Shell to Parliament.

This was what Chalandon and Gandois were unable to do with Chevenement.

Strategy formulation then requires devising a series of steps that make sense in terms of the market, company competence, and the needs of important constituencies and their representatives. There are economic, administrative, and political imperatives and all must be met, usually by some kind of compromise. The challenge is to find a path through this thicket of conflicting demands that does not compromise the strategic integrity of the corporation. Fundamentally, its product and market objectives must be commercially sound even if not optimal, whatever other political accommodation is required.

If this sounds like "manager as superhero," it is a false impression but still closer to the truth than manager as scientist or super-technocrat. The balancing of constituencies, the managing of politically salient issues against long-term objectives, and the formulating of corporate purpose is still an art form that leaders struggle to master. One lesson from petrochemicals is that there is no simple economic solution to the struggle.

NOTES

1. See, for example, a discussion of the phenomenon in French companies in John H. McArthur and Bruce Scott, *Industrial Planning in France* (Boston: Division of Research, Harvard Business School, 1969), 232–39.
2. Interview with Finsider management, spring 1983.
3. In one instance known to the author, after the sirens had alerted the workers to an impending explosion of a polyethylene unit, a worker ran from his bunker to try to adjust the machinery so that it would not blow up. He was the only casualty in the accident. The tragedy in Bhopal emphasizes just how critical is this commitment to safety and efficiency. If the workers had done their job and not had tea before running away, the tragedy might have been averted.
4. Alfred North Whitehead, *Adventures in Ideas* (New York: Reprint, Free Press, 1961), 90.
5. Henry M. Strage, McKinsey & Co. of London, remarks at "Strategic Management Conference" Barcelona, Spain, October 1985.
6. See, for example, "Sam Heyman's Hopeful Script for Carbide," *Business Week,* 23 December 1985, 30–31.
7. One German manager, on hearing a presentation of the findings in chapters 5–11, said, "That is quite fascinating, but it would be better for everyone if you don't publish. It will only give governments grounds for interference."

Glossary

Acetylene A gaseous hydrocarbon containing a triple bond that is explosive when compressed but safe if diluted with nitrogen or acetone. It is made by the action of water on calcium carbide, by pyrolysis, or by oxidation of other hydrocarbons. It is used in welding and soldering, for removing paint, for illuminating, and for many organic syntheses.

Acrylic fiber Any of various synthetic textile fibers made by polymerization of acrylonitrile, usually with other monomers. Because they are quick drying and resistant to moisture and moths, they are used in clothing fabrics.

AMOCO Standard Oil Company of Indiana.

ANIC A chemical subsidiary of the Italian National Oil company, ENI, now part of Enichemica.

Bulk plastics Commodity plastics.

Butylene A by-product of the ethylene production process. This C4 compound is a basic raw material for a wide range of valuable products, especially rubbers and specialty chemicals.

Capacity swaps When two companies trade production facilities so that one exchanges plant capacity with the other.

Caustic soda A synonym for sodium hydroxide. A brittle, white, deliquescent solid that dissolves readily to form a strongly alkaline and caustic solution. It is made by the electrolysis of common salt or by treating soda ash with hydrated lime. Used to make other chemicals, soap, detergents, rayon and cellulose film, pulp, paper, and in petroleum refining, bleaching, and mercerizing.

Combinato A complex in which several companies locate in one area to take the output of a single cracker. It is a Japanese phenomenon.

Comecon countries Nations of Eastern Europe joined in a common market led by the Soviet Union.

Commodity plastics Those polymers whose cost and properties are so attractive that they are manufactured in vast undifferentiated volumes. They are readily transported and extensively traded. The thermoplastics discussed in this book—LDPE, HDPE, PVC, PS, and PP—provide important examples.

Copolymers Secondary chemicals added during production of olefins to make different forms of plastics with special properties, e.g., benzene with ethylene makes styrene.

Crack To break into simpler chemical compounds, usually through heating.

Cracker Short for "steam cracker," the facility used to make ethylene.

DG III The Directorate of the European Commission concerned with developing industrial policy for Europe.

DG IV The Directorate of the European Commission responsible for the enforcement of the Common Market's antitrust laws, articles 85 and 86 of the Treaty of Rome.

Downstream In or toward the latter stages of the industrial process, e.g., in oil refining gasoline is downstream from crude oil.

EDC Ethylene dichloride, the precursor for vinyl chloride. A heavy, toxic liquid compound made by the direct union of ethylene and chlorine. It is used as a solvent and as an insecticidal fumigant.

Ethanol A volatile, flammable liquid manufactured by the hydration of ethylene. Used as a solvent, antifreeze, fuel, and as a raw material for many organic chemicals.

Ethylbenzene A liquid hydrocarbon most often made from benzene and ethylene used to manufacture styrene.

Ethylene A flammable gas used only as a raw material to make plastics and other chemicals such as ethylene glycol (antifreeze) and ethyl alcohol. It is cracked from ethane or naphtha feedstock in giant facilities called steam crackers. Its simple chemical structure of two carbon and four hydrogen atoms clearly defines its products. Although ethylene is completely standardized, it is difficult to transport and seldom traded. It is best thought of as the first stage in a chain of production, rather than as an independent process.

Ethylene glycol A thick, liquid alcohol made usually as the end product of the hydration of ethylene oxide from ethylene. It is used as antifreeze and as a raw material for polyester.

Ethylene oxide   A colorless, flammable, toxic gaseous or liquid compound used especially in synthesis (as with ethylene glycol) and in sterilization and fumigation.

Feedstock   The basic raw materials used in olefin, polymer, and copolymer processes. The most commonly used feedstocks in making ethylene are ethane from natural gas, and naphtha and gas oil from petroleum refineries. When naphtha and gas oil are used as feedstocks, many more by-products are made than when ethane is used.

First stage petrochemical derivatives   Intermediate petrochemical products such as vinyl chloride or ethyl benzene.

Formaldehyde   Usually made by oxidation of methanol or of gaseous hydrocarbons. It is used as a disinfectant and preservative and in the synthesis of phenolic and other synthetic resins.

GATT negotiations   The General Agreement on Trade and Tariffs governs trading relations among the major nations. The most recent agreements were negotiated during the "Tokyo Round" (1974–77). The previous ones were negotiated at the "Kennedy Round" (1964–69).

Gatti-Grenier Report   A 1983 report that attempted to study Europe's petrochemical capacity problem. It was intended to provide the basis for collective action.

Greenfield facility   A totally new plant complex as opposed to a new unit of an old complex.

HDPE   High-density polyethylene. A variant form of polyethylene and a tough thermoplastic polymer suitable for blow-molded bottles.

Hydrocarbon   Any of a large class of organic compounds containing only carbon and hydrogen. Occurring in many cases in petroleum, natural gas, coal, and bitumens.

Integrated facilities   A group of production facilities for related products, the output of one process being the input for the next.

ISAC   An industry sector advisory committee, called for by the U.S. Trade Act of 1975.

Isopropyl alcohol   A volatile, flammable, liquid secondary alcohol. It is made by hydration of propylene by means of sulfuric acid and is used as a solvent, rubbing alcohol, and as a source of acetone by dehydrogenation.

Kartellamt   The German government's antitrust division in Berlin which functions as an independent ministry.

Keiretsu In Japan, a family of companies related to a trading house.

Laggard plant An olefin plant built before the 1970s; generally smaller and less efficient than newer plants.

LDPE Low-density polyethylene. A variant form of polyethylene and a flexible thermoplastic polymer suitable for use as a packaging material.

Leader plant An olefin plant built in the 1970s and 1980s; generally larger and more efficient than older plants.

LLDPE Linear low-density polyethylene. An intermediate form of the polymer polyethylene, it produces a stronger product than that produced by the conventional polyethylene molecule. This allows less material to be used in achieving the same properties.

Methane A flammable, gaseous, saturated hydrocarbon. It is used as a fuel and as a raw material in chemical synthesis. It occurs naturally as a product of the decomposition of natural gas and is also formed in the carbonization of coal.

Methanol A light, volatile, flammable, poisonous liquid alcohol formed in the destructive distillation of wood but now usually made synthetically (as by catalytic reaction of carbon monoxide and hydrogen under pressure). It is used as a solvent, antifreeze, and as raw material in the synthesis of formaldehyde and other chemicals.

Monomer A simple molecule that can form polymers by combining with identical or similar molecules, e.g., ethylene, propylene, VCM, or styrene.

Naphtha Any of various volatile, often flammable, liquid hydrocarbon mixtures. They are used as solvents, diluents, and as raw materials for conversion to gasoline.

"The nine" A reference to nine petrochemical producers organized through the efforts of Viscount Davignon of the Industry Directorate to hold discussions concerning capacity reduction. The nine were Ato-Chloe, Rhône-Poulenc, ENI, Montedison, DSM, Solvay, Shell, Hoechst, and ICI.

OCITA Organization of Chemical Industry Trade Associations, an umbrella organization founded in 1974 to bring together five different chemical industry trade organizations in order to manage the industry's interests during trade negotiations.

Olefin plants Chemical plants that yield other olefin chemicals as by-products, such as propylene and butylene, in the process of producing ethylene. These plants are huge, costing up to half a billion dollars, and are complex to run.

Olefins Simple petrochemicals that can be processed further into a variety of higher-valued chemicals.

On stream Operating.

Organic chemicals Hydrocarbons.

PE Polyethylene. A thermoplastic resin made from the polymerization of ethylene. This organic intermediate is used to make packaging, insulation, and containers.

Petrochemical A chemical isolated from petroleum or natural gas or a derivative produced from such a substance by chemical reaction.

Phenolic plastic A plastic consisting of a thermosetting resin of high mechanical strength and electrical resistance. It is characterized by resistance to water, acids, and organic solvents and is used in molded, cast, or laminating products, such as adhesives or coatings.

Plastic Any of a large group of materials of high molecular weight that usually contain as the essential ingredient a synthetic or semisynthetic organic substance made by polymerization or condensation (like polystyrene) or derived from a natural material by chemical treatment. They are molded, cast, extruded, drawn, or laminated under various conditions (as by heat in the case of thermoplastic materials) into objects of all sizes and shapes including films and filaments.

Polymer One or more chemicals fused together in long molecular strands. Not easily defined by neat chemical formulas. Polymers display great variety in terms of density, strength, melting point, clarity, thermal and electrical conductivity, ability to take colors, and many other properties. Each set of properties makes a polymer more or less suitable for a particular purpose, and determines how it can substitute for natural materials or for other plastics. It is usually formed by mixing monomers (such as ethylene, propylene, or styrene) in a solution, heating and then removing the polymer by filtration or condensation.

Polymerization The process of changing a compound into a polymeric form with different physical properties by joining two or more like molecules to form a more complex one. The

.process is one way of adding value to an olefin by differentiating a product.

Polyolefin A polymer of olefins, such as polyethylene, that contains many double bonds.

PP Polypropylene. A heat- and water-resistant thermoplastic polymer, suitable for use in appliances.

Propylene A primary product from naphtha, it is a by-product in the ethylene production process. There is a larger merchant market for it than ethylene because it is easier to transport and store.

PS Polystyrene. A thermoplastic polymer which, depending on the final stage of the production process, can be made into either expandable form for making Styrofoam or into high-impact forms for solid objects.

PVC Polyvinyl chloride. A thermoplastic polymer that has excellent electrical properties and that can be made flame-resistant, making it useful in construction (piping, flooring, and siding).

Rationalization Modifying process and structure of facilities to make them as efficient as possible.

Resin Any of a large class of synthetic products usually of high molecular weight that have some of the physical properties of natural resins but typically are very different chemically. They may be thermoplastic or thermosetting. They are made by polymerization or condensation. They are used as plastics or as essential ingredients of plastics, in varnishes and other coatings, and in adhesives.

Specialty chemicals Products designed for specific uses.

Spheripol process A method of producing polypropylene developed by Montedison.

Steam cracking A process in which feedstocks are mixed with steam and heated under controlled, pressurized conditions to transform them into olefins and other petrochemicals. The simpler, more direct process in ethane crackers tends to make them more economical than naphtha crackers, provided the plant has a convenient source of natural gas. A cracker designed to process ethane could not process naphtha and vice versa. But naphtha crackers can be designed to process gas oil, helping to minimize raw material costs when feedstock prices fluctuate.

Styrene A mobile, liquid, unsaturated hydrocarbon that polymerizes in the presence of air or peroxides to yield polystyrene.

It is used to make synthetic rubber, resins, plastics, and in improving drying oils.

Synthetic fiber Man-made textile fibers usually including those made from natural materials as well as fully synthetic fibers like nylon or acrylic.

Synthetic rubber Various products that resemble natural rubber in physical properties and ability to be vulcanized. Synthetic rubber is made by polymerization of butadiene or similar unsaturated hydrocarbons or by copolymerization of these hydrocarbons with styrene or other polymerizable compounds.

Unipol technology A method of producing linear low-density polyethylene developed by Union Carbide.

Upstream Toward a portion of the production stream closer to basic extractive or manufacturing processes.

VCM Vinyl chloride monomer, a monomer for polyvinyl chloride. It is a transformation of ethylene molecules produced by adding chlorine to the production process.

Vinyl acetate A flammable, polymerizable liquid that is prepared by catalytic addition of acetic acid to acetylene. It is used mostly for the production of vinyl resins and in making other vinyl esters by reaction with other acids.

Vinyl plastic Tough, durable plastic based on vinyl resins often compounded with other substances. Vinyl plastic is used in films and sheetings, coatings, tile and flooring, foams, sound records, and other molded and extruded products.

Zaibatsu Giant privately owned and family-controlled industrial groupings organized around a bank that dominated the Japanese economy before World War II.

Ziegler process Until very recently, the leading process for making polypropylene.

Index

This book was set into type electronically using a Mergenthaler Linotron in Bembo, a recutting of an incunabula type face attributed to Aldus Manutius. The book was printed by offset lithography on acid free paper.